A TALE OF
12 KITCHENS

A TALE OF
TALE OF
12 KITCH

LE OF
KITCHENS

A TALE OF
12 KITCHENS

**FAMILY COOKING
IN FOUR COUNTRIES**

JAKE TILSON

To Bennie

Happy Best
Birthday ever!

much love
Kim, Syras
Rahim & Sier

ARTISAN | NEW YORK

Dedicated to my family

Writing a domestic family cookbook is akin to selling the family silver. The words "thank you" seem small words indeed for my wife, Jennifer (Jeff) Lee; daughter, Hannah; parents, Joe and Jos; sisters, Anna and Sophy; mother-in-law, Mary Lee; Susie and Bill Robson; and Ernie Lee for all their love, patience, kitchens and recipes and without whom this book would not have been possible.

Published by Artisan
A Division of Workman Publishing Company, Inc.
225 Varick Street
New York, NY 10014

Library of Congress Cataloging-in-Publication Data
Tilson, Jake, 1958–
A Tale of 12 kitchens : family cooking in four countries
    / Jake Tilson.
p. cm.
Includes index.
ISBN-13: 978-1-57965-320-0
ISBN-10: 1-57965-320-0
1. Cookery, International.   2. Tilson family. I. Title.
II. Title: Tale of twelve kitchens.
TX725.A1T547 2006
641.5—dc22   2006045866

Printed in Singapore
Published by arrangement with Weidenfeld &
Nicolson, London
First American edition, September 2006

10 9 8 7 6 5 4 3 2 1

Other books by Jake Tilson
Light and Dark (1979)
8 Views of Paris (1980)
Exposure (1980)
Excavator-Barcelona-Excavador (1986)
Breakfast Special (1987)
The Terminator Line (1991)
3 Found Fonts (2003)

NO MICROWAVES HAVE BEEN
USED IN THE PRODUCTION
OF THIS BOOK.

FOREWORD

NANCY HARMON JENKINS

Upfront and without any qualifiers, *A Tale of 12 Kitchens* is a wonderful book. It's about food, about cooking and eating, about sharing and seducing and drawing closer to each other through the appetites. It has loads of recipes, most of which are easy to reproduce, but it's not by a famous chef or restaurateur. Jake Tilson doesn't have a television show, nor has he coursed the farther reaches of the globe in search of a thousand never-before-published recipes, and he's not a food writer diligently cultivating bylines and public appearances. In fact, if you're like most Americans, you've probably never heard of him at all. Once you've dipped into his book, however, I predict that you will want to know more about him, and you'll dip again. And again, and again.

Who is this Jake Tilson, then?

Jake—I can call him by his first name because I've known him since he was a lad—is, above all, an artist, like his father and mother before him, his two sisters and his wife to this day. And he brings an artist's sensibility to what is obviously his first love, food. By "artist's sensibility," I mean the ability to make connections and to express them for the rest of us who don't always appreciate or understand the extent and intricacy of the links that bind our lives in time and space. In Jake's mind (and in my own), food is a concrete, irreducible and powerful expression of that connection.

But lest you think this is a philosophical-anthropological tome filled with obtuse statements of the obvious, let me reassure you. On the contrary, Jake's book is about joy and passion: the joy of cooking, the passion of eating and the thrill of discovering something you hadn't known existed before you stopped at that taco stand in Los Angeles, or thrust your nose through the door of that diner in Manhattan, or shared a plate of pasta in that Tuscan farmhouse kitchen. Jake Tilson takes us through all that and then recounts for us in witty and consummate detail how he learned to make *börek* or blueberry pancakes or the ragù for a *pasta al forno* such as our neighbors make in our hidden village in Tuscany.

Jake is an inveterate collector of information, as well as of physical bits of things. Like all the Tilsons, he keeps notebooks that are more like scrapbooks than anything else, full of scribbled notes and drawings, arrows that connect one thought to another, along with all those collected bits and pieces—labels from cans and boxes and bottles of wine, old menus, postcards, ticket stubs, receipts. Each bit resonates with meaning, and meaningful resonance is part of the charm of a book that itself is part collage.

Like Jake's own life, his book begins in the English countryside, where he grew up in a rambling, slightly crumbling manse called (somewhat improbably, considering the activities that took place there) The Old Rectory. From there he went to Italy most summers and then to London where, as an art student, he took control of his own kitchen and began to experiment with cooking and feeding friends, lovers, family. It was a way, he says, of beginning to understand who he was, how he could be at home in himself: "Home occurs in a scattering of locations and in varying degrees," he writes, "forming a personal atlas that acts as an embedded touchstone connecting these disparate locations, expanding my sense of what and where is family and home. Food and cooking are pivotal to building this sense of identity."

London led to New York, marriage led to Scotland and many other parts of the world. "Marriage refills the kitchen larder," he says, as marriage to his Scottish wife refilled the Tilson larder with Cullen skink and Atholl brose, with full-flavored kailkenny (potatoes and cabbage in rich country cream), and refreshed memories of his own Scottish grandfather. Then back to New York and on to Santa Fe, Los Angeles, a Persian deli in London and a myriad of places in between, all to be honored in recipes and memories.

Above all, Jake's book is a romantic celebration of people and places. I defy you to find anyone who captures so well the romance of food in New York—not at Le Cirque or the Union Square Café but in diners, luncheonettes, places like Veselka's, the Kiev, Elka's Coffee Shop (of the last, he writes, "Their blueberry pancake stack is like a pile of fresh zombies"), speaking to the ethnic panache of a New York that is closer to Woody Allen and Martin Scorsese than to the likes of Donald Trump, a New York of character, dazzle, excitement, and all of it tied up in the foods served at Sam Chinita on Eighth Avenue or the Westside Coffee Shop with its Dominican-Mexican-American menu. It took Jake's vision to show me that those dusty, diminutive New York supermarkets, their long narrow aisles crowded with a jumble of toppling cans and boxes and bottles, were just old-fashioned corner groceries in a different guise. Who knew?

To New York, to Scotland, to London and Palm Springs and points in between, Jake Tilson brings not just his eager tongue and palate, but his wide-open eyes and ears, and yes, all of his full-bodied heart. So cook a little, eat a little, but above all celebrate with him as you wend your way through his book.

SIXTIES POTS AND SEVENTIES PANS

FOR AS LONG AS I CAN REMEMBER I HAVE ALWAYS WANTED TO COOK

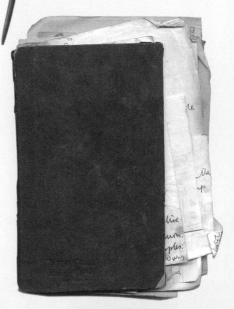

15p PER 1 lb.

BUT WHY DO WE COOK WHAT WE COOK? WHAT HAS THE DEEPEST EFFECT ON OUR CULINARY HABITS? IS IT CHILDHOOD, MARRIAGE, THE NEIGHBORHOOD OR WHAT WE SAW ON TELEVISION LAST NIGHT?

Cooking and eating are so inseparable from our daily routines that we tend to ignore the significance of what we choose to buy, prepare, cook and serve to ourselves, family and friends. Increasingly what we eat tends to reveal a lack of time made available for anything culinary. Ignore cooking at your peril!

Investigating domestic cooking makes you acutely aware of a household cook's position within a family of families—one cook among many, spanning generations and crossing borders. For me, mother, father, sisters, grandparents, wife, daughter, in-laws, relations and friends are all intertwined and immovable from how, why and what I cook. By exploring my own gastronomic roots and influences, I hope this book will act as a mirror to yours. You may value or discover some aspect of your own personal "cuisine" that lay pushed to the side of your plate. Happy cooking!

A LIVE-IN KITCHEN

An entry in my mother's 1958 notebook records what she cooked the day before I was born—shepherd's pie and sprouts for lunch and a light supper of onion soup and pancakes. They tended to eat large lunches, pasta alla Bolognese, fish and sprouts— less for supper, perhaps a simple soupe Catalane. Earlier in the day from the market she had bought: milk, fruit, cheese, vegetables, meat, eggs, bread, flour and cigarettes. Each item carefully priced. I did the same as a student: it must be genetics or a careful pocket. Our first family kitchen was a disused Victorian dairy shop in Notting Hill Gate in 1950s London. Although the shopfront window was whitewashed, people

SUBMARINE MELTS
HOT BAGUETTE SANDWICH

Crunchy, steaming, moist and melting—easy to prepare and quick to cook. Reminiscent of New York deli sandwiches wrapped in extra-thick commercial-grade aluminum foil with hospital corners. Also an evocation of roadside picnic lunches in France—with the assistance of an oven. Definitely pitched as a kid's lunchtime meal. I enjoy the sogginess from the tomatoes, but if you want a crisper sandwich, seed the tomatoes first.
SERVES 4

4 individual-portion baguettes
4 plum tomatoes, sliced

16 slices garlic sausage (or salami, coppa, mortadella, or ham)
16 slices cheese

Preheat the oven to 425°F. Split open each baguette and fill with the tomato slices, garlic sausage and cheese. Don't overfill the baguettes, or the bread will frazzle before the filling has a chance to cook. Wrap the filled baguettes in foil, place directly on an oven rack, and cook for about 20 minutes. The tomatoes need to be steaming hot, the cheese dripping. Unwrap and cut each sandwich diagonally into 3 pieces. As teenagers, we would eat one small baguette each. They're also wonderful filled with artichokes, salami and a sprinkle of crushed red pepper flakes.

would constantly knock on the door, step in, and say "One pint, please." They wouldn't see a starched-aproned shopkeeper cutting rounds of cheddar—in place of the marble display cabinets were stacks of half-finished canvases leaning against the dairy walls, large palettes loaded with oil paint, buckets of water, tomato cans full of turpentine and a baby stuck in the corner playing with empty egg boxes on the black and white tiled floor. At the back of the shop an orange-crate table held up shelves and a single electric cooking ring; pots and pans hung on the crumbling walls. This was our rather makeshift kitchen. Although the room possessed the components of a shop, our random shoppers would realize their mistake and leave. My parents, Joe and Jos Tilson, were young artists, recently married in Venice. My father was teaching at St. Martin's School of Art and fellow ex-Royal College of Art students such as David Hockney and Robyn Denny lived nearby. My grandfather, Alastair Morton, was thrilled with our first family flat, saying, "That's the way art students should live."

We cooked, painted, ate and slept in this one room. A cramped toilet was shared with the upstairs flat. The orange crates used in our furniture were scavenged from nearby Portobello Road market—a winding quarter mile of brass, copper, used clothes and crockery stalls that gave way to wooden barrows piled high with carrots, potatoes, onions and leeks. In 1958, pre-carnival Notting Hill Gate was still a relatively poor neighborhood; many children ran around the streets in bare feet. My parents had just returned from living in Spain with the artist Peter Blake, where they had fished, painted, cooked outdoors and ridden on Lambrettas and mules. Their only reading matter in Spain was *A Book of Mediterranean Food* by Elizabeth David, published in 1950. I still refer to the recipes weekly and I have rubber-stamped her *salsa di pomodoro* recipe on our kitchen wall. My mother brought this southern gastronomic influence back to our 1950s London kitchen. British regional cuisine was in its black-hole phase, extinguished by the Second World War and hidden from view by thirteen years of food rationing. Britain was also undergoing a slow culinary invasion from mainland Europe and was ripe for the taking. I imagine Ada Boni's *Talisman Italian Cook Book*, 1950, was extracting a similar influence on postwar North American kitchens, although their international recipe map is more complicated and requires a degree in migrant history to understand it fully.

London was on the cusp of change, still flavored with postwar austerity, before the Pop Art 1960s. Babies were left outside in their prams by the doorstep in smog, fog and snow, or so my mother had been taught. None of her friends from college had children. I promptly caught pneumonia, not a good prospect at the age of one, but thankfully I survived to taste 1960s London.

Nora's Xmas Pudding
<u>HALF IT —</u> this is for 2.

1lb	raisins
"	sultanas
"	currants
½ 2lb	chopped mixed peel
"	chopped stoned prunes
4ozs.	chopped sweet almonds
	grated nutmeg 1 lemon
3 measures	sherry/madeira/brandy
¾ lb	S.R Flour
½ tsp.	salt
¼ tsp	ground ginger, cinnamon + nutmeg
½ lb	breadcrumbs
¾ lb	Demerara
¾ lb	shredded suet
1lb	peeled cored grated Bramley apples.
6	eggs+milk, or guinness to mix.

Day before clean fruit.
Put fruit, peel, lemon rind, almonds in mixing bowl + pour wine over. Cover.
Sift flour, salt, +spices together. Add crumbs, sugar + suet.

Next day mix fruits, dry ingredients, grated apples + eggs. Pour in enough liquid to make a mixture which drops easily from teaspoon, when jerked. Turn mixture into well greased bowls to within ¼ inch of top. Cover with double greaseproof paper. Boil for at least 6 hours. (water ½ way up) Reheat for 2 or 3 hours on Christmas Day.

_____ Pudding
1 _____ each of _____
Demerara sugar
2 vinegarbo Bordeaux
A few pinch cinnamon.

Put _____ sugar + cinnamon + _____ cover with wine.
_____ cook in _____ oven for 45 minutes _____ low to get all.
Serve with _____ cream + _____ fingers.

ELSIE KITAJ'S MOROCCAN KEFTA

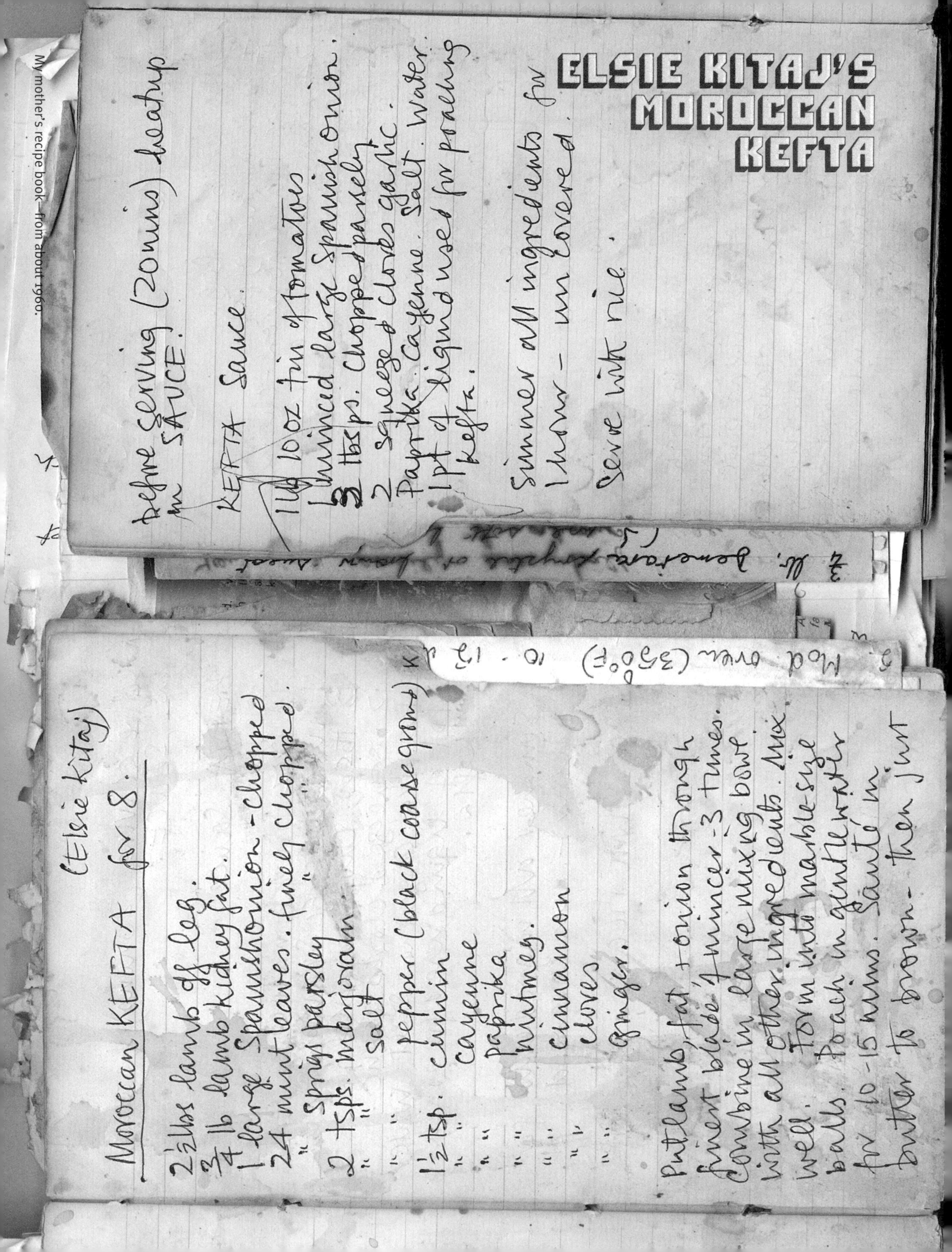

before serving (20 mins) heat up in SAUCE.
KEFTA Sauce.
1 lb 10 oz tin of tomatoes
1 minced large Spanish onion.
3 tbsps. chopped parsley.
2 squeezed cloves garlic.
Paprika. Cayenne. Salt. Water.
1 pt of liquid used for poaching kefta.
Simmer all ingredients for 1 hour - un covered.
Serve with rice.
¾ lb. Demerara
Mod. oven (350°F) 10 - 12
(Elsie Kitaj)
Moroccan KEFTA for 8.
2½ lbs lamb off leg.
¾ lb lamb kidney fat.
1 large Spanish onion - chopped
24 mint leaves. finely chopped
" sprigs parsley " "
2 tsps. marjoram.
" " salt
" " pepper (black coarse ground)
1½ tsp. cumin
" " cayenne
" " paprika
" " nutmeg.
" " cinnamon
" " cloves
" " ginger.
Put lamb, fat + onion through finest blade of mincer - 3 times. Combine in large mixing bowl with all other ingredients. Mix well. Form into marble-size balls. Poach in gentle water for 10-15 mins. Sauté in butter to brown - then just

My mother's recipe book—from about 1960.

the little
red
school
book

Bassett's
LIQUORICE
Allsorts
1/- PER QTR. lb.
Made in England by
Geo. Bassett & Co., Ltd., Sheffield, England.

BIRD'S
CUSTARD
buy now!
SAVE

Ty-Phoo TEA
KEEP AWAY FROM SCENTED GOODS
FOR QUALITY ECONOMY

Chocolate Fudge.
1lb granulated Sugar.
1 oz butter
½ pt condensed milk (unsweetened)
5 oz plain chocolate
2 tabs water
1 teas vanilla essence.

Put all the ingredients except
vanilla essence into a pan.
Stand the pan on a slow heat until
the sugar has melted. Then turn up the
heat & boil fairly rapidly for 25-30 mins
Stir occasionally. Take pan off heat
then in vanilla essence & beat the
mixture with a wooden spoon until it
Thickens a little & creamy. Turn out as
quickly as possible on to a greased tin
while it is almost cold, cut food pieces
pieces with a sharp knife. When quite
cold put on to greaseproof paper.

My learn
to cook book
A Children's Book for the Kitchen

KUP KAKES
KUP KAKES
LYONS   KUP KAKE

POP ART KITCHEN

This was our second kitchen, a busy place. It had a long, broad, wooden table, school homework at one end, chopping board at the other. As a birthday culinary treat my mother cooked me *escargots*, prepared in typical French Relais Routier truck-stop style, as experienced on our annual treks to Italy. I assisted by opening the can and pushing the rubbery molluscs into their reusable snail shells which were stored in an old sweet jar. For most of the year they resembled gnarled toffees high on the top shelf. The smell of melting garlic butter on snails was heaven, I could almost see a French linen tablecloth materialize under my plate. I have yet to try the snail cooking method of burning a stretch of snail-laden hedgerow and then picking off and eating the cooked snails once the fire dies down.

One of the important places to be was around Joe Tilson's family table in his farmhouse-style kitchen just off High Street Ken, which was a [Pop Art] forum, a place where you would bump into writers and artists.

ALLEN JONES, ARTIST,
TALKING ON BBC RADIO 4, 2004

Food was important to our family. My parents entertained most nights and the phrase "and we would go to the Tilsons' for supper" appears in many autobiographies. As children these after-hours suppers were first glimpsed by my sister Anna and me from the top of the dark, twisting staircase, catching phrases of conversation as jackets were piled onto the curlicue Victorian coat stand. Aromas escaped from the kitchen as we crouched in cold pajamas on hard carpet. For larger parties or film nights we helped arrange ordered rows of cocktail glasses, primed with their first ingredient before guests arrived. We divided out imported stuffed olives or candied cherries. One gray morning after a particularly frenzied party, which had filled our entire house for what had seemed like all night, I snuck out of my bedroom window, stepping carefully across the moss-covered fire escape onto the roof. Torrential rain beat down on the flat asphalt. Among the detritus of snaking cables, flaking cement and bent television aerials, I found an overturned hostess trolley that had spilt its load of salami sandwiches sometime during the early hours and now lay sodden, edging toward the brink of the brick parapet. Fritz Lang's film *Metropolis* had been shown the night before from a rattling cine-projector to four hundred people squeezed into our open-plan living room. Food as part of a celebration was introduced to us early on.

SEEDS OF CHANGE

High Street Kensington contained all the classic ingredients of a postwar British high street, pre-chain-stores, pre-globalization—but not for long. A similar pattern spread throughout the villages of London. There were department stores such as Barkers,

Pontings and Derry & Toms alongside independent butchers, greengrocers, electrical stores, a fabulous Lyons Corner House, hardware shops, banks, boutiques, a cinema and a few restaurants. We also shopped in the Sainsbury's food hall—a deep, tiled rectangular space, flanked with wooden-framed glass display counters festooned with regimented produce. Straight-back chairs were provided for weary shoppers. The air was larder cold. Clerks stood behind the counters ready to serve. Butter was patted into rectangles to order and sugar was weighed into blue paper bags. Unknown to us at the time, Sainsbury's was the first company to open self-service supermarkets in 1950, out in the suburbs. I don't recall which shop occupied the corner of Argyll Road and High Street Kensington before 1968 but what came next changed everything. A small piece of Americana dropped on our doorstep, a supermarket opened at the end of our road—the Californian chain Safeway. Designed as a vast single-room interior, it had a large selection of low-cost produce, minimal staff help and a large turnover. Britain wasn't quite ready yet for the super-sized stores being built by Ralphs in North America as early as the 1930s, but Safeway were the masters of medium-sized stores that penetrated deep into the urban fabric. North American friends full of foreboding warned us our local greengrocers, butchers and market stalls would be forced out of business, as they had been in their neighborhood back in Los Angeles. They were right. But for many households supermarkets brought fixed low prices, no haggling, less hassle and the promise of fresh produce. To shop in small stores had required bargaining and negotiating skills and there was often no competition to encourage higher standards. The long-term monotonous effects from supermarkets standardizing produce certainly affected the agricultural landscape, city centers and the taste of food, but that is changing.

The back-street side of Safeway was en route to our bombsite playground by the library. I would sit and watch boxes of produce disappear down a small escalator as lorries disgorged their contents into the back of the shop. The pavement was dirty with the oily breakages. However, as a child, I found the long, stacked aisles of bright, repeated packaging as thrilling and modernistic as the shiny color covers of imported Batman and Superman comics. The shop looked like a film set. The beginning of a long love-hate relationship.

SUBCULTURE SCHOOL

The politics of 1960s London had a direct influence on schoolchildren through *Oz* magazine, *The Little Red School Book*, the underground subculture, and from the wide mix of family backgrounds in the recently built Holland Park Comprehensive

Joe, Jos, Jake, Anna, 1964.

School. Although pocket money was spent on buying LPs by Cream, Led Zeppelin, Jimi Hendrix and the Velvet Underground, as ten-year-olds we were also involved in direct action politics. A profusion of protest badges, sticker packs, antiwar posters, joss sticks and alternative magazines came from exotic shops such as Kensington Market and Biba. Safeway bore the brunt of my school friends' anti-apartheid campaign. Dressed in our army-surplus trench coats, we would attach skull and crossbones stickers reading, "Warning—Don't Buy This Produce—Anti Apartheid" onto stacked cans of South African peaches. Eventually weary security staff caught us and escorted us off the premises. I don't think charges were ever brought.

URBAN GRAZING

On sunny weekends we ran down the terra-cotta-tiled steps of our white stuccoed house and piled into our yellow Jaguar to hunt out restaurants in Chelsea. My father had special arrangements with two local Italian restaurants—San Frediano and the Meridiana, both on the Fulham Road. A meals-for-art exchange. Similar agreements later took us to San Lorenzo, Pizzeria Condotti, the Caprice and the Ivy. In the sixties the Meridiana was opened by Enzo Apicella, who had designed the early Pizza Express restaurants. Expansive Italian lunches on round tables with starched tablecloths, drinking San Pellegrino mineral water and Barolo. Bright white plates surrounded by tall grissini, fresh *michetta* rolls and heavy cutlery overlooked by walls of Pop Art. Occasionally we ate in a dark, deep Chinese restaurant next to the Commonwealth Institute, a muffled interior of carpets, drapes and heavy yellow tablecloths. A Wimpy hamburger house opened on the Earls Court Road—as children we were tempted by the photographs of finished dishes, and chips. Photography hadn't sold food to me before in a restaurant and was only just being introduced on food packaging. Our recipe books were text only, with an occasional drawn illustration heading up a new chapter.

Thankfully to counteract bland British Wimpy Bar burgers, North American hamburger restaurants opened in Chelsea, twenty years before the Hard Rock Café phenomenon and six years before the portent yellow "M" arches arrived in Woolwich in 1974. Yankee Doodle and The Great American Disaster were stylish hamburger restaurants brimming with sixties graphics that resembled album cover designs and urban diners rather than train station toilets. Turmeric-colored French's mustard, large succulent burgers in poppy-seed buns, branded jars of red, green and yellow relish and slim French fries. Exotic and strange, a teasing glimpse of what I would discover in New York twelve years later.

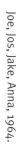

DOODLE

★ ★ ★ ★ ★ ★ ★

t soup.

★ ★ ★ ★ ★ ★ ★
DOGS

ut.

heese.

★ ★ ★ ★ ★ ★ ★
FRIED CHICKEN

ome-baked bun
stard.

★ ★ ★ ★ ★ ★ ★

ick, golden fried in
dill pickle and relish.

★ ★ ★ ★ ★ ★ ★

aise dressing.

MENU

FROM SEED TO PLATE

Becoming a small part of the ecological movement in 1971 forced us to make the uncomfortable move from reading books about "growing your own" to actually getting out a spade and digging all day. We were complete novices. As we came home from school, my mother would look up from weeding carrots and wave before we disappeared into the attached stone cottage for tea with our grandmother. Some crops flourished, others failed fantastically. The physical side of changing your life from theory to practice was exhausting. And then everything dies or goes wrong and it doesn't seem worth it. Eventually we pick, dig, prepare and consume an entire lunch of homegrown produce and taste what all the fuss is about. Homegrown potato salad with chives and vine-picked tomatoes so fresh they flap about on your plate—these tastes stay on your palate forever.

Our parents had moved us from the urban ferment of London to a vast, rambling Old Rectory in a small village in Wiltshire, a move from consumerism toward rural self-sufficiency. Back to the land. The house had cold, uneven flagstone halls showing a century of use, delicate floor-to-ceiling Georgian windows framed with fine, thin moldings and lawns that receded into fields like an ocean. Its thirty drafty rooms were damp, wet and cold, linked by leagues of creaking corridors and surrounded by ten acres of land. In the depths of winter it took a ton of firewood to keep us warm and a glass of water would freeze overnight on my bedside table.

We experimented with ways of planting and tending fruit and vegetables, tried new seed varieties and shifted bed locations. Discovering mulching and companion planting seemed momentous—the former meant no more weeding and the latter

Elderberry Wine (Eliza Acton)

Boiling water
2 gallons to 3 gallons elder.

Cover for 24 days.

Seive. then mush with more water brought to the boil.
to every gallon
3 lbs sugar

3/4 oz ~~ground~~ cloves ?

2 tsp 1 oz ginger ground

Boil for 20 mins
Skim.

Elderflower Champagne

6 heads of freshly picked elderflowers in full bloom
1 gallon cold water
1½ lb sugar
2 tablespoons white wine vinegar
Juice and rind of 1 lemon

Squeeze the juice of the lemon, then cut the rind into ¼s and put this with the elderflowers in a large basin. Add the sugar + vinegar, then pour over the cold water + stir well to dissolve sugar. Cover and leave to steep in a cool place for 24 hours. Strain off and bottle in screw topped bottles. This makes 1¼ gallons. Foams alot and can be drunk in 3 weeks. Best left for 2 months.

Laurie Clark's elderflower champagne.

fewer bugs eating our cabbages. For a teenager it was immensely empowering to grow your own food and help out in the kitchen. Having direct control over a part of your food chain leaves you with a lifelong love and appreciation of fresh fruit and vegetables. We erected commercial greenhouses, reared chickens, ducks and bees, made bitter beer, sharp preserves and delectable rhubarb and elderflower wine, which occasionally double-fermented, becoming an intoxicatingly fruity champagne. I don't think the local county council has applied for *appellation d'origine contrôlée* quite yet. My grandfather, Alastair Morton, had commissioned Patience Grey as a textile designer for Morton Sundour before she wrote her inspiring cookbook, *Honey From a Weed*, and my mother corresponded with her. Her book led us to forage and harvest from the hedgerows. Another impetus to our gardening and cooking was seed catalogues and books on organic husbandry such as *Grow Your Own Food* by Lawrence D. Hill, the incomparable *Companion Plants and How to Use Them* by Helen Philbrick and Richard B. Gregg, and the imported North American *How to Have a Green Thumb Without an Aching Back* by Ruth Stout. My mother, Jos, published a journal, *Catalyst*, for artists to communicate and share information. This brought her into contact with *The Mother Earth News* and *The Whole Earth Catalog—Access to Tools*, founded by Stewart Brand in North America. These journals had a utopian view reminiscent of the early years of the Internet, in which Brand also played an important role. They were equally concerned with freely shared information and expertise to help others— bypassing conventions. Alternative living! Rather like the Western pioneer Sears, Roebuck mail-order catalogues, from which you felt you could buy anything, from an entire prairie house with livestock to a pail full of roofing nails. The difference being that *The Mother Earth News* told you how to build the house from wood on your land and forge your own nails.

As a companion to these publications, a suitably offbeat recipe book was needed to reflect our increasingly agrarian circumstances. *Food in England*, the seminal big red book by Dorothy Hartley, seemed perfect. A book for English kitchens where a fire burns gently all day, it embraces seasonal variety and the need to pickle an over-abundant crop. And in *The Mother Earth News* fashion, there are countless diagrams advising the reader, including how to fill a medieval cauldron with suspended linen bags full of pudding, or earthenware jars of poultry and beef which rested on birch twigs. Or the construction of hearthstone cooking that utilized peat, an iron pot and stone on which to bake bread. Inspirational. Our kitchen became rather Elizabethan. Most of what we ate was either grown by ourselves or bought from local organic farmers or the butcher Reg Love & Son in Chippenham. The Aga provided a continual source of heat

QUICK BROWN BREAD

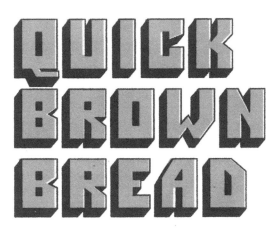

Making your own bread seems to epitomize the spirit of going back to nature and trying to be self-sufficient. We tried different types of flour, ground our own wheat, and one year a lodger planted a small field of wheat and reaped a few loaves from the crop. With at least five hungry people to feed, my mother seemed to be making bread constantly—adding that unique rhythm of baking to our kitchen. This is her quick brown bread recipe, only proofing the dough once.

MAKES 2 LOAVES AND 8 ROLLS

10^{1}/$_{2}$ cups (3^{1}/$_{4}$ pounds) whole wheat flour, or as needed

Two ^{1}/$_{4}$-ounce packets active dry yeast or 1 ounce fresh yeast

5 cups warm water

2 tablespoons olive oil

A large pinch of salt

Heap the flour in a large bowl, and make a well in the center. Whisk the yeast in a bowl with a few tablespoons of the water and then pour into the well. Add the olive oil and salt. Begin to mix the dough with your fingers, adding the remaining water a bit at a time. When I was testing this recipe with my daughter, she had to phone my mother to ask advice on stickiness—"not too sticky" was the reply. We had to add a few extra tablespoons of flour to get the right consistency. Knead the dough for 10 minutes, or until it becomes smooth and springy. I like to finish the kneading on a lightly floured board.

Oil two loaf pans and a baking sheet. Divide the dough into thirds. Put one-third into each loaf pan, then make 8 small round rolls to fill the baking sheet. Leave them all to proof somewhere warm for 45 minutes. Preheat the oven to 450°F. When the bread has risen, bake the loaves for 35 to 45 minutes. The rolls will take less time, about 25 minutes, and might need moving up and down in the oven for even baking. Take the baked bread out of the pans and leave the bread and rolls to cool on a wire rack. Make sure you sample a hot slice or two—a rare treat.

for cooking, warming and raising yeast. Hartley's comments on fuel-orientated recipes rang true—as anyone who has vainly attempted to use a wok on an Aga would know. Next to useless. Each type of fuel developes a unique and natural set of recipes and procedures for cooking. Hartley's book also described the medieval cooking methods still being practiced by neighboring farmers on our visits to Italy—spits, cauldrons, swing irons, trivets and iron dogs.

A CHICKEN-PECKED KITCHEN

Kitchens are the hospitable hubs of most homes, but country kitchens open unique culinary gateways to the growing produce beyond. No matter what one does to an urban kitchen, it always lacks that potentially threatening edge of encroaching nature, a wintry battering or some summer soothing from the changing seasons outside the kitchen door suggesting what and how to cook. Beyond are fields and farms. Sometimes it can feel like living in a vast factory—the comedian Peter Cook said the only thing the country was good for was for keeping towns apart.

Unfortunately the previous owner of our country kitchen had allowed the room to lapse into a domestic non-place, a pitiful dark utility room. The final blow to this character assassination was to build a toilet in the corner. Rather than gutting the room and starting from scratch, we searched for traces of its past. My father discovered clues rising above the old sideboard on the blackened plaster walls. Layers of disturbed plaster revealed the original placement of the shelving—thicker lines denoted deeper load-bearing shelves. From these guides my father reinstated the old dresser shelving system. He then built a double-width draining rack above twin Belfast sinks, similar to racks we found in Italy. This would house all of our daily crockery and glasses—no need for cupboards. Over the years the kitchen walls slowly developed a mottled yellow hue from successive decorating, below which a gritty flagstone floor was pecked at by the occasional chicken. I overheard a mother once strictly warn her child not to pick up anything from the floor, for fear of catching some terrible disease. A large flour-grinding mill sat under the window next to a hand coffee grinder. The coal-fired Aga sat comfortably in a wide fireplace under fermenting demijohns of wine. A disused cooking range in the corner was left undisturbed, a reminder for us of previous cooks. In the back hall stood large wooden apple racks the size of large vending machines, next to which was propped a keg of homemade beer, a lethal place to linger before going into town with friends. Disused cold attic rooms were also used to store vegetables and apples, laid out on old newspapers on dusty floorboards.

FORK AND SPADE

As our gardening became more ambitious, we bought farm equipment from agricultural auctions, including a chaff cutter to create mulch and to help feed our five, huge movable compost boxes. With this expansion we needed help. Fortunately The Old Rectory became part of WWOOF— Working Weekends on Organic Farms. This wonderful project was established by Sue Coppard in 1971 and is still in practice today, now called World Wide Opportunities on Organic Farms. Ten willing city folk would visit to work on our organic land most weekends. They would stay three nights and dig and mulch in the expanding garden. Visiting a family trying to be self-sufficient was as much part of the WWOOF experience as toiling on the land. Long days spent chaff cutting, digging new beds, dredging the pond or clearing woodland would be followed by preparing, cooking and eating long evening meals. Many WWOOFers became close friends and some stayed on as residents. There were often three other families lodging in various parts of the house, much to

OLD RECTORY HONEY · CHRISTIAN MALFORD, WILTS.

the bemusement of other villagers. The lodgers tended to be art students from nearby Corsham, where my mother had also been a student, or artists, teachers, musicians and poets—an extended family, and other hands to help mow the soccer-field-sized lawns, and new cooks from whom to learn.

SHIFTING SHOPPING

As you drive west out of London down the M4 motorway, Wiltshire envelops you suddenly. Silhouetted groups of trees clump together atop curving hills. The rolling land is stratified with circling sheep paths resembling multiple tidemarks. There is a strong resonance of the past from the Bronze Age. This ancient view changes as you take the motorway exit for Chippenham, a sprawling market town. Only one hundred miles from London, and not yet considered as commuter belt, Wiltshire made us feel as if we had immigrated to a mysterious country. In the 1970s there was still a farmers' market, regional butchers, greengrocers and even independent electrical shops—few brand stores. Pig farms seemed to be everywhere. Over the following years we sadly witnessed the endemic plague of shop franchises and multinationals spread their graphic goo across Chippenham, until it slowly became the same as anywhere else. The demise of independent traders also struck many blows against regional produce and culinary traditions. In parallel to this the green movement produced the first organic produce shop we had seen, Harvest Natural Foods, which opened in nearby Bath. It's still there. As with other alternative shops at that time, they had a holistic approach to retail. In a tall elegant Georgian shop, Harvest was as much an information center as somewhere to buy tubs of organic peanut butter, the likes of which we had never tasted before, deep and nutty, not too sweet. Harvest also sold journals, newspapers and books. This relaxed, multifaceted approach is something larger chain stores now try to emulate, resulting in a dull ersatz experience. Retailtainment! A great loss to our food landscape was the closure of all the Wiltshire bacon factories, including the C & T Harris bacon factory in Calne. Pigs had long been driven in droves from Ireland to London through Wiltshire and there are references to "old" Wiltshire bacon from 1794. The Harris family had patented the Wiltshire Cure, a sweet-tasting, low-salt bacon cured in brine without added water. Harris, after visiting America in 1847, brought back the idea of cooling the factory with ice, which enabled year-round production, and also reduced the salt required, creating a milder taste. Harris also made the spectacular treacle-cured Bradenham Ham. Thankfully workers from both Harris and the Royal Wilts Bacon factory in Chippenham found employment with local farms such as Sandridge Farm in Bromham. Sandridge Farm rear their own pigs for bacon and ham to cure the local way.

A constant reminder of the price-driven food-buying habits of Britain engulfed the center of our neighboring village, Sutton Benger. Behind an unassuming set of metal gates stretched the multiple barns of a sprawling abattoir for battery chickens that was fed daily by long white lorries. Driving into Chippenham we would encounter lumbering juggernauts racked with squalid cages of squawking birds. Following these leviathans of greed, my mother occasionally spotted a chicken fall out on the road ahead, dazed but alive. She would pull over quickly, jump out, throw the bird in the back of the Land Rover and take it home to introduce to our growing flock.

LOCAL SPECIALITY

Viewing as we did the demise of so much culinary heritage in Wiltshire, I wonder why I find regional food so important and mourn it when it vanishes. What makes certain food regional? The book *Traditional Foods of Britain* by Laura Mason and Catherine Brown (Prospect Books—if you have a deep interest in food buy all their books!), published the findings of a report on regional food in Britain. The report used a 1992 European Parliament directive as a guide. The directive allows food producers to register products with geographical names if they can show that their region of origin bestows special characteristics on the product. There are two levels of classification: PDO—Protected Denomination of Origin; and PGI—Protected Geographical Indicators of supply.

Legal protection of name and location is something the wine trade has propagated for centuries. The ancient Romans set wine production areas geographically. Laws were passed in France in 1936 for their *appellation d'origine contrôlée*, and in Italy in 1963 for DOC, *Denominazione di Origine Controllata* (Denomination of Controlled Origin). *The Traditional Foods of Britain* lists 396 products in a single volume; the French version runs to 26 volumes (size not specified). To qualify for inclusion, foods with regional association had to pass four tests: (1) region; (2) history—three generations; i.e., 25 years times three; (3) savoir faire—specific knowledge required to make the product; (4) marketing it to the public. The French have a term used in viticulture, *terroir*, that goes some way to describe an inimitable regional product, what the wine critic Matt Kramer calls "somewhereness." *Terroir* is a good subject to provoke heated discussion between lovers of wine. A shifting description of ecological factors that form the character of land, climate and vegetation specific to one region, vineyard or row of vines—and also the winemaker's art. The soil is considered to hold

a vineyard's soul, yet some studies look to the geological strata below to understand a region's true *terroir*. The *terroir* of Burgundy is supposed to impart a particularly strong influence on its wines—shining through regardless of maker. I discovered an Australian website that offers a geological survey to assess the viticultural suitability of your land, enabling you to pair it with specific grape varieties. However, the effect of *terroir* alone on a wine might produce a great wine only every eight years. Some wine commentators would add vignerons and winemakers to a definitive equation of *terroir*.

The discussion of *terroir* in food production is problematic since each case throws up its own quirks and anomalies. Regional food and culinary customs remain important because they are a collective communal expression of a location from the lives of the people who have lived there. Like sourdough starter, such customs and products need to be nurtured, keeping a part of their past in the present—without which they fail. In Wiltshire many recipes and products were inextricably linked to the locality, such as lardy cake. Its prime ingredient was the lard produced by hundreds of local pig farms. The French have been accused of being protectionist as Europe integrates. They have elevated their rural traditions, especially food, bolstering the regional collective identity to a point where they are often reconstructing their own past. If only the British had been so clever. Hopefully it's not too late.

POTS AND PLANS

Being thrown in at the deep end is a sound tactic for learning something fast. When I was 14 and 15, my sister Anna and I spent two summers gardening and cooking for ourselves, watched over by our grandmother. Our parents and sister Sophy were in Italy. During the day school routines continued at Hardenhuish in Chippenham; a pink and white Hatts coach took us home to cook supper for ourselves. Daily chores included stoking the Aga with coal, feeding chickens and some light gardening. Mr. Love, the butcher, delivered meat twice a week. Through the front door he came, stamping across the flagstone hall, whistling to let us know it was only him, and placing the delivery directly in our fridge in the back hall. Chops, mincemeat, bits of steak, chickens and bacon. By July the vegetable garden could have supplied a small grocery store. Additional food cupboard items were bought either at the village shop or on Saturday bicycle trips to Chippenham. I began to make beer, which I either bottled or added to a large oak barrel outside the kitchen door. The wine cupboard was full with last season's vintages from the garden. Aged 14 it was liberating to plan, prepare, cook and eat our own meals. School friends often came over—we squeezed a record player next to the bread box so we could listen to Roxy Music and David Bowie

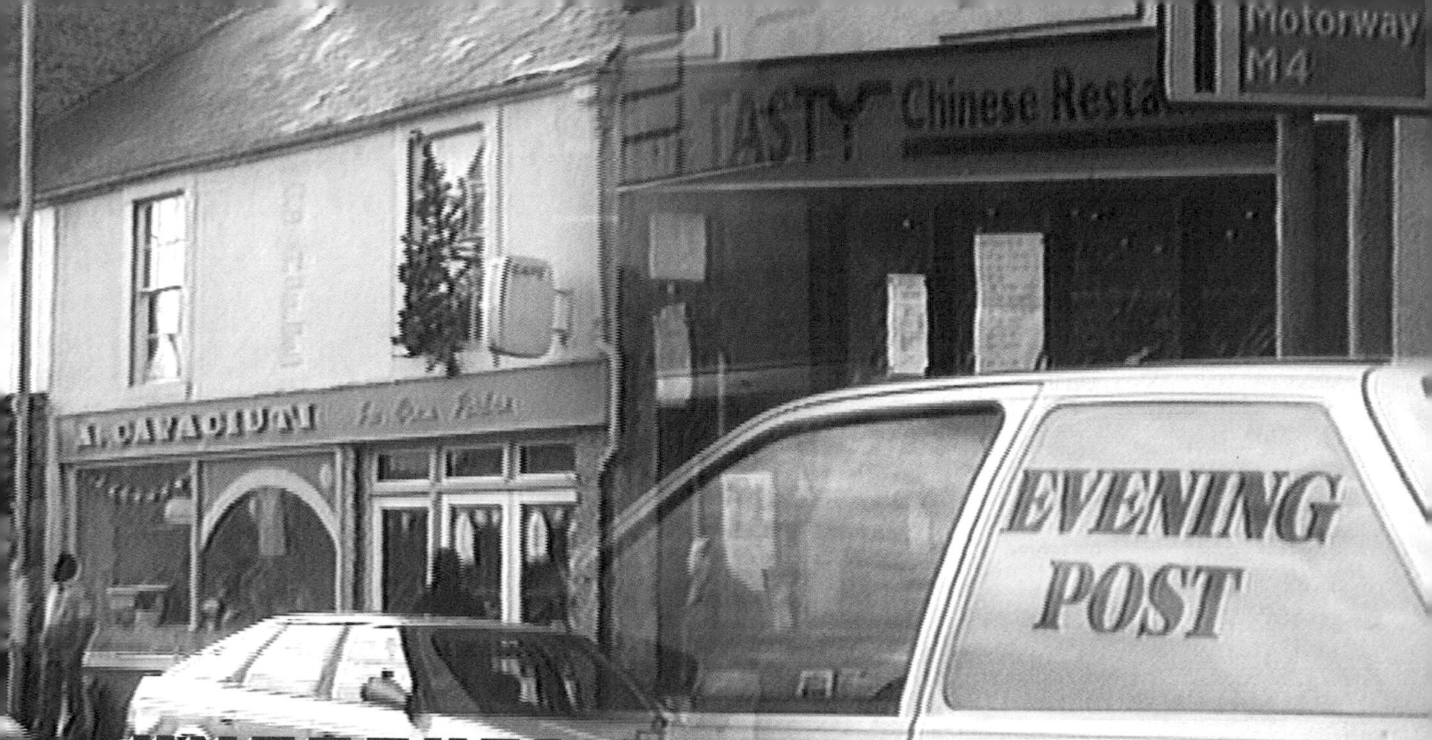

UNCOOKED CHOCOLATE CAKE

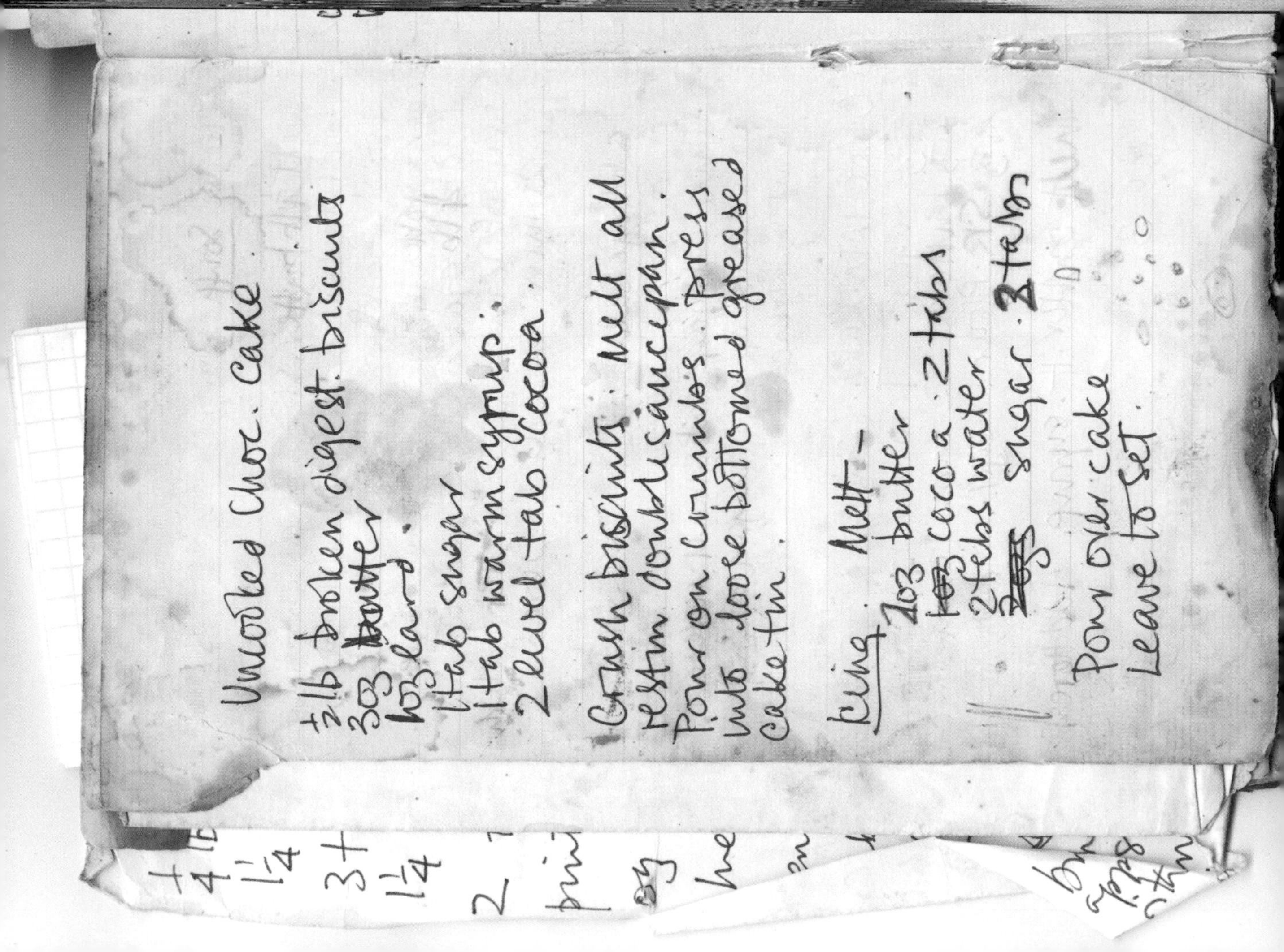

Uncooked Choc. Cake

½ lb broken digest. biscuits
3oz butter
1oz lard
1 tab sugar
1 tab warm syrup
2 level tab Cocoa

Crush biscuits. Melt all
rstm double saucepan.
Pour on crumbs. Press
into loose bottomed greased
cake tin.

Icing. Melt —
2oz butter
½ coco a . 2 tbs
2 tbs water
2oz Sugar . 3 tabs

Pour over cake
Leave to set.

while we cooked. Heaven (this was pre-Walkman). I lugged our mammoth rented television set through to the kitchen, but the reception was lousy. We froze cartons of yoghurt as a trial dessert, aiming for a spoonable consistency. One large meal went terribly wrong, with everyone suffering a bout of food poisoning. I had the leftovers tested by Sainsbury's customer services. They found the problem to be the canned tomatoes—the metal date-stamp had pierced the can. For years afterward I checked cans until they replaced metal stamping with a permanent ink. A great deal of experimental cooking was attempted in our teenage kitchen as we grappled with how to cook, use cookbooks and plan weeks of meals. There were many mistakes— overseasoned, bizarre mixtures. Food also crept in as a subject matter for art at this point: I painted and drew as well as chopped and stirred. A rock band I was in, Saffron, would practice in my bedroom, so we fed Martin, Steve, Jeff and Louis too. Anna and I had to keep our own bedroom fires lit and did our own laundry and sheets. Chopping, stacking and wheeling in firewood was a continual job in the winter. Occasionally some floor sweeping was done but we had a rather bohemian notion of dusting—we just didn't do it. Unlike the grime of city dust, country dust seemed to reach a certain thickness and then stop.

My mother was recently re-reading her diaries. Large numbers of guests ate with us at least three times a week, often more. Growing, shopping and cooking were done on a large scale. Cooking wasn't taught at school, although my two sisters did cook as part of home economics. Our kitchen skills were learnt from watching and helping our mother. To be almost expelled from school for cooking must be rare. My friend Louis and I climbed the thin branches of a crabapple tree outside the headmaster's office window. The apples were cleared by ground staff and thrown away otherwise—at best a few birds might get some. We made crabapple jelly with the bagfuls we took home. Unfortunately our clambering had been witnessed; luckily the headmaster let us off— punishment was to hand over a single jar of the beautiful pale red jelly to him. He complained it was rather cloudy. Cheek! Other school friends were equally interested in food. A great friend, Jeff Bateman, talked of our opening a restaurant. This was partly due to the severe lack of restaurants in Chippenham—it seemed sensible to open our own. White-tiled fish and chip shops dotted the town alongside cafés such as Cavacuiti's. However, for a three-course sit-down meal in a wood-lined room with a full array of cutlery and after-dinner drinks I went with school friends to The Jolly Huntsman on New Road. It had all the characteristics of what children's comics call a nosh-up meal. I ate a heavily garnished trout armed with French beans and French fries, dessert would have involved cream, we drank port after dinner and smokers indulged in thin cigars. We drank wine with our meal, but being teenagers probably downed a few pints of brown ale beforehand. If the food wasn't Relais Routier quality, the event still conjured up a sense of occasion and bon viveur. Eating out in public with peers was rare, an art to be mastered when becoming a student. Sadly a lone Indian takeaway arrived shortly after I had left home for college.

OTHER MOTHER COOKS

Observing and helping in home cooking is often a tangential influence. Apart from my mother's cooking, there were three other significant cooks, Betsy Smith, Ela Machnik and Julia Hodgkin. Dick and Betsy are my godparents, and lived nearby in East Tytherton in a vast old schoolhouse. Dick's painting studio, a low lying wooden classroom, stretched out from their house in an elegant L shape. A flurry of small outbuildings full of gardening paraphernalia behind the house led to a long, expertly tended vegetable garden humming with pristine produce destined for Betsy's kitchen.

As a teenager I missed out on Betsy's French haute-cuisine-inspired dinner parties but instead tasted her American festive cooking at Thanksgiving and Halloween. Betsy is American and made mouthwatering hamburgers that were wonderful, loose, open meaty affairs—not the hard rubbery patty variety. To achieve this she was the only patron of Reg Love & Son Butchers in Chippenham to ask for her prime steak to be minced. Betsy tells me that English butchers made hamburgers with beef scraps, lights, and melts—ground twice with a medium blade—producing a horrid mess that stuck to your hands as you tried to form a hamburger. Betsy persuaded Love's to buy a fine blade and mince skirt, flank or prime to make her hamburgers. Reg Love was equally pleased with the results. Her burgers were served with real Boston baked beans, tasting dark and rich. It was an otherworldly experience. Betsy would go to Love's on Mondays to buy offal for pig's liver pâté, or faggots (a type of uncooked sausage). Mr. Love found the caul fat for her—as she says, Chippenham was the country's best meat market. They would grind up the liver, bellies and other pig parts for her, and would then clean out the whole grinder on Monday nights. As well as Dorothy Hartley, Betsy cites *British Cookery* by Theodora Fitzgibbon as being an influential book. She also recalls Caroline Conran's excellent *Poor Cook*, showing how to cook cheap cuts of meat. It's a book I still use. By the time the paperback came out the wording had changed to buy these cheap cuts before they became unavailable.

School friends' mothers provide an informal view of kitchens in action. My friend Louis lived in a tall stone mill at Lower Long Dean surrounded by steep oak and elm woodland, green pastures and a fast-flowing river crammed with delicious crayfish.

His mother was Julia Hodgkin, married to the painter Howard Hodgkin. Julia cooked in the style of my mother—albeit with a Provençal influence, because the Hodgkins often spent summers in France, had kitchen cupboards full of French crockery and Louis and his brother Sam had been to the French-speaking *lycée* in London. The keen eye of their friend Terence Conran needed only a glimpse into his friends' kitchen drawers full of market-bought implements from small European towns for them to surface in the kitchen department of his new shop Habitat. I know some people who would hide a certain item they had discovered in an Alsace or Umbrian hardware store for fear of finding it in the King's Road Habitat the following week. That outward big-bang retail explosion seems to have reached the outer Pacific rim by now. You can buy almost anything anywhere. I conducted a test after finding a particular parmesan grater on a market stall in Cortona, Italy. I kept watch on kitchen shops and culinary catalogues. It took about five years for the grater to make it into the U.K. Cucina Direct catalogue.

Our extended family of lodgers sometimes added three extra busy kitchens from which to observe and assimilate kitchen skills. The house resembled a small grow-and-cook culinary school at times as everyone had vegetable plots in the garden. Every now and then a house meal for fourteen would be arranged, dishes brought from all kitchens. At Christmas all three kitchens went into action to feed a table of twenty. Tasks like plucking pheasants were made easier with so many hands. We worked at the long kitchen table, a heady gamey aroma brought on by the heat of the low-slung lamps hovering above the discarded feathers. Watching and helping art students cook, eat and drink gives an eighteen-year-old many ideas—I was about to be a student myself. Advance fieldwork. Ela and her partner Mac, both students at the local Corsham art school, used the kitchen next to ours and were great cooks and hosts. My sisters and I sometimes ate with them after a walk to the local pub in Foxham. Ela's parents were Polish, so I observed how ancestry affected the way she cooked. At Christmas she had to cook a twelve-course fish meal, to match the apostles, for her granny. She also cooked a wonderful Polish stew called *bigos*—a dish I learnt to cook as a student.

The other inseparable element that makes cooking so important is company and location. A great lesson to learn. Not just how to cook good food using local produce with the aid of complementary food writers, but to whom you serve it. How and why are just as important. A picnic attitude, relaxed and informal, a coming and going of dishes. The dinner table becomes the focus of your hospitality and conviviality, a place to convert strangers into friends.

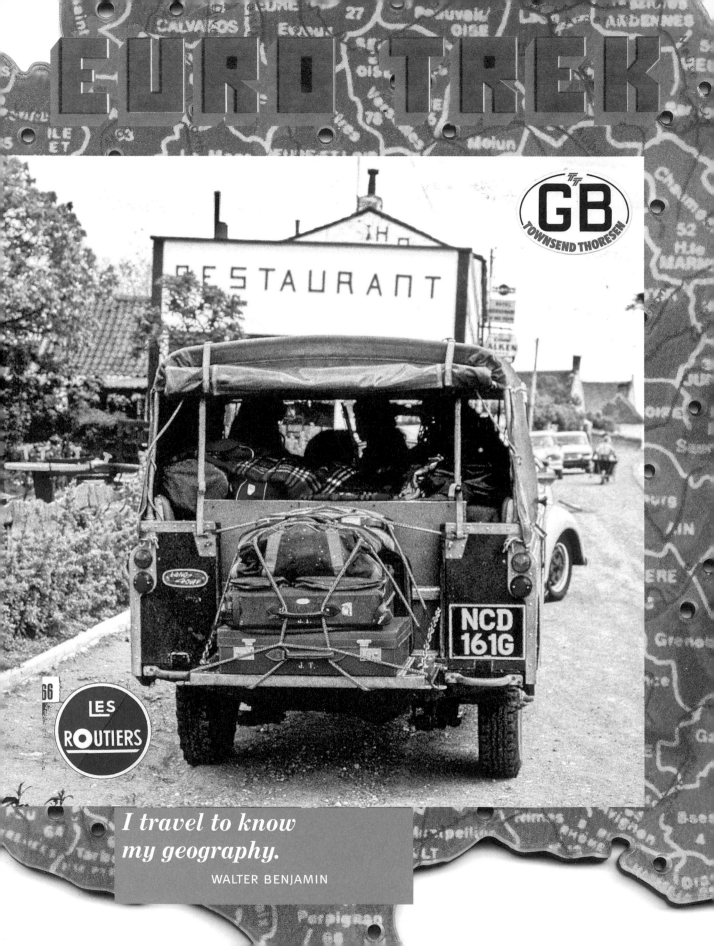

EURO TREK

GB
TOWNSEND THORESEN

RESTAURANT

NCD 161G

66

LES ROUTIERS

I travel to know my geography.

WALTER BENJAMIN

Holidays for our family were always an adventure—as much about traveling as arriving at a destination. An inseparable mixture of work and fun. Leaving 1960s Britain to travel through the heart of Europe was a gastronomic revelation. Regional food in France and Italy still flourished, untainted by international cuisine or the logo-food of fast-food multinationals. Coca-Cola had made some inroads, but otherwise everything was different and new. Mass tourism was in its infancy, menus were in the local language and didn't cater for what-I-eat-back-home palates. I definitely caught the travel bug from my parents. The potent virus was administered annually as we packed drifting piles of bags, tools, instruments and toys and filled up our Land Rover, leaving only two small spaces in the back for children to squeeze among shoulder-high mounds of luggage—Sophy sat up front with our parents. Even the tailgate was laden down with extra luggage, held in place by an elastic octopus strap. We set off for the ports of Folkestone or Dover, hoping for a smooth sea crossing. Aboard the Chantilly car ferry we would eat a last hideous breakfast of soggy toast and pallid coffee. Huddled on damp, salty bucket seats, we became slowly deafened by the shuddering rattle of racks of crockery and cutlery vibrating in time with the ship's engine.

We passed through the poppy fields of northern France, past local markets shaded with umbrellas and roadside truckers' restaurants with the magical Relais Routier signs serving *potage du jour* and local specialities. Dusty medieval town squares to maneuver through. Disused farm buildings facing the oncoming traffic on the elm-lined Roman roads still bearing brightly painted advertisements for coffee or colonial-sounding liqueurs. If the sky was clear we would shop for a picnic lunch bought from small town patisseries and boulangeries. The lack of motorways forced you to drive through each town. I could gauge where I was by the contents of my baguette—a particular cheese or cold cut of meat. From market stalls we bought seasonal fruit and vegetables in the Loire, Ardèche or perhaps in the Vosges. Hotels, pensions and auberges acted as punctuation, pauses en route. A small connection to the great travelers of last century. Somewhat utilitarian. A vague route was half the fun, not knowing where we would spend the night. As the afternoon wore on, we would be on the lookout for hotels or promising towns and villages ahead on the map. Changing geology might make us detour toward a likely looking gorge so we could enjoy hotel with food, with view. In the cool of the evening we usually ate in the hotel restaurant, three courses. Our route was marked out by the changing antipasti menu as we got closer to the sun, driving south. Often hotels would be full, expensive, or both, so we'd drive on, my mother still clutching the map as she gave a thumbs-up after surveying the pension's menu and rooms. But only once in fifteen years did the five of us sleep in

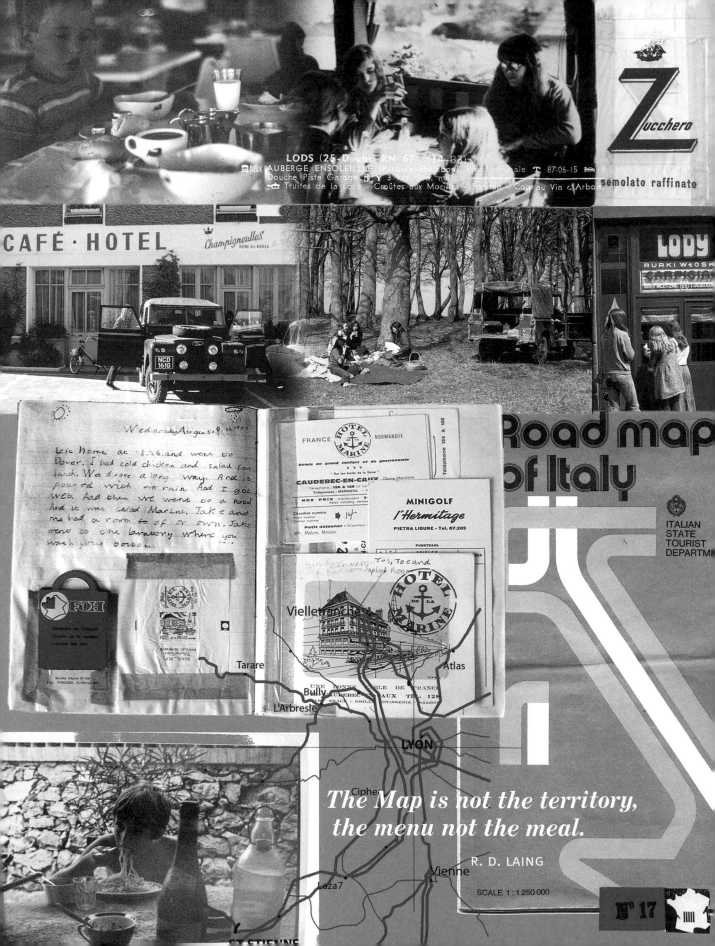

The Map is not the territory, the menu not the meal.

R. D. LAING

the Land Rover—it was on the beach in Cannes. I admire my parents' lack of planning. I don't know if I could travel across Europe, annually, with three children, not knowing there were multiple hotel rooms waiting for us booked in advance. It was an open-ended sense of exploration, even though the destination was set—Italy. Some years there would be a loose plan, such as visiting as many Romanesque churches as possible or a particular museum or artist's house—this created a seemingly erratic route on our dog-eared road maps.

The art historian Lucy Lippard notes that walking in a landscape or city allows a certain mental freedom which translates a place to a person kinesthetically. It unlocks a deeper understanding of the environment. Cycling offers a similar viewpoint. The passing ground is felt through the tires and saddle, your body feels physically connected to the space you are experiencing. Trapped in a ton of steel and glass, cars dull the senses, pacifying and excluding the speeding viewers from their landscape. Fortunately our open-topped Land Rover was rather like a motorized tent, letting in windswept views, smells, insects and all. The entire back section and side panels would roll up, leaving only the top roof for cover—we felt connected to the passing vistas and bumpy roads. Driving through the Camargue, we took off the canvas roof to reveal the aluminum frame of the car and the car became like a go-cart dodging dragonflies in the tall grasses. Each evening we would all contribute to that year's travel diary, adding whatever it was that interested us. This ritual is well described by Michael Compton in his book on my father, *Joe Tilson* (Thames & Hudson):

He and his family record in scrapbooks the places they have visited. They assemble words, dates, photographs and ephemera such as printed bills, menus, leaflets, and wrapping papers, all of them epitomising the imagery and character of a place and many asserting the continuity of its past and present. The travel itself may itself have the character of a family pilgrimage. It may include not only the contemporary, lay rituals of tourism, especially photography, but conscious atavistic rituals of marking, touching, consuming and libation. The making of the scrapbook too, has its rather cheerful element of ritual. It may contain not only found images but the first sketches of works that will come out of it.

The progression of border controls culminated in that year's chosen route over or through the Alps. We would spend up to three months a year in Italy, shopping and cooking with an occasional visit to a beach.

APRONS & ASPIRINS

The Pauper's Cookbook
Jocasta Innes AIR MAIL

MorningFresh Mushrooms

BROOMWOOD ROAD S.W.

SAXA SALT

No one teaches students how to shop but you'll probably get a few cookbooks as presents for your first solo kitchen. I received *The Pauper's Cookbook*, by Jocasta Innes, Elizabeth David's *Italian Food*, Claudia Roden's *A Book of Middle Eastern Food* and Kenneth Lo's *Chinese Food*—I still use them today. For Christmas I asked for a wok and in teenage fashion was annoyed that it lacked a lid. Typical. I shared my first student kitchen with friends of my parents. They were usually out so I cooked and ate alone. It was a large converted Victorian front room with broad bay windows, a gas cooker, small fridge, kitchen units and sofas. Cupboards to fill and a fridge shelf to call my own. I marked my provisions with territorial airmail stickers. Shopping for groceries must be an ability we attain through osmosis, an urban survival skill learnt from observing countless shopping ventures. On the lookout for mold and items that should be soft and not firm, or vice versa. A weekly trek to Shepherds Bush market provided carrier bags full of vegetables for experimentation aided by my new box of spices. Small convenience shops on the King's Road near college added canned foods and legumes to my concoctions. Being an art student helped legitimize the self-exploration I was undergoing as a teenager—and materialize it as actual exploration. Out into the city. Timber yards, bookshops, metal merchants and to Covent Garden market when it still sold fruit and vegetables. In the kitchen I cooked *bigos*—good bachelor food. I started a fresh batch most Sunday nights, adding new ingredients as the week progressed, refreshing it slightly, maybe an extra onion, a little more cabbage, a spiral sausage, or a glass of beer. The last plateful eaten with rye bread was always the best. Atrocious coleslaw was another speciality, with an onion-to-cabbage ratio of 50-50. Hanky inducing. It took an honest friend to make me seek out a decent recipe.

A student moving from flat to flat stumbles into new kitchens frequently. I suddenly found I was shopping at the same butcher my great-grandmother had used, Doves in Clapham. The kitchen and cooker in our small terraced house were probably similar to hers; we also found gaslights, carpet stair rods and an outside toilet. Student houses soon fill up with girlfriends, sisters and a stream of visitors—the joys of communal cooking returns. Food fanatic college days also opened up cheap restaurant eating in London, expanding our culinary horizons. Cypriot doner kebabs, Chinese soft-shell

crab, and idli, rasam and masala dosai from Kerala. To attempt some of these dishes at home we looked at cookbooks by Dharamjit Singh and Madhur Jaffrey to help us decode the wares on offer at local Indian markets in Tooting. A friend named Ruth showed me my first mortar and pestle full of fresh Indian spices bought in Brick Lane—black cardamom pods, cumin seeds, fresh curry leaves and coriander seeds. Grinding these spices filled the air suddenly with aromas from a spice warehouse. When they were toasted, I felt I could live off the wafting spicy vapors alone it was so heavenly. I had witnessed a conjuring trick, a gastronomic revelation.

In Clapham we planned the week's meals ahead, scouring recipe books for new ideas, and then actually created a shopping list—amazing. Our favorite pushcart at the Saturday market in Northcote Road provided seasonal vegetables, and having a butcher three minutes from the kitchen table was convenience itself—no need to store meat ourselves. The package store on the corner, owned by Young's Brewery, sold everlasting cans of Special or Regular bitter—which were in fact ludicrously large eight-pint cans—dangerous fuel for students.

Creative experimentation sneaked into our kitchens, which served up themed events, complete with fake menus, restaurant decorations and fittings found in Dumpsters or bought at my new favorite type of shop—a professional catering/restaurant suppliers, Dentons in Clapham. I enjoy any shop aimed at trade customers, goods on display, no hard sell, but for me a restaurant supplier is like a toy shop to a child, full of unadulterated wonder. My brain short-circuits contemplating the endless possibilities. There were World Cup parties, Beef Fest, Moroccan Feasts, Burns Night and the annual 3 Bears Barbecue hosted by myself, Bruce and Ed. The back garden was kitted out with a fake porch-style environment of old telephones, real fridges, homemade barbecue and a crackling television, all relocated for 12 hours under a huge tarpaulin in case of rain. To share our enthusiams further, I set up a literary arts magazine, *Cipher*, with a fellow student and friend, Stephen Whitaker. Issue 5 provided an outlet for our food passions with a cooking supplement—recipes commissioned from the novelist David Plante, Nikos Stangos, food writer Paul Levy and other artist friends. Local legend tells of one fateful year in which thousands of City workers received massive end-of-year bonuses. They all bought houses in Clapham, every last one of them, a yuppie invasion. The secondhand shops became wine bars and bistros. The understocked corner shop became a pretentious burger bistro. On Saturday nights the lights in their conservatory extension flashed as the drunken crowd sang "Jerusalem"; the restaurant was aptly named the Inebriated Newt—themed sauces and microwaved buns. Abysmal. It was time to move.

BIGOS POLISH HUNTER'S STEW

A rich stew, best eaten a few days or even a week after cooking. The pot of *bigos* is added to and eaten from throughout the week. As a student, having a waiting pot of *bigos* in my fridge saved me from raiding the corner kebab shop too often. The perfect dish for cooks who like to tinker with recipes.

A great dish for a student to learn on too, there being no right way to make it, and there will always be something in the fridge to add and eat at the end of a day—achieved quickly. After time you'll discover whether you're a 3-day-*bigos* person or, like me, a 5-day-*bigos* person. When making *bigos,* make sure you have enough to last a few meals. The tastes develop after a few reheatings and mature well. The must-have ingredients are cabbage and sauerkraut—to which can be added many variations of sausage and bits of meat. A fruit element is important to the flavor, as is a little alcohol. In a local Lithuanian shop I found both *dzuku uzkanda,* hot smoked pork, and kielbasa pork sausages. In Poland, *bigos* was stored in stoneware pots or wooden casks for traveling.

SERVES 4, WITH LEFTOVERS

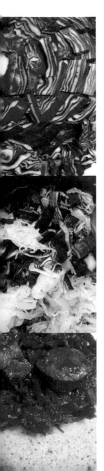

2 tablespoons thinly sliced dried mushrooms

4 handfuls chopped or shredded red cabbage

4 handfuls sauerkraut, chopped

1 cup chicken stock, or as needed

2 large onions, finely chopped

2 tablespoons butter

3 handfuls cubed, trimmed smoked ham, (trim off the skin, leave the fat)

3 smoked pork sausages, sliced

10 pitted prunes

2 tart apples, cored and chopped

1/2 cup red wine

Salt and pepper to taste

Sugar (optional)

Boil the dried mushrooms in a small pan of water for 10 minutes; drain and put aside. Combine the cabbage, sauerkraut and stock in a large pot and simmer gently. Meanwhile, sauté the onions in the butter until golden. Add the onions, mushrooms and all the other ingredients to the cooking cabbage. Stir gently and leave to simmer for 40 minutes. Some cooks like to add a little sugar. Keep an eye on it and stir occasionally—extra stock may be needed. Serve with large slices of rye bread. Resist the temptation to eat it all at once—save some for later in the week.

Pot au feu in Paris, 1980.

BONJOUR CHEF

For a young person, developing a culinary obsession when living abroad for the first time is like white-water canoeing. A bombardment of the senses. After college I spent a gluttonous cinematic year in Paris; shopping, cooking, writing and going to afternoon movies—rather decadent. My train pulled into Gare du Nord on *est arrivé* day. Beaujolais nouveau poured into heavy *ballon* glasses from barrels hastily propped outside wine shops along every boulevard—what a welcome. The cavernous, Art Nouveau eating halls I had eaten in with my parents were beyond the francs in my pocket, so no more clattering plates of *escargots* or steaming *coq au vin*. Instead I turned colonial, Algerian and Réunion cuisine. Living at first in the Hotel Telemaque in Montparnasse without a kitchen, I learned the delicate art of urban eating. Being 25 took care of surplus calories. College friend Bruce Johnson, German sculptor Uli Lindow and I slowly ate our way round the local restaurants: French, Algerian, Vietnamese, Korean and Japanese. Many had terrazzo floors, treacle-colored woodwork, nicotine walls, dangling luminescent globe lighting, aprons, cigar smoke, unfussy tableware and utilitarian furniture—all good gastronomic ware. The

backstreet couscous restaurants we habituated were like community meeting rooms, as much part of the street as part of a building, an atmosphere permeated with cumin, preserved lemon and frying briks. Although I have eaten couscous in Tangiers and Fez, I tend to prepare and serve it backstreet Parisian style. I practiced cooking the dish in Paris on an extended invitation to share the kitchen and flat of my friend Tony Alcock, a specialist decorator. I would shop and cook between writing and going to the cinema while he was out at work on a chateau in the suburbs. Nearby Montparnasse had a regular outdoor food market. At first I mistook it for a film set from a regional French town; in fact, it was real and you could shop there. The local supermarket Eno stocked mainly French ingredients as did Chez Ed, with its plain wholesale-style approach. Small Algerian and Tunisian shops sold me tinned harissa, couscous grains, merguez sausages and the North African spices I needed to practice with. Young French friends in Paris were fanatical about their food and cared greatly about what they cooked—this was a shock coming from 1970s London. Many were not Parisian and exhibited pride in regional dishes from their home provinces. They ate in restaurants in a casual, unfussy way. When shopping they bought ingredients rather than meals, pointing out a distinctive cheese or a special cut of meat from back home. They would ignore several inferior pâtisseries en route to their preferred baker's baguette. If a friend is traveling back from Paris I still request a baguette and croissant. It's worth meeting them off Eurostar to sample the bread fresh.

DON'T GO TO ANY TROUBLE BACKSTREET COUSCOUS

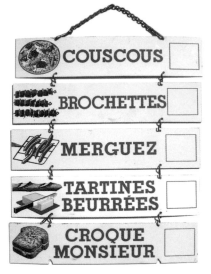

COUSCOUS

BROCHETTES

MERGUEZ

TARTINES BEURRÉES

CROQUE MONSIEUR

A dish that encourages interpretation and invention. I assemble mine with the assimilated memories of smoke-filled Tunisian restaurants in Paris and three memorable meals in a frenzied visit to Morocco in my youth. In Paris they tend toward the separation of the meat from the stew. This becomes an inspiring triad of tastes and texture—soft, dry couscous, crisp roast meat, accompanied by the wet vegetable stew. *Couscous* is the name for both the semolina pasta and the dish itself. Serve with roasted meat, chicken, lamb, fish or sausages.

SERVES 8

5 carrots, sliced into rounds

5 zucchini, sliced into rounds

3 onions, roughly chopped

3 large cabbage leaves, shredded

3 cups canned chickpeas

2½ cups of chicken stock

3 cloves garlic, chopped

3 tablespoons of tomato paste and/or
  one 14-ounce can of tomatoes, crushed,
  with their liquid

spices

1 cinnamon stick

1 teaspoon ground cumin

1 teaspoon ground coriander

1 teaspoon ground ginger

1 teaspoon ground cumin

10 saffron threads

15 sprigs fresh cilantro, tied in a bunch

15 sprigs fresh parsley, tied in a bunch

Vegetable stew—quick method

To achieve a backstreet Parisian-Tunisian-style vegetable stew, adopt a nonchalant approach. Put all the ingredients in a large pan, cover with water and simmer for 30 minutes. Done. Serve with the couscous and roasted or grilled meats.

Variations

You could add the harder root or other vegetables first and the softer ones toward the end of cooking for a more consistent bite. Some cooks first sauté the spices, onions and garlic until the onions are translucent, before adding the remaining ingredients. The key items are carrots, zucchini and chickpeas. Improvise with endive, shredded cabbage, diced squash or even a cut-up stray potato.

Couscous

I use a medium whole-grain couscous from our local Iranian store. Barley couscous is also good, with a nutty flavor. I use a quick method for preparing the couscous taught to me by a Parisian friend. A medium-grain couscous is easier to cook than fine.

SERVES 8

2 cups medium-grain couscous
Pinch of saffron threads (optional)
Salt

1 tablespoon butter
30 golden raisins for garnish

Put the couscous into a bowl with a few strands of saffron, if desired, and a little salt. Gently pour boiling water onto the couscous until the water just breaks the surface of the grains; do not stir. Leave to soak for 20 minutes. Melt the butter in a large frying pan. The bowl of soaked couscous will appear to be a solid mass. With a fork, gently plow the top layer of grains off into the hot buttered pan. Gradually loosen all of the grains into the pan. Heat through, stirring with a flat-ended wooden spoon or spatula, for a few minutes. You can also cover the pan and reheat later.

Heap the cooked couscous in a pyramid on a warmed round plate and dot a ring of raisins around the edges.

Accompaniment

Any roasted meat or fish forms the final point of the couscous triad. Country chicken (page 76), *agnello scottadito* (page 59) without the sage. Merguez sausages, grilled fish or fried sardines. A leg of lamb rubbed with cumin, coriander and a teaspoon of harissa, then roasted on a bed of outer cabbage leaves sprinkled with caraway seeds. A *couscous royale* in Paris is a mixed platter of chicken, lamb and merguez.

To serve

Transfer the stew to a deep serving bowl. Each plate requires a heap of couscous, meat and a ladle of vegetable stew. Throughout the meal, the couscous seems never to diminish on your plate if replenished with enough liquid stew.

FRESH HARISSA

A search for a lost taste and texture I remember from a small, hot and crowded streetside restaurant in Tangiers. I only ate one meal there, but the harissa sauce that accompanied the couscous almost made me extend my stay in Morocco. Harissa originated in Tunisia and is also used in Libya and Algeria, as a condiment and an ingredient. The canned or tube variety produced in Tunisia is smooth and powerful, but there was a looser, grittier desert taste in my Moroccan memory. Recipes for harissa seem to swing between North African traditional and European bistro. I bought 12 large Kenyan chiles in Brighton and had a jar of roasted piquillo peppers in the cellar from an inquisitive shopping trip. Hidden in my chile rack I found a can of smoked Spanish paprika, so I was set. I made two sauces with variants on the ingredients and methods. It does take a while, so make extra for the freezer. Keeps well in the fridge for days too.

SERVES 8; WITH A FREEZER BAG, FOR 4

7 ounces large, long red chiles
4 cloves garlic, chopped
Olive oil
1 teaspoon ground coriander
2 teaspoons ground caraway seeds
1 tablespoon plus 1 teaspoon tomato paste
1 teaspoon ground cumin

1 teaspoon cumin seeds
2 teaspoons Spanish smoked paprika, hot or sweet
1 large roasted red pepper, preferably a piquillo pepper
Splash of red wine vinegar

Use rubber gloves to handle the chiles. Slit each chile lengthwise in half and scrape away the seeds and ridged veins. Roughly chop the chiles and garlic, then pureé in a food processor until smooth, adding a little olive oil. Remove half of the mixture to a bowl to make Harissa 1.

Harissa 1—Traditional North African
Add a teaspoon each ground coriander, ground caraway, tomato paste, water and olive oil to the puréed chiles. This produces a fiery, simple, yet elegant harissa.

Harissa 2—European
Toast 1 teaspoon each ground caraway and ground cumin in a small dry skillet and add to the food processor containing the remaining chile mixture. Add 1 teaspoon ground coriander, the Spanish paprika and the roasted pepper. Blend well. Transfer to a bowl. Add 1 tablespoon tomato purée, the red wine vinegar and 3 tablespoons olive oil. This makes a piquant, sweet and smoky-tasting sauce positioned somewhere off the Straits of Gibraltar, where the salty Atlantic Ocean meets the calmer Mediterranean.

JUDGING BY THE ACRES OF SHELF SPACE DEVOTED TO
FRENCH COOKING, THE GASTRONOMIC WORLD HAS
LOVED FRANCE FOR CENTURIES. PROFESSIONAL CHEFS
SEEM TO BE DRAWN LIKE SHEEP TO FRENCH COOKING—
PERHAPS IT'S THE STRICTNESS AND STRUCTURE
INVOLVED. ALMOST MATHEMATICAL. I PREFER A MORE
DOMESTIC TOUCH, WHERE MEASUREMENT IS DONE BY
EYE OR HANDFUL AND IS NOT CRITICAL TO A DISH'S
OUTCOME. ALTHOUGH I WAS LUCKY ENOUGH TO DINE
AT MICHELIN-STAR TABLES AND ART NOUVEAU GEMS
IN PARIS, OUR TRAVELS IN FRANCE WERE JUST THAT,
TRAVELS—ALWAYS EN ROUTE TO ITALY. FOR SOMEONE
OBSESSED WITH COOKING, AS WELL AS EATING,
INFLUENCES AROSE FROM WATCHING PEOPLE COOK.
IT WAS IN ITALY WHERE I SPENT TIME ASSIMILATING
THE KITCHENS OF ARTISTS, WRITERS, BUILDERS AND
FARMERS. FOR HOME-COOKED FOOD MAYBE YOU NEED
TO DECIDE ON WHICH SIDE OF THE ALPS YOUR BREAD
IS BUTTERED—MINE IS DEFINITELY TOWARD AOSTA,
TO ITALY, AND SO TO OIL RATHER THAN BUTTER.

Seppie in umido—squid stewed in red wine.

Light and Dark

TUSCANY

A FARMHOUSE KITCHEN IN A HIDDEN VALLEY

FOR THIRTY YEARS A RUSTIC FARMHOUSE DEEP IN CHESTNUT WOODLAND HAS PROVIDED A FAMILY HOME IN WHICH TO COOK AND EAT. OPEN HEARTH COOKING AND AN OUTDOOR WOOD STOVE. RECIPES ARE DICTATED BY LOCAL MARKETS AND NEIGHBORS' SURPLUS, PROMPTING AN IMPROVISED CUISINE UNHINDERED BY URBAN DISTRACTIONS.

§ Cucina Toscana

The home-cooked food we experience during childhood has a profound effect on what we choose to cook for ourselves as we become providers. Recollections abound: what we ate, where our parents shopped, which recipe books they read, how food was prepared and cooked—even how they served it. Travel also has a strong influence on a young cook. Revisiting the same country, town or village you observe culinary customs, perhaps over decades. Add to this a second home abroad and the gastronomic influences multiply exponentially. To fully enjoy a foreign home requires integration with the community. My sisters and I were lucky to have parents who were steeped in everything Italian. In 1949, our father, Joe, had hitchhiked around Italy amid the ruins of World War II. After winning the Prix de Rome for painting, he lived and worked in Italy. There he met our mother, Jos, who was studying sculpture at the Brera in Milan. In 1956 they lived in Cefalù, Sicily, and then moved to Giudecca in Venice, where they were married at the Comune Palazzo on the Grand Canal. Since then, half their professional careers has revolved around Italy. Joe represented Britain in the XXXII Venice Biennale in 1964. Thirty-two years on, in 1996, he painted the winner's banner for the Palio, the great Sienese horse race, won that year by the *Bruco* contrada. Italian neighbors came to see the painted banner in his studio; for them it was a holy object. In Siena the banner had been blessed in the Duomo, witnessed by a football crowd of cheering Sienese. Family holidays in the 1960s and 70s had been spent driving up and down the length of Italy eating in *rosticcerias* and visiting museums and churches. When I was eleven we bought a remote farmhouse on the border of Tuscany and Umbria, at the end of a steep logging road near Cortona, and settled in. With my sisters, Anna and Sophy, we spent summer months there in the mountain heat. Electricity eventually reached the valley in the mid-1970s, there wasn't a regular water supply and the road required four-wheel drive so our early visits were rather basic. We would spend our days clearing back a year's growth from ivy-covered walls and along woodland paths. Grapevines required tying back, fruit needed to be gathered, trees pruned, shutters oiled and hinges greased against bitter winters. Living half the year there, my parents made the slow transition over thirty years from stranger to tourist and from visitor to becoming locals. Our family roots in rural Tuscany extended out across the rural Apennines into humid medieval piazzas, to the shifting Italian art world of Milan, Venice, Imola and beyond.

Now I visit with my wife and daughter. Italian gastronomy has crept into my heart. Continual visits to the Mediterranean and watching Italians cooking and eating helps focus my kitchen and reset my palate, steering culinary explorations in new directions. The workaholic routines of middle age have limited our recent stays to a few precious

Sophy, Jake and Anna cooking lunch, 1977. 1976. Girarrosto—a clockwork roasting spit. Trivets and other hearthside cooking implements we found in our house.

summer weeks. Becoming parents has shifted our household contribution to cooking. Rather than read a novel or sit by a pool, which we don't have, I'd rather spend an absurd amount of time shopping, preparing and cooking food. A full day's work eaten in minutes—bliss. More than anywhere else, this is where I have shared the family obsession with food and have cooked side by side with my mother and father for decades, without the teenage distractions of an English household—no television, school or friends (although some teenage distractions were portable).

They have created a setting that is both holiday and home—also a place for work, with studios. A home for well-thumbed cookbooks to be used. Many of the books are written by neighbors. Anthropologists looking back at our small rural idyll will have at least four books I know of to help reconstruct forty years in the life of our small village. Nancy Harmon Jenkins's wonderful and evocative book *Flavors of Tuscany* (Broadway Books) is in part a chronicle of our farming neighbors—the magnificent Antolinis—whom we grew up with. Burton Anderson wrote one of the first in-depth studies of Italian wine there, *Vino: The Wine and Winemakers of Italy* (Little Brown). *Before the Palio* (Arti Tipografiche) by Martin Attwood includes a memorable description of how local farmers prepare and roast whole pigs stuffed with fennel plants and garlic—creating the spectacular *porchetta*, sliced and eaten in buns. There must be a literary bug in the local wine, or in the *porchetta*.

A kitchen with a view §

Arriving tired from work and travel I step into the stone coolness of our house, smelling the warmth of cedar wood from a table made thirty years ago. I stumble out through the kitchen door toward the edge of the piazzale and renew the visual imprint of a special mountain. The paw-shaped mountain is imprinted on my mind from long days spent looking. I have drawn it, painted it, walked on it and cooked on it. Like a degenerated image I notice slight changes. A distant stretch of forest felled, taller willow trees sway up into mid-ground, nearby oaks now obscure the edge of my vista. The deep, inner peace of the mountain remains. It appears near enough to eat.

It is late August, and we're hampered on our foraging mountain walks by kamikaze horseflies and housebound by the midday sun. Arriving a month earlier, the scene is different. Flowers, insects, birds and spring food linger. But to see a bird beyond breakfast is rare. Like a beached ship our terra-cotta-roofed farmhouse appears caught in the embrace of a giant cherry tree set in swaying woodland. The stone farmhouse is built for rural survival—keeping warm and staying fed. There was a large outdoor

Roasting chickens outdoors on Monte Ginezzo. Roasting chickens indoors at home on a girarrosto.

bread oven, a room stained black from years of chestnut smoking, open hearths for cooking, ground floor stabling for animals and a *cantina* for storing produce. Swifts' nests set into the façade of the house were once accessed from inside, to take the young for eating. Radiating out from the house were pigsties. Wild boar and porcupines eat the fallen nuts, porcini grow in the speckled shade. In thirty-five years nature has slowly encroached over unfarmed terraces, extending the woodland with unbroken tracts of dense cover. Local farmers grow olives, grapes and, recently, tobacco. They all have extensive kitchen gardens, expertly tended, constantly watered and fenced off against the wildlife. We found the old Roman vine system still intact on our land, rows of field maples with grapevines growing over them. The mountainside is a wild, untended larder to which we have added a few items but leave to their own devices. Within a hundred yards of the kitchen door are wild fennel, six types of cherry, walnuts, hazelnuts, olives, greengages, pears, apples, six types of fig, *susini* (wild plums), blackberries, pomegranates, elderberries, cardoons, mushrooms, chestnuts, wild mint, sage, oregano, bay, rosemary and four grape varieties. We tried growing potatoes and root vegetables in the early years but the *cinghiali* and *istrici*— wild boar and porcupines—got to them first.

A house built for food production and surrounded by ingredients begs to be cooked in. During the heat of the day an Italian kitchen is the only place to be. The fabric of the house hasn't been altered greatly and so it's still kept cool by thick stone walls and half-closed shutters. It's a rustic kitchen, sparsely furnished with few implements and no gadgets except for an impossibly small food processor—with the capacity for a small pesto. A white metal cooker sits alone, fed by a gas bottle. Outside, a cook's view of the fig tree and mountain. Next to the cantina door rests a rickety marble-topped table with flaking wooden drawers. It's used for food preparation, storing bottles of olive oil, wooden spoons and produce about to be cooked. Above are shelves made from old book crates. A wood-burning range is ready for winter use as are the walk-in fireplaces upstairs in which we roast chickens on a clockwork spit. The agrarian fixtures and fittings of plate racks, *metti tutto* (dresser), *madia* (bread-making cupboard), benches, tables and chairs are all either original or made by my father and a local carpenter to complement what had been in the house. After thirty years they have all melded as one, it's hard to tell which bench was made thirty years ago or ninety. Outside is the summer kitchen, under a terra-cotta overhang and a canopy of pine trees. A simple wood-fired stove flanked by deep stone lintels on which to chop and place trays brought from inside. The stove fires up quickly with a few small logs and cooks beautifully—a perfect place to cook and catch the evening sun while enjoying a glass of cold *cantina sociale* wine.

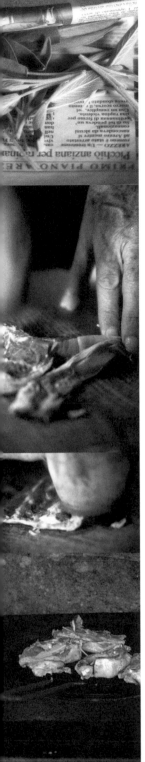

Agnello scottadito seared lamb

If you only use your grill pan for a lone zucchini or eggplant, try *agnello scottadito* for a treat. Crispy-edged, thin, moist lamb chops with sage. I often eat *agnello scottadito* in restaurants as the major player in a mixed grill. Italians tend to like lamb rather well cooked. I prefer it moist and slightly pink, browned in places and the fat slightly crisp along a few edges. It's a matter of taste.

SERVES 4

24 fresh sage leaves
8 lamb chops
Olive oil

About 1/2 cup red wine
Salt
Lemon wedges

Heat a grill pan or cast-iron or other heavy frying pan over medium-high heat. Place a few sage leaves on each lamb chop and flatten the chops with a smooth meat mallet.

When the pan is smoking hot, brush the chops with oil and place in the pan, in batches if necessary. Cook for 2 minutes on the first side, 1 1/2 minutes on the second—or more or less, depending on your taste.

After all the chops have been cooked, I splash a glass of red wine onto the grill pan to gather up the juices, reduce slightly and pour over the heaped chops. Serve as soon as humanly possible with salt and wedges of lemon and eat with thin green beans and thick bread. A great excuse to open your best bottle of red wine.

A Turkish version—Kuzu Pirzolasi
Use thyme and onion juice as a marinade. Grate an onion into a bowl, salt, and leave for 10 minutes. Extract the juice by squeezing the onion in your hands—add some olive oil and chopped fresh thyme. Marinate the lamb chops for a few hours, then cook as above.

Salsa di Pomodoro

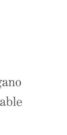

COOKING A SIMPLE TOMATO *SUGO* FOR PASTA ONCE A WEEK FOR THIRTY-FIVE YEARS MAKES ONE THOUSAND, EIGHT HUNDRED AND TWENTY TIMES, PERHAPS MORE. AFTER COOKING TOMATO *SUGO* EIGHTEEN HUNDRED TIMES, IT BECOMES AN AUTOMATIC ACT, RITUALISTIC AND COMFORTING. I REMEMBER THE LAST TIME I PREPARED IT, REGRETTING TOO MUCH SALT BUT ENJOYING A NEW VARIETY OF CANNED TOMATOES, BUT I'VE FORGOTTEN THE FIRST TIME.

To cook and eat *sugo* weekly, you need to build in small variations. Some parameters are determined by season, others by location. Canned tomatoes are fine out of peak tomato season. Try cutting the onion in different thicknesses, crush or chop the garlic. Add the bay leaf to the hot oil, or instead to the bubbling sauce. Take out the bay leaves and purée the mixture, or leave it coarse. The quantity of each ingredient can be adjusted. I aim for a *sugo* I tasted as a child the night my sister Sophy almost drowned in our Italian host's swimming pool. The sauce was bright orange, sweetened with fresh garden carrots and served in a deep green bowl.

I asked Alan, a mathematician friend, to help with the math involved in a simple variations scenario. He replied: "Re the variations. There is 1 way of using all four ingredients. There are 4 ways of choosing three out of four. There are 6 ways of choosing two out of four. There are 4 ways of choosing one out of four. Total : 15 ways. With a choice of one to five ingredients, there are 5 x 15 = 75 possibilities. Obviously this is completely unrealistic. You can't make *salsa di pomodoro* out of carrots alone! A more realistic scenario is where you select a recipe using each of the four ingredients but where each is available in quantities from say, 1 to 5 units. In this case, the total number of permutations is simply 5 x 5 x 5 x 5 = 625. If you add time, there are 625 x 5 = 3,125 permutations. If you make *salsa di pomodoro* twice a week, you'll still be testing permutations 30 years down the line!" Thanks Alan.

SERVES 4

1 onion, finely chopped
1 large carrot, finely chopped
1 stalk celery, finely chopped
Olive oil
8 fresh tomatoes or one 14-ounce can of tomatoes
1/2 teaspoon sugar
Salt and pepper

variations
Fresh plum tomatoes
Red or white onions
Dried/fresh basil or oregano
Stock—chicken or vegetable
Tomato paste or sauce
Red or white wine

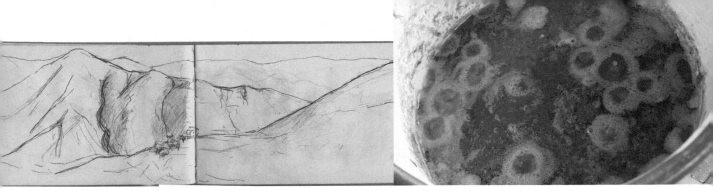

Sauté the onion, carrot and celery in olive oil in a large frying pan until the onion is translucent. Add the tomatoes, along with the sugar. Season with salt and pepper, cover and simmer gently for 30 minutes. Remove from the heat. Put the sauce through a food mill fitted with the coarse disk. This reduces the vegetables without smashing them to a pulp. Return the sauce to the pan and simmer again to reduce until thickened.

Variation
A time-saving trick to imitate that long-cooked velvety taste is to add 2 tablespoons tomato paste, a dash of soy sauce and 2 tablespoons red wine. Boil off the alcohol and simmer for 5 minutes. Use white wine if you don't want to darken your *sugo*'s color.

Signora Frati's *sugo* recipe from my mother's recipe book, 1971.

Signora Frati's Spaghetti Sugo.

One big onion.

½ kg tomatoe

Parsley
Celery
Basil
Carrot
garlic

Boil for one hour. Salt. Pepper. Salt.

Fiori di zucchine fritte

A plateful of delicate morsels. Deep-frying looks so tempting. Spluttering, fast, furious and slightly dangerous. Luckily, this recipe can be achieved by shallow-frying in a quarter inch of olive oil. Deep-frying is one of those culinary practices I normally leave to restaurants so I can remain blissfully ignorant of the actual quantities of oil required to make perfect *suppli* or *fritto misto*. Be sure to allow time for the 2 hours the batter needs to stand.

SERVES 5 AS AN APPETIZER, ALTHOUGH THEY ARE QUITE FILLING

For the batter

1/4 cup olive oil

Scant 1 cup Italian "00" flour, sifted

Generous pinch of salt

About 1/2 cup tepid water

1 egg white

To fry

15 zucchini flowers

5 small sage sprigs—the 4 top leaves joined on the stem

5 wild fennel tips (top 2 1/2 inches; optional)

Olive oil for shallow-frying

For the batter, I go straight to *Italian Food* by Elizabeth David for her *pastella* frying batter. In a medium bowl, add the olive oil to the flour and salt and mix together. Slowly whisk in the water until the batter is the consistency of heavy cream—not too thin, or the batter won't stick. Let stand, covered, for 2 hours. Whisk the egg white and gently fold it into the rested batter.

To reduce the amount of oil needed, I use a small frying pan and about 1/4 inch of oil. The oil needs to be hot—test with the occasional drip of batter. In batches, generously drench the flowers, sage and fennel tips in batter and carefully place in the hot oil. When the ragged edges of the batter become golden, turn and cook the other side until pale golden. Drain well on many paper towels.

As I write in London after cooking this last night, I am suffering indigestion from not draining off the oil from my half of the fried booty—too hungry to wait—so don't hold back on the paper towels.

There was a little batter left over, so I tried battering onion, carrot slices and arugula leaves. Also with some Pecorino Romano and a little anchovy stuffed into a zucchini flower.

Some cooks add a splash of brandy to the batter.

Fried zucchini flowers

§ What's to hand

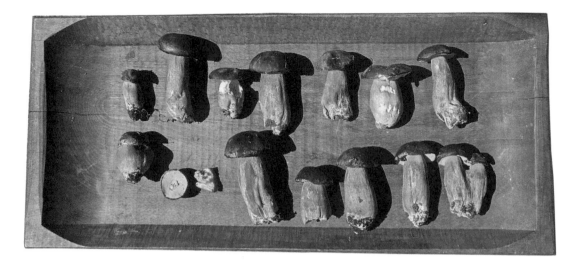

As the heat builds outside, the desire to cook from scratch lessens with each climbing degree on the kitchen thermometer. Yesterday we cooked all day. Gutting birds, chopping vegetables, guests arriving, cooking outdoors, late-night dish washing— the full works. Today leftover combinations are all my heavy brain can grapple with. My eyes rove across a blue bowl of succulent *faraona*, guinea fowl, deep in the fridge; somehow they've survived the night unmunched. The Antolinis, our neighbors across the valley, kindly gave us a huge basket full of vegetables which are now stored in our stony cold *cantina*. In the fridge, hidden under zucchini, I spy large tomatoes and wide red peppers. Stuffing seems in order. This slightly unplanned approach is how we tend to cook in Italy. One day of intense cooking providing enough leftovers to become ingredients for improvised dishes for the next day or two. A creative use of leftovers is encouraged as the house is forty minutes from the shops, down in the heat of the Val di Chiana. My mother has collected new recipes for us to cook, gathered from waiters and friends over the spring. I bring recipes from London to test. A library of Italian cookbooks is consulted to fill in gaps or to help suggest what to do with the main gastronomic inspiration here—fresh, Mediterranean ingredients.

Faraona in umido con zucca gialla
Guinea fowl & pumpkin stew

GUINEA FOWL HAVE BEEN EATEN LOCALLY FOR CENTURIES. AN ENTIRE CHAPTER IS DEDICATED TO THEM IN BARTOLOMEO SCAPPI'S SIXTEENTH-CENTURY COOKBOOK OPERA.

This stew occurred from the coincidental meeting of a guinea fowl and *zucca gialla* —a deep orange-colored pumpkin—in the bottom of our fridge. The guinea fowl was a gift from the Antolinis. The Co-op pumpkin came vacuum-packed with a sprig of parsley added for color. Mita Antolini complained about her guinea fowl being tough, so I decided to stew it.

SERVES 5

1 guinea fowl or hen, cut into 14 pieces (legs in 3 pieces each, breasts in 4 each), giblets and bones reserved

Stock vegetables—1 stalk celery, 1 onion, 1 carrot, cut into chunks

2 bay leaves

A few peppercorns

Olive oil

5 cloves garlic

1 onion, finely chopped

2 stalks celery, finely chopped

6 shallots, sliced

1/2 small pumpkin, seeded, peeled, and cut into cubes

1 teaspoon ground cinnamon

1 cup white wine

Salt and pepper

Preheat the oven to 400°F. Put the reserved bones, wing tips and giblets into a small pot with the stock vegetables, 1 bay leaf, the peppercorns and a pint of water. It's satisfying to have some stock puttering away while cooking.

Brown the guinea hen pieces in olive oil in a Dutch oven over medium heat. Add the remaining bay leaf to splutter and spit, adding a tree-fresh bitterness. Remove the browned meat to a bowl; discard the bay leaf. Add a little more oil to the pan and sauté the garlic, onion and celery. Add the shallots, pumpkin and cinnamon and stir for a few minutes. Add the browned guinea fowl and wine, along with the strained stock and enough water to half-cover the guinea hen. Season with salt and pepper.

Cover, put the pot into the oven, and cook for 1 1/2 hours, or until the guinea hen is tender.

To make use of the oven being on, you might roast a tray of potatoes. Cut several large potatoes into small chunks and soak in cold water for 1 hour. Heat 3 tablespoons of olive oil in a smooth roasting pan. Spread the drained, dried potatoes evenly in the pan and add a generous sprig of rosemary. Shake in the hot oil, sprinkle with sea salt and roast for about 45 minutes, or until brown and crispy.

F.S.
TARIFFA 1
RAPOLANO TERME

FIRENZE S. MAN
VIA EMPOLI
VALE PER IL
SOLO GIORNO   2°Cl
DEL RILASCIO   £900
LIRE

B 0876

Cortona - Via Nazionale

§ Shopping

In Italy the emphasis on regional ingredients and quality makes the shopping experience a pleasure to all the senses. Most Italian shopkeepers and stallholders have an intuitive touch when displaying their wares, allowing the natural beauty of the produce to shine. All achieved with a lightness and ease that supermarkets elsewhere fail to reproduce when attempting a Italian-themed promotion. Above all it's the taste that matters, whether it's produce from the stacked precision of the Rialto market in Venice or boxes of irregular-shaped vegetables bought in the local village shop.

The urban cook's perception is that you can buy anything anywhere—be it vegetable, fruit, meat, fish or fowl—particularly in cities such as London or New York, whose melting pot populations have imported such wondrous customs and ingredients. I'm always surprised, relieved and reassured at how different the produce looks, feels and tastes in Italy from what I have been used to in London. The same can be said for restaurants. In London I don't tend to eat Italian food, except for perhaps at San Lorenzo's and in the past at Apicella's or La Meridiana. I would rather wait for Italy itself. Perhaps food changes its molecular structure at an altitude of 30,000 feet, making no ingredient truly exportable. Asparagus was not put on this planet to travel club class from the Far East to London. Thankfully food is experienced by all the senses and is powerfully affected by circumstance, memory and association. Maybe the varying electric current on two bread-kneading machines creates minuscule changes, so bread using seemingly identical ingredients cooked in both Cortona and Cambridge can taste completely different. Perhaps the kneader's hands add to bread's individual and inimitable taste, or it's affected by what the baker ate last night, the salt, water, air or something that we've yet to discover. All these elements conspire, allowing differences to coalesce and remain.

When trying to re-create our Italian kitchen back in London, the results are an entirely different cuisine, wonderful but different. The nearest we've come to a successful replication meal was with the help of a large, dusty oval Cortonese pane Toscano loaf, herbs picked the day before on the mountain, a bag full of San Marzano tomatoes from the Mercato delle Erbe in Bologna and a freshly bottled Vino Rosso di Topello made by our neighbor Arnaldo Antolini. Ingredient X was the resonance of Italy on us, lingering on our skins and nestled in our clothing. It transported us back, or allowed what was still with us to surface. After a trip I find that I have about three weeks of heightened sense awareness when I can truly judge and pinpoint these differences. Perhaps that's why I like to buy Mediterranean ingredients in London from an Italian freshly returned from visiting relations near Piacenza, such as the fantastic Lina Stores in Soho. Other shops and magazines persuade you that the correct tableware will invoke the essence of Tuscany in your pallid garden or cold, wintry kitchen. Crank up the central heating for three days. It still isn't the same—ersatz Esperanto food. Go to Italy and beg or borrow a kitchen and cook. After the first bite you'll be hooked for life. You may even have to move there.

After I spend the winter in London staring up at Elizabeth David's *Italian Food* on a cold shelf, it's a joy to cook her recipes in the country of origin with sympathetic ingredients. Eating a dish in a trattoria or an Italian friend's house also engages, informs, immerses and extends my thoughts about something as simple as preparing, cooking and serving a tomato sauce. The experience becomes a barometer or touchstone with which to judge the dish when cooked back home.

We shop everywhere, from small grocers perched in hill towns that appear hewn out of the medieval stone walls, to umbrella-covered sprawling markets held weekly in Cortona and Camucia. Our local supermarket in Camucia, the Co-op, has grown since we first used it in the seventies, and moved location. To the casual user it may appear like any other supermarket, but it has blossomed into a remarkable store and is a socially responsible company, not only to its 5 million members and customers but also to its supply chain and the environment. Various measures to reduce the impact of packaging include biodegradable carrier bags. Much of the exceptional produce is seasonal and regional, supporting local producers such as the uncle of Arnaldo Antolini, who supplies beef and pork to them. The meat can be seen being butchered on the premises, viewable through a glass window.

Until unification in 1870, Italy was a group of small municipalities, and, since cultural independence is prized, the twenty regions today remain fiercely autonomous. A city's gastronomy doesn't often spread beyond the city limits, let alone into another province. Although the gastronomic landscape of Italy today can appear static, its past reveals a culinary flux of exotic influences from the early trading routes into Venice, Genoa and Messina, assimilated over centuries. Italy seems to be naturally "slow" and en masse, not always an active political strategy. The seepage of multinational taste is evident, so there is still a continual battle to retain what is regional, traditional and produced with care. What might seem a culinary straitjacket fortunately allows for continual invention and improvisation at home and in restaurants, retaining an Italian feel. So although one may be worried that Italy might become the world's first Gastronomic Place of World Heritage Interest, it's still very much alive and rightfully wary of external influences whose motivations are not at all concerned with excellence of ingredients or developing national identity. Personally I don't travel thousands of miles to arrive at Florence station to eat a Magnum ice cream or a croissant.

FESTA della CORTONA

The Co-op, Camucia. Grocers displays in Cortona. Breakfast at Bacchetti, Cortona.

Artigianato

1989

DOMENICA

ORE 9 - Pro

S.

con PROSCIUTTO e F

POPOLARI e BALLO LI

«LA NUOVA IDEA»

LA PRO - LOCO

Anatra arrosto con finocchio
Roast duck & wild fennel

There's a wild duck in the fridge. It's August so some of the swaying fennel plants can have their flowers harvested and face a roasting pan. Succulent blackberries still clamber over the shaded path to the well, time for a forager's supper.

SERVES 4

1 large wild duck

4 thin slices fresh ginger (optional)

2 oranges, 1 cut into segments, the other sliced

1 wild fennel plant, roots removed

Salt and pepper

A handful of blackberries

About 1/2 cup chicken stock

Preheat the oven to 425°F. Stuff the duck with the ginger, if using, orange segments and as much of the fennel as you can squeeze in. (One was growing outside the kitchen door. Be careful if you take fennel from roadsides—they belong to someone, so ask first.) Rub salt and pepper into the skin of the duck.

Fill a roasting pan with half an inch of hot water, add a spray of fennel and the blackberries. Set a wire rack above this mixture, toss on the orange slices and pop the duck on top. Carefully place this arrangement in the oven. Roast for 20 minutes. Reduce the heat to 375°F for 1 hour, or until the juices of the thigh run clear when pierced. Transfer the duck to a platter and let rest for 15 minutes, to keep warm.

To make the sauce

Meanwhile, remove the fennel and oranges from the roasting pan, leaving the berries, and spoon off the fat. Add the stock, and simmer over medium heat until slightly reduced.

To serve, carve the duck or cut into portions with poultry shears and pour on the sauce.

Anatra alla Scappi
Scappi's duck

A Christmas aroma of fruit, duck and spices engulfs the hot afternoon kitchen—like mulled wine. The Antolinis are coming for lunch, so I want a special recipe, something Italian yet from the past. I find a recipe from 1500 by Bartolomeo Scappi that requires many local ingredients, plus a few that would have been imported by sea from the East. Many Renaissance recipes are heavily spiced. Next time I would roast one of the ducks to eat alongside Scappi's duck.

SERVES 12

1 pound thick-sliced pancetta, roughly chopped

Olive oil

1 teaspoon ground cinnamon

1 teaspoon ground ginger

1/2 teaspoon ground nutmeg

2 large ducks, cut into 10 to 14 pieces each, skin removed

8 ounces plums, halved and pitted

9 cloves

2/3 cup raisins, soaked in water until plumped

3 tablespoons red wine vinegar

Salt and white pepper to taste

1 bottle good local red wine

Preheat the oven to 400°F. Sauté the pancetta in a little olive oil in a large frying pan until crisp. Add the cinnamon, ginger and nutmeg and cook, stirring, 1 minute more. Take off the heat.

Arrange the duck in a large flameproof casserole, and add the pancetta mixture, plums, cloves, raisins, vinegar, salt and white pepper, and enough wine to almost cover the duck. Place in the oven and cook, uncovered, for 1 hour, turning the pieces of duck occasionally.

Remove the duck to a warm serving dish. Simmer the sauce over medium heat to reduce slightly, and pour over the duck. Serve with roast potatoes, farro or skirlie (page 129).

Country roast chicken

*Pollo gi
2003*

I hate carving chicken—it gets cold and loses flavor and moisture. I like the meat attached to the bone in great chunks. Like so much farmhouse cooking, this requires little preparation for a wonderful result. Make sure it can be eaten as soon as it is ready as it doesn't like hanging around.

SERVES 6

A bed of vegetables, such as chopped celery, onions, carrots

3 sprigs fresh rosemary

6 cloves garlic, left unpeeled

1/2 cup white wine

1 large free-range organic roasting chicken, cut into 12 pieces (legs cut into 3 pieces each, breasts cut into 3 each)

Salt and pepper

3 tablespoons olive oil

Preheat the oven to 400°F. Spread the bed of vegetables in a large roasting pan— I often use Swiss chard stalks, large sliced onions, halved carrots and whole celery stalks. Add the rosemary, garlic and white wine. Place the chicken pieces skin side down on the vegetable bed. Season with salt and pepper, and drizzle with the olive oil.

Roast the chicken for 1 1/2 to 2 hours, basting occasionally with the pan juices, particularly toward the end. After 1 hour, turn the chicken pieces over and add a little water to the roasting pan if it's become dry. The chicken is cooked when the thigh juices run clear when pierced. Transfer the vegetables to a wide hot serving dish. Cut the larger chicken pieces in half, and place on top of the vegetables. You should have portion-sized pieces of succulent browned chicken. No carving knives, no fuss, just mouthwatering chicken. Serve with the platter of roasted seasonal vegetables—finely cut beets or thin slices of turnip and zucchini.

§ Chickens & pigs

Italian chickens look individual and unique. They've seen some life and possess a natural skin color from white to an umber-tinged yellow—no fake corn-fed tan. Lean without being scrawny. No hidden clumps of fat between the thighs and chest or slugs of heavy fat pushed into the chest cavity. Feet and head intact. The neck in particular adds great flavor to my stocks, as do the heart, kidneys and liver. Locals often cut up and roast their chickens with their organs attached, fighting over the bits with liver as they do for liver in the local pork speciality *porchetta*—a whole roast pig stuffed with a mountainside of fennel plants and garlic bulbs. *Porchetta* is sold from open-sided vans at markets. Try a large, dusty fresh *pane* filled with slices of moist aromatic pork, sweet break-tooth crackling, a fragment of herb-crusted liver and garlic. To die for. Surely the most rugged, tasty and beautiful sandwich on the planet.

Pollo arrosto alla campagnola

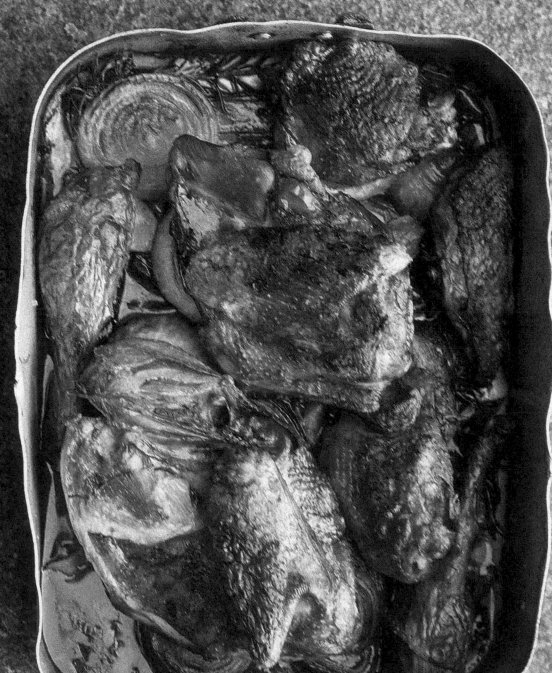

Piante Aromatiche §

Cooking abroad helps ground you in the location—finding ingredients, implements and new ways of cooking to use there or to take home. We stayed at a friend's house in Suffolk last summer, and it was hot enough to swim in the choppy green waves of the English Channel. Their walled kitchen garden overflowed with large zucchini and an orchard of apples fast becoming wasp fodder. Unfortunately, the espaliered fig trees weren't quite ready. My wife, Jeff, made chutney and jam, I designed the labels. We make fig preserves in Italy and always travel home scraping against the HM Customs and Excises laws and baggage weight allowance. Our bags look as if we've been grocery shopping rather than holidaying. When in Italy at the family house, I assemble bundles of hill-fresh herbs to mail out to friends on our return—rosemary, sage, bay and fennel, some planted, some wild. The bay tree stands thirty feet high, nine wide, so it doesn't miss forty or so outer branches being exported. I add a few pine needles and lavender stems for ambience, then wrap tightly in an Italian newspaper—*La Repubblica*—and secure with twine. Pack the bundles into the suitcase. Two days later via a Land Rover, train, Bologna airport, Gatwick Express and the Royal Mail they arrive at friends' houses still "mountain fresh"—use immediately. One year, with the help of Nancy Harmon Jenkins, food writer and friend, we bought a small sack of fennel flowers from Cortona market—worth more than cocaine. I divided the bounty into empty 35mm film containers, designed and attached a label and mailed them out.

Sun-dried fennel flowers, packaged herbs, drying juniper berries.

One year's gastronomic haul.

panzanella

PANZANELLA IS AN ANCIENT ITALIAN RECIPE USING STALE UNSALTED BREAD, TOMATOES, BASIL AND ONIONS TO MAKE AN UNUSUAL SUMMER SALAD. AS VALENTINA HARRIS MENTIONS IN HER BOOK *THE COOKING OF TUSCANY* (SAINSBURY'S, 1992), IN THE PAST THE BREAD WAS SOAKED IN PURE SEAWATER. MAYBE BOTTLED SEAWATER IS THE NEXT FAD FOR SUPERMARKETS. PANZANELLA IS ANOTHER ITALIAN FLAG DISH (*LA BANDIERA* IS GREEN, WHITE AND RED), LIKE INSALATA CAPRESE—MOZZARELLA, BASIL AND TOMATOES.

I've eaten *panzanella* prepared by my mother for over thirty years—many variations. Its origin is said to be Tuscan. A poem written by the sixteenth-century Florentine painter Agnolo di Cosimo, better known as Bronzino, mentions *panzanella*. Bronzino's poem "Rime alla cipolla" places the dish as being Florentine. At that time the recipe used chopped onions, stale bread, cucumber, basil, arugula and *colla porcellanetta*, which is a paste made from the ribs of a female pig. Like other dishes in Italian cooking, *panzanella* is an ancient recipe that predates the introduction of tomatoes. The great Italian cook Aldo Santini has an interesting variation that uses 2 pounds of three-day-old bread. Soak the bread—uncut—in cold water for 1 hour. Then leave the bread to drain—do not squeeze it. (I imagine the warm Italian air would help.) When dry, break the bread into a bowl and add salt, olive oil, a splash of vinegar, three chopped red onions, two slightly unripe tomatoes, two very ripe tomatoes, radishes, basil and some lettuce.

The most useful help and advice came by mobile phone from my parents, who were sitting in the Milanese restaurant Don Lisander. I had mentioned the Bronzino link to them the day before. They had tracked down the name of the poem and the recipe contained in it. They had also bought the Aldo Santini book and were discussing it with the waiters and chef in the restaurant as they ate lunch. Their waiter's mother, who lives in Sicily, makes a hot *panzanella* using yesterday's bread in a large pot, adding water, chopped tomatoes, olive oil and lots of basil, then boiling it to make a thick soup. They call this regional variation *panzanella*, although we might call it *pappa al pomodoro* (tomato bread soup). The Italians have a habit of using the same name for different dishes the entire length of the country. Most confusing.

I plan to test the recipe over the weekend when my wife's mother visits from Scotland. The cusp of winter in London is not the optimum climate in which to eat *panzanella*—rather a warm, soft summer day. Having said that, the farmers' market does have fresh spring onions, end-of-season tomatoes and unsalted bread.

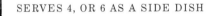

SERVES 4, OR 6 AS A SIDE DISH

1/2 loaf stale unsalted Tuscan bread or
  other rustic bread—it needs to have
  an open texture
1/2 cup olive oil
1/4 cup red wine vinegar
Salt and pepper to taste

1/2 cucumber, chopped
4 scallions, chopped
1 mild onion, thinly sliced
4 large ripe tomatoes, chopped
8 fresh basil leaves

Roughly break the stale bread into a bowl. Add cold water to cover and let soak for
30 minutes. Meanwhile, to make the dressing, whisk together the olive oil, vinegar,
salt and pepper. Once the bread is soft, squeeze out the water. Take handfuls of the
bread and press it firmly between your hands until it's dry. Line the bottom of a
salad bowl with the bread. Add the remaining ingredients and pour on the dressing.
Mix well and set aside for at least 20 minutes, not in the fridge.

Variations
Some people add canned tuna, garlic, celery, peppers and different varieties
of tomato. Others add dried oregano to the dressing. The tomatoes,
cucumber and onions are often sliced rather than chopped.

Coniglio con panna porcini
Slow-cooked rabbit in porcini cream

A two-parter. A delicate simmering pot of rabbit with cream, whose leftovers become the perfect sauce for my favorite pasta shape—pappardelle. If you can't obtain fresh porcini, use either dried or powdered porcini with some light cream. This recipe is made even easier by using one carton of *panna ai funghi porcini* for both dishes.

SERVES 6, OR 4 WITH LEFTOVERS

2 rabbits, cut into serving portions

Olive oil

1 stalk of celery with leaves, finely chopped

1 onion, finely chopped

2 cloves garlic, crushed

1/2 cup white wine

3 fennel bulbs, trimmed and cut in half

Scant 1/2 cup *panna ai funghi porcini*

In a deep frying pan, brown the pieces of rabbit in olive oil. When browned, put aside on a plate. Add the celery, onion and garlic to the pan. Cook gently, stirring for 3 minutes, then add the white wine.

Put the browned rabbit back into the pan, mix with the vegetables and place the halved fennel bulbs on top. Simmer for 30 minutes, or until the rabbit is tender. Remove the fennel bulbs if they cook too quickly.

Before serving, stir in the *panna ai funghi porcini* and gently heat through. Serve with roast tomatoes and roast potatoes with rosemary and bay leaf.

What to do with the leftover rabbit
A classic sauce for pappardelle.

Leftover rabbit

1/2 cup chicken stock

1 onion, finely chopped

2 cloves garlic, crushed

Olive oil

Scant 1/2 cup *panna ai funghi porcini*

Pappardelle

Strip the remaining meat from the cooked rabbit pieces, watching out for small bones. Make a small stock from the bones. Sauté the onion with the garlic in olive oil in a frying pan until translucent. Add the rabbit strips and heat through. Add the strained stock, cover the pan and cook for 5 minutes. Let this cool slightly, and then stir in the *panna ai funghi porcini*. Serve on pappardelle for creamy heaven.

Faraona con uva
Guinea fowl on grapes

What to cook for supper? We have guinea fowl but no pumpkin so I can't test cook recipe number 5647 (see page 68). My mother cooks a fabulous recipe with game and grapes, a classic double—we'll try that. For guidance and inspiration, I leaf through books on Renaissance cookery. Mum looks up Jane Grigson, dad reads from *Le Ricette Regionali Italiane* as I scan the fridge to see what's at hand. Some limp celery, a Bacchus-sized bunch of grapes from Naples. Dad suggests garlic; Mum, some juniper berries. We have a few juniper berries picked on the mountain yesterday by Hannah. I pick a bay leaf from the tree outside the kitchen door. I find ten walnuts in a box of muesli for the finishing touch.

SERVES 4

A large bunch of white or green grapes, halved and seeded

5 cloves garlic, chopped in half

1 stalk celery, finely chopped

10 juniper berries

1 bay leaf

1/4 cup white wine

10 walnuts, roughly chopped (optional)

1 guinea fowl or hen

Salt and pepper

Olive oil

Preheat the oven to 400°F. You'll need enough grapes to cover the bottom of a large baking dish three grapes deep. Then add the garlic, celery, juniper berries, bay leaf, wine and the walnuts, if using.

To butterfly the guinea hen: using poultry shears or a sharp knife, cut down along either side of the backbone and remove it. Open out the bird, place it skin side up on the cutting board and press down hard to crack the ribs and flatten it. Place the guinea hen, skin side down, on the grapes. Season with salt and pepper. Drizzle on a little olive oil. Place on the middle oven rack and cook for 45 minutes.

Turn the bird over to brown the skin, moving the dish to the upper rack of the oven, and cook for 45 minutes longer, or until the juices run clear when the thigh is pierced.

Let rest in a warm spot for 10 minutes before cutting the bird into portions with poultry shears or a heavy knife. Serve with bulgur or soft polenta to soak up the juices.

Strozzapreti or Strangolapreti
Spinach dumplings

I ordered *strozzapreti* in Rome recently, expecting delicate, gnocchi-like, mouthwatering cheesy dumplings—instead I was given the Sicilian version of pasta twists with a deep rich tomato sauce, sumptuous. Another example of the Italian practice of giving dishes from different regions the same name. The gnocchi-like version is slightly fiddly but well worth a try, or two—preferably not for guests on your first attempt.

MAKES ABOUT 22 *STROZZAPRETI*, SERVES 6

1 pound spinach or Swiss chard, trimmed and washed

1½ cups ricotta

4 ounces Parmesan, grated, plus extra for serving

2 eggs

Salt and pepper

½ teaspoon grated nutmeg

About ¼ cup all-purpose flour

6 tablespoons butter, melted and still warm

Steam the spinach or chard until tender. Drain well and finely chop. Put in a large bowl, add the ricotta and mix well. Add half the Parmesan and 1 egg, mixing with a light touch. Season with salt, pepper and the nutmeg. Add the remaining egg and mix gently.

Bring a large pot of water to a rolling boil and spread the flour on a plate. This is the tricky bit. With a tablespoon, scoop up a spoonful of the mixture and form it into an oval shape and release it onto the floured plate. Flour your hands and gently turn the dumpling in the flour, then toss it gently from hand to hand a few times to let the excess flour fall away. Make about 5 dumplings, then drop them gently into the boiling water. When they bob to the surface—about 2 minutes—they are cooked. Transfer to a warm serving bowl while you make the rest.

Toss with the melted butter and serve with the grated Parmesan and perhaps a little *salsa di pomodoro* (page 60).

After boiling the *strozzapreti*, some cooks sauté them in butter with a sprig of sage for a few minutes.

eating out §

Portole, the local family-run hotel and restaurant, stradles a mountain's back, giving views north into the Apennines and south across the plains of the Val di Chiana and the glimmering Lago Trasimeno. We've enjoyed many a wedding banquet in their large cool dining room eating tradtional Tuscan fare. When I was a teenager, between courses nine and ten the monk to my right stood up and sang an awe-inspiring rendition of "Ave Maria" that silenced the 100 guests. He had the voice of an angel.

Portole

VIA UMBRO CORTONESE, 36 - 52044 CORTONA

Castel Girardi

VIA UMBRO CORTONESE
CASTEL GIRARDI, NEAR CORTONA

In the hot Tuscan summer evenings young Cortonese drive or scooter out of town up into the cool mountain air to eat wonderful pizza at Castel Girardi. We visit in the calm of lunchtime to sit under the vines and sample and enjoy the kitchen's latest offerings, perhaps some *sformato*, trios of homemade pasta, *crostini* or *agnello scottadito*, absolutely delicious.

The Tuscan restaurant Cafaggi in Florence has been owned
by the same family for 60 years and cooks produce from
the family estate. It was probably last renovated when I
was five. Luckily it was that classic 1960s everyday Italian
restaurant décor that has been in fashion more often than
not over the past 40 years. Just the right amount of
ornament—often textured, using materials such as terrazzo.
I'm probably served by the children I used to play with on
our first visits—or by their children. Outside, the street
sounds of Vespas and Euro rock music are much the same
today. Cafaggi was one of the first restaurants we took our
daughter to. My wife and I took turns walking around the
block pushing a baby buggy in between courses. Now she
sits through the whole meal. Thank you, grissini!

VIA GUELFA (35R), FLORENCE

Tamburini

RAVIOLI DI ZUCCA
al KG 34 000 17.56
50130

Tamburini, a produce shop and self-service restaurant, is positioned at the heart of a world-class gastronomic square mile in Bologna, in Emilia-Romagna. Founded in 1932, they sell only handmade produce. The shop brims over with it. Pork items are made from animals slaughtered only in winter. Fortunately for visitors lacking a nearby kitchen to cook in, there is a self-service restaurant to taste local wares. Go through to the back room; it overlooks the heat of the street and is flooded with natural light. Sit by the left at the door. This side entrance to the bistro needs to be pushed hard to open—*SPINGERE*—creating chances for chatting to passersby. Stacked chestnut and oak firewood rests near the wood-fired oven as a queue forms quickly at noon with dusty builders, white-collar workers and the occasional foreigner. Check with your local customs department before buying ham to take home, otherwise buy fresh tortellini, *piadina*, an unsalted Tuscan loaf and a bottle of Sangiovese Tamburini.

Tortellini in brodo

A quick, delicate winter soup. Fresh tortellini is so delicious it requires a simple recipe. In Bologna a favorite method is to cook the tortellini in stock, making a light soup. The hot clear broth provides a perfect base to unlock the taste of each individual tortellini, keeping them warm until you eat the last one. A package of fresh tortellini will keep in your fridge for a few days or can be frozen. This pasta is traditionally eaten on Christmas Eve in Bologna. The shape is supposed to symbolize Venus's navel.

SERVES 6

5 cups chicken or fish stock

1 pound fresh tortellini

Salt (optional)

Thick slices of Tuscan bread or
  other rustic bread

1 clove garlic, halved

Olive oil

Grated Parmesan cheese

Bring the stock to a rolling boil in a small pot. Add the tortellini and some salt if your stock is unsalted. Simmer for about 5 minutes, or until the tortellini rise to the surface. Meanwhile, toast the bread. Rub the toasts with the garlic, sprinkle lightly with salt, if using unsalted Tuscan bread, and drizzle with olive oil. Ladle the broth and cooked tortellini into wide shallow bowls. Sprinkle with a little grated Parmesan. Serve the toasts. In Tuscany, bread is often placed in the bowl and the soup poured over it.

Fourth course: ~~chicken~~, Fried chichen with potatoes

Fifth course: Green salad.

Sixth course: fruit

Seventh course: a very good choclate semi-frado

eigth course: a ~~$~~ coffee trifle

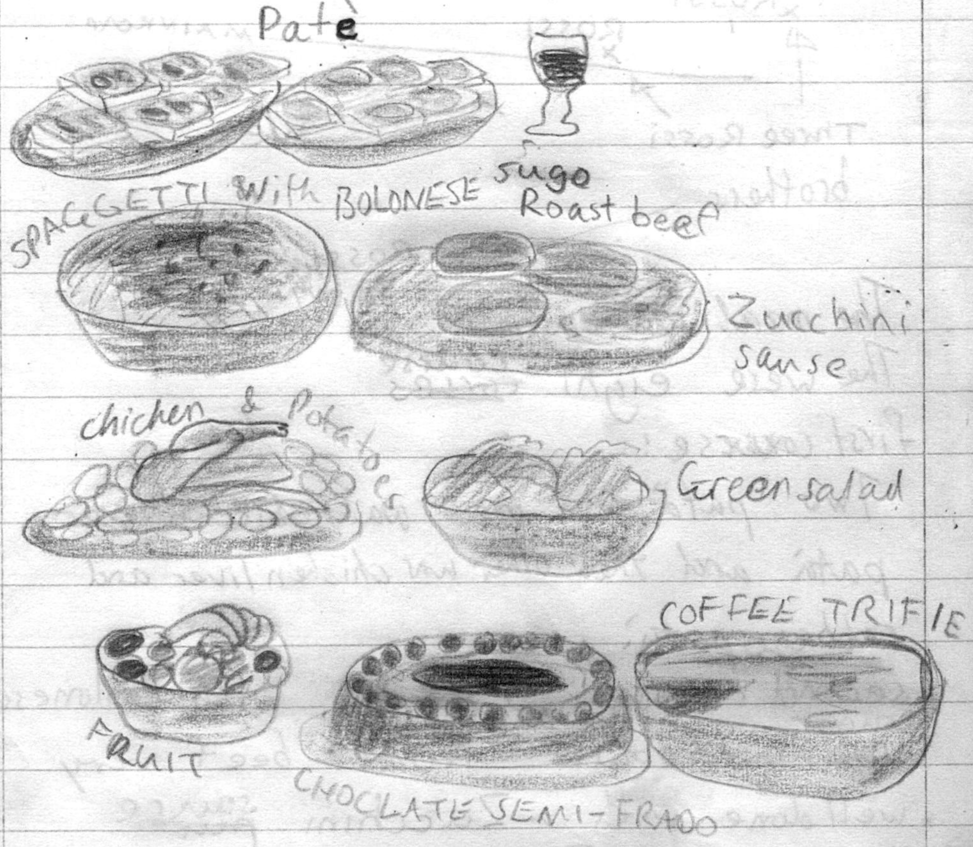

Patè

SPAGGETTI with BOLONESE sugo

Roast beef

Zucchini sause

chichen & Potatoes

Green salad

FRUIT

CHOCLATE SEMI-FRADO

COFFEE TRIFIE

ITALY HAS A LONG, SLOW-BURN EFFECT ON OUR
KITCHEN. THESE DAYS MEDITERRANEAN FOOD
SEEMS TO BE SUPPLANTING FRENCH CUISINE AS
THE DOMINANT INTERNATIONAL STYLE—CERTAINLY
AS A LIFESTYLE GASTRONOMY, GUIDED BY A
HEALTH-CONSCIOUS PUBLIC. I COULD HAPPILY
EXPLORE THE EXTRAORDINARY RANGE OF COOKING
OFFERED THE LENGTH AND BREADTH OF ITALY
FOREVER. HOWEVER, IN THE SAME WAY MY
PARENTS HAD BEEN CAPTURED BY ITALY IN THE
1950S I FOUND SOMEWHERE ELSE THAT BLEW
THE DOOR OFF MY KITCHEN. NEW YORK, NEW YORK.
JUNGLE FOOD. I EAT THEREFORE I AM.

Veselka Restaurant, seen here in 1984.
144 2nd Avenue at 9th Street, New York, NY 10003.
Serving Ukrainian food since 1954.

East
Village
Vendor

NEW YORK CITY

FOR A BREAKFAST LOVER, VISITING NEW YORK IS LIKE FINDING THE SOURCE OF THE NILE

★ CROSSTOWN COOKING

There's nothing quite like the exuberance of youth, a time to consume vast amounts of information and food—sucking it all in like a discerning sponge. I see the same spirit for experimentation and thirst for knowledge in friends who have reached their seventies. For those of us who cook, this youthful openness hopefully manifests itself in the kitchen—developing a real sense of exploration. In my choice of culinary influences New York stands out as the only location I haven't cooked in for any length of time. Yet it remains a second home to me, and so plays a huge role in my outlook toward eating, shopping and living. This temperament needs to be observed, learnt and assimilated early on in life, and refilled at regular intervals.

New York is an assault course for cross-ethnic cooking. Having been a prime destination for immigrants for centuries, the streets are infused with restaurants, grocers, bakers and butchers from every country in the world. The intersections of these gastronomic traditions collide and merge at every street corner and on many a menu. Culinary maps of New York are redrawn almost daily as neighborhoods shift— watch Chinatown sprawl north into Little Italy. Restaurants also change location as they move on up the architectural food chain—often starting from a hole-in-the-wall, perhaps aiming to be a citywide franchise or else being bought out by a "food group" —awful, a fate worse than factory farming.

As a family we treat New York as an urban national park, wandering, climbing, foraging and watching out for bears. A place for observation and picnicking. We spend as much time in kitchenware shops and grocery stores as we do in museums and galleries. But my first visit there was alone. In 1980, stepping off a Freddie Laker Boeing at Kennedy onto a frozen metal gantry leading to the immigration halls, I am struck by everything. All of it. Each rivet and screw, every scrap of paper and fleck of dust appears different and exciting, electrically charged. Decades of watching North America through the filters of television, movies, art, childhood toys, food packaging and comics hasn't prepared me for the full onslaught of New York in 3D. Woody Allen remarked that his films will be remembered only for their off-action glimpses of old New York street scenes. My mental map of New York is already a cinematic

patchwork of Woody Allen, Martin Scorsese, Cagney and Lacey, and Billy Wilder, flavored with the drawings of children's author Richard Scarry. Scarry has drawn every generic machine, vehicle and implement I come across in New York—although not as many of them are driven by beavers as in his books. However, they do possess that flat, graphic 1950s color scheme.

The JFK Express, the best way into the city in that era, had a pale blue and white exterior, chrome trim poking through the spaghetti-like viral graffiti. Inside I find a single, untagged orange bucket seat. We rattle into lower Manhattan. Staggering up the subway exit stairs I step onto a vast, deserted film set awaiting its crew and actors. Everything that rises from the steaming graffitied concrete into the night air is made of metal: pavement edges, public telephones, toilets, buildings and roads— protection against the urban wear of 8 million New Yorkers. It's plastered with stickers and tarnished with dirt. I love it. Ten years later, I get married there in City Hall and have lunch at the River Café in Brooklyn.

To carry out urban fieldwork, a domestic base is essential—not a hotel. My godparents, Richard and Betsy Smith, lived in Manhattan with their sons, Edward and Harry, but so far downtown that cabs griped at taking me. Staying with friends allows a student foodie access to a local fridge and the chance to observe a new family kitchen in action. Betsy is a fabulous cook, her larder brimmed with exciting produce. To live on Warren Street in 1980 was considered pioneering. Twenty-five years later, the gentrification is almost complete. Back then industrial warehouses overlooked cracked empty streets. Artists seem to be drawn out of necessity to edgy commercial districts that provide vast studio spaces and lofts. It was Halloween, so Betsy took me to the top of the World Trade Center to gaze down onto the dark island as night fell. Dick had taken me to see the small farmers' market at the Trade Center earlier. Back in the loft Betsy drew three red lines on my walking map of Manhattan—lines I shouldn't cross. She then made pumpkin pie.

THREE JET-LAG BREAKFASTS

Before the loft-dwelling household wakes, I tiptoe out into a windswept dawn in lower Manhattan for breakfast number one. Glaring light from the Hudson River, still clear of the condos that now line West Street, thrashing the streets. Biting cold wind, deserted, wide and dusty. Weeds grow in cracks between steel and cement. I expect a sand dune any step as I make for either The Three Bears or Square Diner, up West Broadway. Over ten days I will slowly work through their breakfast specials: pancake three-stack, French toast, English muffins, hash browns, Canadian bacon —all assisted by the able diner-style coffee. Fermented in a glass jug for 40 minutes over a low heat creates that unique bouquet, real diner coffee, slightly burnt with a long finish—perfect with pancakes. I tried unsuccessfully to replicate the brew in London. Perhaps I lack the exact catering filter papers or got the pH balance of the water wrong. Breakfast two back at the loft as Edward shows me the Land O Lakes butter package trick as we eat Thomas' English muffins. A long walk uptown to the Met puts me in the mood for a Midtown cheeseburger deluxe platter on

The
THREE BEARS
Coffee Shop
&
Restaurant
125 CHURCH STREET • NEW YORK CITY
Corner of Murray Street
349-2390 -1-2

"HOME COOKING"

Lexington. Waxed tubs of coleslaw and sliced pickles spiked with a cellophane-wrapped cocktail stick. Slipped under the glass tabletop is their cocktail guide; maybe later. New York is an accommodating city for a solo diner. I feel like Jack Lemmon in a black-and-white Billy Wilder movie, jostling past Midtown workers to a luncheonette break from my Park Avenue advertising job. The jam-packed vertical density of offices and shops provide an unending stream of eaters for hundreds of restaurants. Here, as in Italy, eating out in restaurants is considered a necessity rather than a treat. Some eateries are breathtakingly pretentious; luckily for gourmands drawn to the everyday end of the eatery chain, the choice is colossal. I avoid the Pizza Hut, Subway and fast food abominations—as appallingly uniform here as anywhere else—and seek out independently owned and run diners and restaurants. In Midtown this usually requires walking east toward Lexington. London seems to detach its working day from eating. Restaurants tend to be elsewhere. This is changing but London is still a challenging city for a solo eater to dine in, happily seated at a table, without feeling like a complete idiot.

Western European cooking dominates the all-night East Village diner and breakfast trade. For lunch you'd go kosher at 2nd Avenue Deli (now closed), but for breakfast or an early morning treat our friend Susan recommends Veselka's, the Kiev or Elka's Coffee Shop. This really is breakfast heaven. It might even be worth suffering short-term memory loss to enjoy perfect breakfasts all day long, guilt free. Failing that, jet lag also assists. Staying at Susan's apartment-cum-office on 15th Street puts us within striking distance of these Polish-Russian-Ukrainian wonders, as well as a solo-guitarist blues bar. Deep driving snow won't put me off a 6 A.M. breakfast number one at Veselka's: two eggs (scrambled), *challah* bread, *kasha* and *kielbasa*. After I amble around for three hours in teeth-clenching cold, Susan might be up and ready to visit the Kiev for a light breakfast number two of muffins, and two hours on again Elka's Coffee Shop is calling. Their blueberry pancake stack is like a pile of fresh zombies. Real fruit filling causes them to collapse slightly when prodded with a fork. Diners that avoid using canned fruit in their pancakes are hard to find, but worth seeking out. Maybe there's a breakfast special website that lists such secrets?

Pancake Laboratory

FROM THIN DELICATE CREPES TO A FLUFFY SOURDOUGH BUTTERMILK STACK, PANCAKES ARE A GREAT DISH FOR WEEKLY EXPERIMENTATION. WHILE MAKING PANCAKES, DRINKING COFFEE IS ESSENTIAL, AS INSEPARABLE AS MAKING TOMATO *SUGO* AND DRINKING RED WINE, OR BARBECUING AND A BOTTLE OF BEER OR A GLASS OF VINHO VERDE.

I like to have a hot platter warming in the oven onto which I can stack pancakes as they come off the griddle. As well as creating a satisfying stack, it allows everyone to eat at the same time. Don't forget to warm the plates and take the maple syrup and butter out of the fridge well in advance.

Experimentation is made easier by the general rule of equal quantities of flour to liquid for most batters: 1 cup of flour to 1 cup of milk. From this starting point exploration, can begin: mixing flours, fruits, substituting milk for orange juice, using just egg whites or no eggs at all.

Various batter ingredients

All-purpose flour, whole wheat flour, buckwheat flour, yam flour

Baking soda

Salt

Eggs, egg whites, whisked egg whites

Sunflower oil, corn oil, peanut oil

Milk, buttermilk, soy milk, rice milk, orange juice

Additions, either added to the batter or sprinkled on the pancake when cooking

Chopped bananas, apples, peaches, dates, or nuts, blueberries, dark or golden raisins, spices

To serve

Chopped fruit

Sliced bananas

Real maple syrup

Butter

Lemon wedges and sugar

Recently I've been cooking fluffy pancakes. Separate 2 eggs. Whisk the whites into stiff peaks in a large bowl. In another bowl, whisk together 1 cup flour, 1 cup milk, the egg yolks, a pinch of salt, 1 tablespoon oil and 1 teaspoon baking soda. Fold this mixture gently into the whisked egg whites. Smear a little oil

on a hot griddle or large heavy frying pan. Add a ladle of batter per pancake; I like them 6 inches wide. Drop a few slightly squashed blueberries onto the uncooked top of each pancake. Let bubbles form and burst, then check to make sure that there are no stuck edges around the pancake before turning it over to cook the other side. Classic, fluffy 3-stack pancakes.

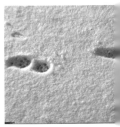

Orange juice pancakes

A simple substitution of orange juice for milk makes a delicious change. Use a thick, pulpy orange juice. The sweet smell of frying fructose wafts up from the pan as you cook these. I keep them to the size of a DVD as they are rather more floppy than a milk-based pancake. Serve with a little maple syrup, no butter.

Snow pancakes

This is one of the few recipes I have found using snow, and it comes from Dorothy Hartley's *Food in England*. The snow needs to be light and fluffy, not hard and icy—the sort of snow that won't roll into a snowball. I've tried various snows and found this to work best.

Prepare a crepe-style batter by combining the flour, milk, eggs and salt in a bowl and whisking together until no lumps remain and some air has been incorporated into the mixture. Smear the griddle with a little butter. Take a half ladle of batter, sprinkle some snow into the ladle and then pour onto the griddle. Cook for a minute or so until the edges begin to brown, then flip and cook the other side. Result: delicious pancakes full of holes.

E TRAIN CHERRY COLA ROAST HAM

MY FIRST TASTE OF THIS DELECTABLE DISH WAS IN THE WINTER OF 1985. SAM'S MOTHER, ELA, LIVED OUT IN QUEENS, AND EVERY MONTH SHE WOULD TAKE THE E TRAIN INTO MANHATTAN TO CHELSEA TO VISIT HIM WITH A HUGE THERMOS PACKED WITH HER SPECIAL ROAST HAM.

Opening the giant flask was like letting a genie escape from its lamp. A sweet smoky aroma filled the cold Chelsea apartment. It smelt like autumn. Ela wouldn't tell us the secret ingredient; we wondered if had been cured in molasses. Sam was eventually given the recipe when Ela was 82, and no longer cooking. A friend, Tony Wilce, tells me he ate many types of meat cooked in cola while living in Africa—including crocodile. Cola is a perfect tenderizer. The cherry cola, mustard and cherries give the ham a deep smoky sweetness—moist and tender. We also often cook ham in pineapple juice.

SERVES 6

One 4 1/2-pound unsmoked ham
1 large onion, cut in half
2 quarts cherry cola
Jack Daniel's whiskey
10 cloves

3 tablespoons dark molasses
Gulden's spicy brown mustard
1 small can (about 9 ounces) dark sweet cherries in syrup

Soak the ham in water overnight in the refrigerator to reduce its saltiness. Next day, throw this water away. Place the ham, skin side down, and the onion in a deep pot. Now the fun part: pour on the cherry cola and watch it fizz and bubble, then add a slug of Jack Daniel's. Add enough water to cover the ham. Bring slowly to a boil. Cover, reduce the heat and simmer gently for 2 1/2 hours. If you have some spare cola, make yourself a quick cook's cocktail with some Jack Daniel's.

Gently remove the ham and fish out the onion. You have a pan of wonderful stock—let it cool, then freeze. Preheat the oven to 475°F.

Lay a long piece of aluminum foil in a shallow roasting pan and place the ham on top. Trim off some of the outer fatty skin—leaving about a finger's depth. With a sharp knife, cut a deep crisscross pattern into the fat and stud it with the cloves.

In a small bowl, mix the molasses and mustard with a little of the syrup from the can of cherries. Pour over the ham and scatter a few of the cherries on top and around. Wrap the foil into a loose parcel and put the pan into the middle of the oven for 15 minutes. Open the foil and cook for another 5 minutes to finish off. Take out the ham and let it rest for 15 minutes before serving.

Serve with fried cucumbers (page 118), mashed potatoes and shredded red cabbage cooked with garlic, onions, apples, golden raisins, caraway and ham broth.

✪ EXCESS BAGGAGE

Another inspirational by-product of visiting New York, other than used rolls of film and that extended sense of excitement, is merchandise and sidewalk flotsam. The flea markets are exceptional, as are the treasure-filled Dumpsters and trash cans. My homebound rucksack would brim with *objets trouvés* destined for my studio, but I also became a one-person transatlantic export company for the larder back home. This slow addiction might start as a solitary purchase from a far-flung duty-free gourmet food display—perhaps a jar of regional chutney slipped in with your two-liter bottle of gin while your partner wasn't looking. More innocent acquisitions follow. Not content with buying suntan lotion in aisle 2, you purchase a bottle of chile sauce you admired in a restaurant the night before, taking a few extras as gifts. Soon you'll not only be seeking out culinary purchases at every conceivable opportunity, but the spare suitcase you brought for the return journey will be full of emblematic foodie gifts and foodstuffs you can no longer live without. A bonus of being a self-confessed epicurean exporter is the guilt-free air-miles you earn as you physically escort your purchases back to base. Although some imported items are available at home, I avoid their extortionate prices, relishing instead the satisfying associations of where I actually bought my produce—which is half the fun.

To prepare for a Manhattan spending spree my gastronomic homework should have included watching the grocery shopping habits of *Annie Hall* and *Taxi Driver*. Supermarkets were endemic in London by 1980, but New York provided a surprise— they were miniaturized. Packed with produce of bewildering choice. An alien graphic language, from tightly packed pharmaceuticals to fifteen varieties of milk. No color coding seemed to tie in with European expectations. Sales clerks packed your grocery bags and delivered them to your apartment door. Amazing. There was still a trace of grocery-store roots in Manhattan's neighborhood supermarkets. A reduced scale, makeshift displays, handwritten signs, personal contact, more akin to an old corner shop. Low ceilings, dense with variety, mist-covered salad displays, fruit in barrels. You rarely saw the whole store from a single viewpoint—sightlines were obscured by canyons of produce. Even though I knew these stores to be utterly profit driven, they seemed apart from the pile-it-high, branded, air-chilled hangar supermarkets whose lack of culinary drama removed any gastronomic possibility. Utility, utility, sell, sell— how boring. But these miniaturized markets, jammed and poured into minute high retail pockets, were and still are a joy to use. The true NYC produce meccas may still be Zabar's, Fairway Market, Citarella, Jefferson Market, Union Square Greenmarket,

Dean & DeLuca and Gourmet Garage but a small D'Agostino or Gristedes supermarket still possesses an inimitable charm, constitutes a neighborhood food experience, and is well worth exploring.

Recently we made a culinary pilgrimage to New York to hunt down old gastronomic haunts, discover new ones and add items to my "best food packaging" collection. Our daughter, Hannah, helped me search out possible contenders—a reward of 50¢ per find. She also discovered that unlike my wife, Jeff, I tend to take numerous hot-dog breaks and cake-testing pit stops en route. So while Jeff went off to check out a Chinese exhibition at the Met, we were left to graze.

Culinary urban guidebooks provide an invaluable historic backdrop but sadly the information dates quickly. Even the Internet lacks the edge over talking to friends who live and shop in New York daily. Dive into their fridges, read the labels, retrieve plastic carrier bags from their trash—then visit the shops. It requires instinct, like choosing where to have lunch from a parade of restaurants. The next evening, conversation during supper turned gastronomic as it often does, and Aimeé tells us of Fairway Market at 74th Street, which years ago had a chilled self-service meat room. Outside this freezing chamber were rows of heavy overcoats on hooks. Before stepping inside to select your meat, you borrowed an overcoat to keep warm. It sounded like a 90s art installation. I had to see it—if the room still existed.

First I investigate changes in the edible cityscape since our last visit, wondering how old favorites are faring. Upmarket food stores in Europe seem to last forever compared to their cousins in the volatile American marketplace, which has seen some serious casualties. Independent stores leaving the family fold seem to be most at risk. The wonder that was the original Balducci's closed early in the new millennium. It resembled a condensed Harrods Food Hall with an Italianate edge, a once quintessential New York gourmet landmark. Some say it was a victim of the dot-com revolution. It had been sold in 1999 when Nina and Andy Balducci retired. Still holding on in Greenwich Village is the inimitable Jefferson Market, a beautiful store, which manages to retain its neighborhood atmosphere and avoid the elite badge of dishonor. Citarella, whose origins were as a fish market, moved into the old Balducci's store down the street and it has grown into a veritable food emporium, awash with beautiful produce bathed in the deep aroma from a Neal's Yard cheese display; massive rounds of Montgomery cheddar and Colston Bassett stilton adding to the throng of smells—a great shop. (Late in 2005 a new Balducci's opened on the northern edge of the Village.) Farther uptown we stroll in awe of the largest, allegedly, supermarket in town, the Whole Foods Market at Columbus Circle, 59,000 square feet of food. From the Time Warner

Center mall an escalator lowers you into the store, providing a slow, cinematic entrance, as the vistas of the shop are gradually revealed—clever. We couldn't buy anything because the queue of miniature solo shopping trolleys at lunchtime was 40 deep, quite extraordinary.

That morning, Hannah had found my working travel diary on which she spotted the printing of Breakfast No. 1 and Breakfast No. 2 on each day. Horror! I had been sneaking out at 6 A.M. or earlier to get in some pancake research without her. Today we'd all have Breakfast No. 2 together at Zabar's, way uptown at 80th and Broadway. Zabar's is our first love of gourmet New York. After one smoked salmon cream cheese bagel in 1980 we were hooked. We hadn't been back for years. With a brother of the Zabar family opening the fabulous Eli's, a three-story deli, over on the East Side, I wonder how the mother ship Zabar's was faring. The produce looked as delectable as ever. The mezzanine kitchenware department was so densely packed it took us over an hour just to browse—we broke for coffee, cakes and spinach knishes and returned to pore over a few more aisles of kitchenalia. I bought a mug, tried on a few T-shirts—the new blue one is brilliant—considered a dishcloth or a Zabar's 9-inch bread knive and took every piece of paper or plastic marketing I could lay my hands on: Thanksgiving order forms, receipts, baguette bags, catalogues, plastic cups, salad containers and coffee bags. All in all a miniature museum of Zabar's packaging, carefully taken downtown to our excess luggage department. I also bought as much food as my backpack could carry.

As a detour from supermarkets we tried bookshops. New York boasts three exceptional cookbook bookshops. For new titles Kitchen Arts and Letters is rather like Books for Cooks in London and well worth the trip uptown. For rare, out-of-print collector's items there is a beautiful Federal building-style shop called Joanne Hendricks, which appears almost cottage-like, surrounded as it is by major redevelopments. Her books often appear at the top end of my book searches on abe.com. For people who want to cook from their out-of-print books rather than put them behind glass, there is Bonnie Slotnick's wonderful shop full of books—arranged thematically. When my wife saw me shaking with delight as we entered, she kindly took Hannah and herself off for an hour to leave me to rummage. I could have happily spent a week there. With a cheap shipping deal and reasonably priced books, it was hard not to buy a boxful—so I did. Bonnie had just received a shipment of African cookbooks from an enthusiast who supplies her culinary goodies from abroad. I also bought a Persian cookbook once owned by the food writer Nika Hazelton, which is a real delight.

Many of the high-end culinary purveyors in Manhattan had a singular starting point as perhaps coffee importers, fishmongers or ice cream makers. In an interesting phenomenon, as affluent dwellers fill up formerly commercial districts, companies such as Bazzini, who have been roasting nuts for more than 100 years in their downtown warehouse, evolve into an elite general food store. Bazzini operates from a gray Hopperesque corner building with an awning to shelter goods as they were unloaded from horse-drawn carts in the past. I might have to add an entire nut category for my "best packaging" survey due to Bazzini's bold graphics. The shop's interior is a classic downtown conversion, raw at the edges with exposed brickwork, paint-encrusted pillars, arterial plumbing, industrial floors and ceiling. Everything else is uniformly immaculate and considered—no expense spared. A look pioneered by Dean & DeLuca and perhaps Zona now copied citywide and worldwide. Which was the first food emporium to pipe in Mozart and use stainless steel rod shelving?

★ THE COLD ROOM

It was with some trepidation that I jump between Broadway express and local trains up to West 137th Street. Harlem. My slight unease on the street has more to do with unfamiliarity rather than any real threat of violence; it's not 1980. In spite of that I rush down an abandoned zig-zag stone staircase from Riverside Drive to the broad expanse of 12th Avenue. Above me the elevated section of the Henry Hudson Parkway thunders. Facing an icy stretch of the Hudson River are rows of block-built warehouses huddled along the shoreline. Announced in twelve-foot-high letters is the fabulous Fairway Market. It appears locked and shut, deserted sidewalks, empty roads. As I round the corner, the scene comes to life, a forklift unloading produce from a line of laden trucks and juggernauts. A ramp leads to the entrance of the warehouse interior, dark and cavernous, smaller hallways leading off into the gloom. As my eyes adjust, I see tall stacks of superb fruit and vegetables, great bins of squashes laid out on the rough uneven concrete floor. Ceilings vary from low, matte white-encrusted insulation to high-ducted expanses. They droop like stalactites, laden shelving reaching up toward them as stalagmites. Thankfully no Muzak, just a faint whispering of other customers elsewhere in the labyrinth. Uptown Fairway is an inclusive store catering to both Upper West Side foodies and its local Harlem residents. An unfussy approach. I feel at home here and wish I had a pickup truck waiting outside to take

me back to Tribeca so I could make use of this wondrous produce. Our friends Adam and Cindy from upstate would stop off for a buying expedition before driving on downtown; I wish they were here today. Floor-to-ceiling shelves packed with packets, cans and boxes—dense and thick, perfect for foraging. No daylight makes it in this far. The splendidly haphazard displays look as if they found their perching on the uneven floor on opening day. Wonderfully tangential, explanatory signs inform and entertain you as you browse *"Vare (Vah-ray), from the hills of Asturias, Spain, produced by a farmer who has 200 goats and five houses." "To use bottled salad dressing is to miss the point of salad altogether."* These esoteric musings are not the product of focus groups or advertising agencies; they are not beautifully printed—their success is a typically New York retail phenomenon. A layered approach that matures with time and can't be reproduced in a branded way. It reveals a mercantile intuitiveness and a passion for food, selling and communicating with customers. Steven Jenkins, the employee who writes the witty signs, says, "We heap scorn on anything that passes for gourmet. We heap scorn on Tuscan ethno-centrics. Maybe some East Sider thinks it's OK to pay $40 a liter for olive oil, but anyone who says it's worth it is a fool. We celebrate peasant food."

Deep in the store I reach a rotisserie area next to which are swing doors that resemble the entrance to an operating theater and a row of overcoats on hooks. The Cold Room. I was expecting a small room, like the legendary old meat room at the 74th Street Fairway, but this is like the cold store in Stanley Kubrick's film *The Shining*—10,000 square feet at 40°F. Once inside I see receding shelves of pre-packed meat through my billowing, frosty breath. Fish counters tended by cocooned staff. Prime 21-day, dry-aged beef. Every mega store should have one. In August it must overflow with loitering customers avoiding the humid summer heat outside. After an hour exploring I approach the line of checkouts and notice daylight again—it hasn't grown dark outside during my visit.

Out-of-state supermarkets are fast changing the dynamic of Manhattan shopping, with the arrival of Californian chains such as Trader Joe's and the introduction of website food delivery companies. All of these larger non-native outfits lack the disheveled charm of the smaller local chains such as D'Agostino and Gristedes, and the larger stores such as Fairway and Zabar's. Hopefully they can cohabit and the new stores may roughen at the edges with time, learning a few lessons from the grand epicurean masters.

Tony's Peanut Butter
Pancakes ← "meken"
see N"

...aten egg.
...water.
...½ liquid
...until smooth + bubbly
stir in rest liquid lightly.

JOS TILSON'S
PUMPKIN PIE

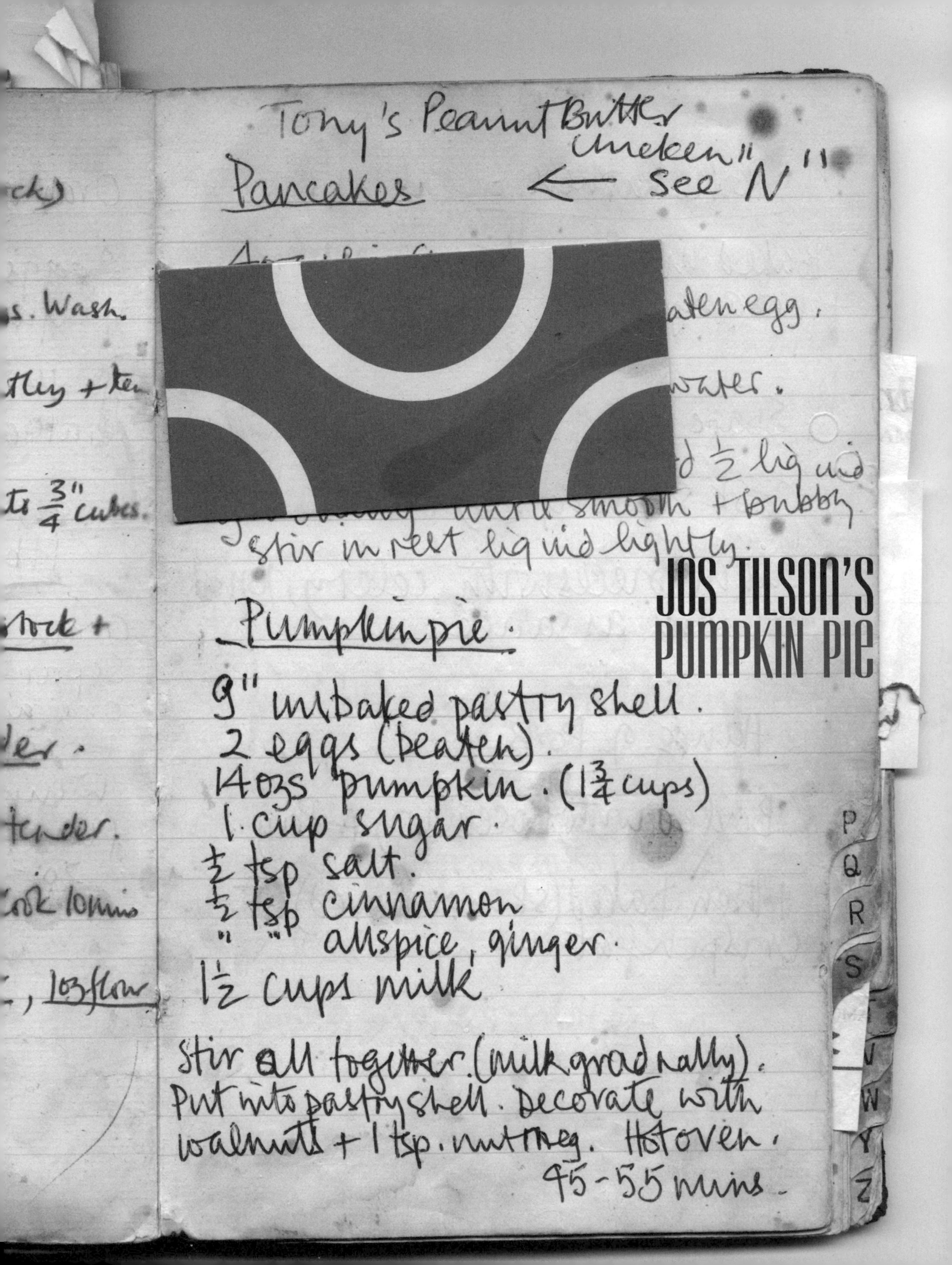

Pumpkin pie.

9" unbaked pastry shell.
2 eggs (beaten).
14 ozs pumpkin. (1¾ cups)
1 cup sugar.
½ tsp salt.
½ tsp cinnamon
" " allspice, ginger.
1½ cups milk

stir all together. (milk gradually).
Put into pastry shell. Decorate with
walnuts + 1 tsp. nutmeg. Hot oven.
45-55 mins.

Welcome to: Bienvenidos a:

WESTSIDE COFFEE SHOP
RESTAURANT

SERVING:
LUNCH - DINNER
ALL OUTGOING ALUMINUM PLATES .25¢ EXTRA

- FREE DELIVERY -

323 CHURCH STREET
(Corner of Canal Street)
New York, N.Y. 10013
Phone: (212) 334-0185

323 CHURCH STREET
(CORNER OF CANAL STREET)
NEW YORK NY 10013

WESTSIDE ★

If I thought London in 1980 was a colonial culinary collage, New York's immigrant kitchens redefined the phrase *melting pot*. Old diners, with stainless steel kitchens and wooden-boothed laminate tables still intact, attracted a new generation of owner-chefs. Some, such as the marvelous National Café Cuban Cuisine diner on 1st Avenue at 13th, cooked from a singular culinary tradition. Adam and I asked for recommendations and then snaffled up some *mofongo* with fried chicken and beans. I didn't have to eat again for at least three hours. Moving up the fusion food chain is Sam Chinita, the incomparable Chinese-Spanish diner on Eighth Avenue. Tripe, hot sauce, rice, beans and *bofongo* or chicken *yat kamein*. This is not haute cuisine fusion, not a coriander coulis or Vietnamese dipping sauce for your chips to be found anywhere. Their menu is just packed with single dishes continents apart. The fusion occurs on your table, on your plate and then on your palate—the mixture is yours. My favorite destination for multi-ethnic cooking is the Westside Coffee Shop, a Dominican-Mexican-American diner on Church Street, just below Canal, opposite a post office. It used to be on Canal Street itself, so coming out of the post office I double-take and remember the new location.

My lunchtime needs veer away from valet parking toward laminate tables and basic fare. Westside offers great food and a serious New York atmosphere—heavily uniformed cops line the lunch counter. I've never seen a uniformed policeman eating lunch out in a London café. Other Westside clientele include students, neighborhood eaters and the occasional stray tourist or suburbanite. I love the place so much I used it as a fictional location in my book *The Terminator Line*, at its Canal Street location. Since then I've recorded the sound of the diner, photographed it and eaten much of the food, up and down the menu. The menu is like a strange novel, starting at breakfast with emblematic American fare, home fries and the like. The Mexican infiltration occurs somewhere around side orders when on *Miércoles y Viernes* (Wednesday and Friday) you can order *arroz con gandules* (rice with pigeon peas). The temptation to theme the burger selection is thankfully overlooked, staying with the usual bacon, swiss cheese and deluxe combos. The full-blown Mexican platter combinations are a solid display of *enchiladas, burritos, empanadas, tacos, tostadas* and *quesadillas*—done in Tex-Mex style. I go for the back page—*Especial del día*, where the Dominican influence is in full flow. On a Wednesday I'll eat the *chivo guisado*, goat stew, served with thick black beans, slightly yellow rice and rich fried plantains. It's worth suffering seven hours economy air travel (fourteen if you include the ride home), just to sample these unfussy delights. I must make a Saturday trip next time to try the *sopa de mondongo*, beef tripe soup.

Fried Cucumbers

Simple and mouthwatering. You'll never look at a cucumber the same way again. Don't make soup with those cucumbers in the fridge—fry them! Best cooked in the summer as you might want to leave the window open while frying.

SERVES 6

About ½ cup cornmeal

Salt (optional)

2 English cucumbers, cut into long slices, ¼-inch-thick slices

Corn oil for shallow-frying

Heat a heavy frying pan over medium heat. Throw a large handful of cornmeal into a paper bag and salt if you like; add a few pieces of cucumber and shake until well covered with cornmeal. Pour a thin layer of corn oil into the pan and let it get good and hot. Fry the cucumber slices, turning once when golden on the first side. Remove the burnt cornmeal from the pan between batches. Drain the fried slices onto paper towels and cook the remaining cucumber slices. Eat quickly.

DOMINICAN SPICED GOAT STEW
CHIVO PICANTE

A Dominican dish from the northwest region of the island, La Linea. I eat it in New York alongside fluffy golden rice (page 177) and thick black beans (page 120)—perfect food for a frosty day spent digging in Canal Street junk shops.

SERVES 6

4 1/2 pounds goat meat, cut into cubes
1 onion, halved and roughly sliced
3 green bell peppers, coarsely chopped
2 green chiles, finely chopped
A handful of fresh oregano sprigs
Juice of 2 lemons

3 cloves garlic, crushed
1 tablespoon olive oil
1 teaspoon sugar
4 tomatoes, quartered
2 tablespoons tomato paste
Salt

In a large bowl, mix the goat with the onion, peppers, chiles, oregano, lemon juice and garlic. Heat the olive oil in a large frying pan, add the sugar and brown it, then add the cubed goat. Stir and brown the meat. Add 1 cup water, cover the pan and simmer for 35 minutes, adding extra water if needed. Put in the tomatoes, tomato paste and a little salt. Continue to simmer the stew, reducing the liquid with thickener.

THANKSGIVING WATER TOWER STACK

I came across this strange Chinese meal for two in New York in the 1980s. We often find ourselves there at Thanksgiving—the perfect time to visit. We celebrate it uptown, downtown, West Side and East Side, most often with my godparents.

SERVES 2

8 to 12 ounces boneless turkey breast, cut into thin strips
1/2 onion, finely chopped
A chunk of fresh ginger, thinly sliced
1 teaspoon sesame seeds
1 teaspoon soy sauce
1 red chile, seeded and thinly sliced
10 Brussels sprouts

8 canned or cooked chestnuts
A strange succotash
1/2 onion, finely chopped
1/4 cup cooked or canned flageolet or small white beans, chopped
1/4 cup corn kernels, chopped
2 small sweet potatoes, peeled and sliced
4 marshmallows

Use a four-tier Chinese steamer: compartment 1—turkey, onion, ginger, sesame seeds, soy sauce and chile, placed in a small metal pan; 2—sprouts and chestnuts; 3—succotash ingredients wrapped in foil; 4—sweet potatoes and marshmallows wrapped in foil. Steam the whole weird stack for 45 minutes. Serve with plain rice.

Dominican Black Beans
Habichuelas Negras

BASED ON THE CLASSIC *FRIJOLES DE OLLA*, BOILED BEANS, BUT INSTEAD OF USING PINTO BEANS, I USE BLACK TURTLE BEANS OR BRAZILIAN BLACK BEANS.

I adore a good plate of black beans, dark in color and rich in taste. The key to success is not soaking the beans and long, slow cooking. They are best eaten a few days later, when the flavor has fully developed, and even better frozen for a month or so and reheated.

SERVES 6

2 cups small dried black beans, picked over and washed

8 cloves garlic, chopped

1 teaspoon minced fresh epazote or oregano

1 dried chipotle chile

2 onions, finely chopped

2 tablespoons lard or corn oil, plus a little extra

Salt

2 tomatoes, chopped

In a large pot, combine beans, garlic, epazote, chipotle and half the onions. Cover generously with water, bring to a boil, then reduce heat and simmer gently for 30 minutes. Stir in the lard or oil and continue cooking until the beans are soft. Add boiling water as necessary when the pot gets low. Add salt only when the beans have softened and cooked.

Cook the tomatoes and the remaining onions in oil in a frying pan until the onions are translucent. Add a ladle of the cooked beans and liquid to the pan, and mash it with a potato masher or the back of a spoon. Add this mash back to the large pot of beans and stir to thicken the remaining liquid.

Variation

To transform your leftovers into *frijoles refritos*, refried beans, sauté 3 cloves chopped garlic and 1 chopped onion in peanut oil or lard. Add a pinch of ancho chile or crushed red pepper flakes and the beans, mash them, and then cook until pasty, stirring often. Serve with crème fraîche or cheese.

AS A CHILD OF THE SIXTIES I WAS DRAWN TO
NEW YORK, FROM MAX'S KANSAS CITY WHERE
THE VELVET UNDERGROUND PLAYED, TO KATZ'S
DELICATESSEN. ITS SYNTHESIS OF ARCHITECTURE,
ART, MUSIC AND FOOD WAS EXTRAORDINARY TO
EXPERIENCE FIRSTHAND IN THE 1980S AND 90S,
PRE–RUDY GIULIANI. I BOUGHT KITCHEN UTENSILS,
PLATES, GLASSES, BOWLS AND COOKBOOKS—
IN PARTICULAR, *THE SILVER PALATE COOKBOOK*,
THE SILVER PALATE GOOD TIMES COOK BOOK AND
THE NEW BASICS COOKBOOK ALL BY JULEE ROSSO
AND SHEILA LUKINS. GOLD'S REAL HOME-STYLE
HORSERADISH, PEPPER, SPICE MIXES, PANCAKE
MIX, ZABAR'S SPECIAL BLEND COFFEE, MEXICAN
CHILE SAUCES, WHOLE DRIED CHILES, JIFFY CORN
MUFFIN MIX, BAZZINI'S RAMS HEAD PISTACHIO
NUTS, HERSHEY'S KISSES AND HALLOWEEN CANDY.
WE LOVE THE CITY SO MUCH WE GOT MARRIED
THERE—MARRIAGE LED TO ANOTHER UNEXPECTED
CULINARY TREASURE TROVE—THE WILD HILLS AND
BAKERIES OF SCOTLAND.

Hunters wallpaper in the farm office.

WHIRLIES AND SKIRLIE

SCOTLAND

HOW MARRIAGE REFILLS THE KITCHEN LARDER

THE X-RAY SECURITY EQUIPMENT AT ABERDEEN AIRPORT OFTEN HALTS TO LOOK AT THE FRAIL SKELETAL OUTLINES OF GAME OR FISH BURIED IN OUR SOUTHBOUND HAND LUGGAGE. MY WIFE, JENNIFER, IS SCOTTISH AND ON VISITS TO HER PARENTS' FARM I HUNT DOWN REGIONAL PRODUCE, COOK FAMILY RECIPES ON THE AGA AND EXPERIMENT WITH PHEASANT AND DUCK SHOT ON THE FARM.

AA

THROUGHROUTES
to and from
ABERDEEN

ABERDEEN

SOMEWHERE ELSE
TO CALL HOME

The food writer Claudia Roden relishes the continual involvement that researching a culinary tradition brings with it. My research also keeps me in daily contact with what she calls *"the area which holds my roots."* As with most people, these roots stretch far and wide. Here I am on a wet autumn day in London surrounded by restaurant menus from New York and Paris, dusty branches of Tuscan bay leaves, a bottle of Arnaldo Antolini's *Vino Rosso di Toppello* for which I need to design a label, and half an Aberdeen buttery I cooked on Monday. These items can appear as mementos creating links to places and other times, but I also view them as utilitarian objects— raw material for art and design.

Marriage or any long-term partnership brings together not only two people but also different cultures, varied customs and diverse cuisines. Choosing an occasional summer holiday destination or deciding whose in-laws to spend Christmas with is a small consideration against the question of what you will cook together day in day out, 'til death us do part.

My fading Scottish roots were reawakened by marriage in my thirties to Jennifer, called Jeff—a shortened version of Jeffiner, her brother's childhood name for her. She possesses the equal unbounded energy of our daughter, Hannah. It's like living with two jet engines. Above all, Jeff is Scottish. My mother was born in Edinburgh and her father, Alastair Morton, was the artistic director of Edinburgh Weavers, a firm set up by his father, James Morton. Alastair, who was also a painter, invited artists such as Ben Nicholson and Barbara Hepworth to produce work for the firm. So Scotland had been lurking, dormant, in my subconscious for years, and although connected by a little Scottish blood, I felt the benefits of being married to a foreigner.

Culture and cooking—entirely different. Years later, I'm learning new Aberdeenshire Doric expressions, such as *cushie*, which means pigeon, or *trachled* (worn out, troubled, exhausted). Scotland also entered our kitchen, its cuisine a mystery to me.

As a gastronomic destination Scotland possesses much that a casual tourist might overlook. Fortunately, to enter an alien culture at a domestic level is far more revealing and rewarding. I begin to feel an ancestral resonance triggered by our visits there. Regional food cooked away from the homeland creates a connection in our London kitchen—a potent reminder of identity, a direct link for our daughter with Scotland and Italy, where her grandparents live. Unlike Italian food, which has assimilated itself into my being over decades, Scottish fare will require research. What do Scottish people eat? What are their kitchens like? I own a few books on Scottish cooking, mainly the "Scotland told in food and pictures" variety with grainy, historic photographs of ol' Aberdeen and crofters in the 1800s. These static images of careworn folk and empty, car-free streets unfortunately often lock the books' recipes in the past. I want to taste what is cooked today and see how it relates to the past. Like many agrarian-based cuisines, the best food was, and still is, cooked at home on small family farms. This is where the culinary heritage stems from and can still be found today. Necessity and poverty produced recipes of speed and immediacy as did cooking agents and available fuel. In older kitchens butter is found; olive oil lurks out in the scullery, little used. Anyone immersed in a nation's cooking finds himself researching ancient customs and traditions as well as soaking up recent influences. Classic Scottish cookbooks portray a rich and varied cuisine reflecting bountiful local produce from the sea, glens, fields and lochs. Past influence from France, Flanders and Scandinavia crept into both their vocabulary and recipes. Scotland's deeply rooted culinary history is wonderfully described in encyclopedic fashion by F. Marian McNeill in her 1929 book, *The Scots Kitchen: Its Lore and Recipes*, which has an entire appendix dedicated to Franco-Scottish domestic terms: Scottish *ashet*, a large serving dish from the French *assiette*; *gigot*, leg of lamb, from *gigot*; *tasse*, a cup, from *tasse*; *chauffen*, to warm, from *chauffer*—140 terms in all. I found the book rummaging in a run-down secondhand book shop in Brighton. To aid my research I also bought any book by Catherine Brown, who brings a great passion and knowledge of Scottish food and historical detail to all her works. Sadly, many great cookbooks tend to get superseded with each generation and knocked off bookshop shelves. Anyone seriously interested in books on food will have to hunt in secondhand shops, or online, to fill in the culinary gaps on their bookshelves. As my Scottish shelf lengthened, I eventually sought out specialist cookbook dealers. I'm well and truly hooked.

[handwritten recipe page:]

...pt stock hot. Place in roll & season. Stew
gently 1½ hrs. Thicken gravy, using 1 tablsp
blended flour. If water used add a little carrot
turnip, onion & garnish.

Scalloped Livers.

Boil the liver, cut into small cubes, mix with a
all cooked white sauce. Put into scalloped shell.
...inkle with brown crumbs & bake in hot oven.

Skirlie.

...cupful oatmeal.   Chop onion finely. fry
1 onion.   pale brown in dripping.
2 tablsp dripping   Add oatmeal. Cook lightly
Salt & Pepper.   5–10 mins. Season well.

Along with barley, oats have been a staple part of the Scottish diet for centuries. Oatmeal is used in porridge, brose, mealie jimmies, haggis, baking and the wonderful skirlie. Recipes that employ sparse ingredients require them to be of the highest quality. I also find this to be true of many Italian recipes—nowhere for a poor ingredient to hide. Fortunately, traditional milling methods in Scotland have survived and produce exceptional oatmeal. Oatmeal from Alford, at the Montgarrie Mills near Alford, Aberdeenshire, has been milled there since Jacobite times—in view of the craggy slopes of Bennachie. Powered by a water mill built in 1882 (see Supplies, page 245).

This Aberdeenshire dish of oatmeal cooked with onions is a great accompaniment to game, meat or fowl or to serve with mashed potatoes. It can also be used as stuffing. *Skirl-in-the-pan* is the noise made as butter sizzles in a pan—or rather screeches. You also hear the *skirl* of the bagpipes, and some say the haggis *skirls*. You'll make double portions the second time you make skirlie because it's so good.

SERVES 4

4 tablespoons butter, margarine or
   dripping
1 onion, finely chopped

2 cups medium oatmeal
Salt and pepper

Melt the frying fat in a pan and gently sauté the onion until golden. Stir in the oatmeal with a wooden spoon and cook the dry mix for 5 to 10 minutes. Season well.
Skirlie is best served with gravy to moisten it.

SWEETHEART 👉 PHEASANT STEW

TODAY I WANT TO COOK WITH A CAN OF SCOTTISH STOUT AND A PHEASANT THAT MY FATHER-IN-LAW REARED AND SHOT. A BEFITTING RECIPE IS NEEDED. WITH A VAGUE RECIPE IN MIND, I CONSULT SEVERAL BOOKS.

I stumbled upon *The Poacher's Cookbook* by Prue Coats in a used bookshop in Notting Hill Gate. One of her pigeon dishes is a casserole based on Carbonnade, a Flemish beer and beef stew. This seems in keeping with Scotland, as French and Flemish influences abounded in Scotland in the 1600s and 1700s. This took me to *Escoffier: A Guide to Modern Cookery* (1907), found in a junk shop in Hampstead. Unfortunately most of his *faisan*/pheasant recipes involve foie gras and truffles. However, his *à la Carbonnade* uses powdered sugar—and a sweet Scottish stout combines both ale and sugar. I'm on the right path. More helpful is Jane Grigson's *Good Food*. Her rendition of *à la Normande* leads me to consider cinnamon; I shall avoid the cream. *The Reader's Digest Cookery Year* recipe *faisan au verger* offers bay leaf, parsley and celery—I won't use the apples or cider. Their Carbonnade suggests a bread topping with garlic butter. Finally, Elizabeth David in *French Provincial Cooking* recommends fennel as an addition. I poach ideas from here and there, and the result is a warming, sweet winter stew with a hint of cinnamon and a garlic bread topping. Can be cooked in advance—adding the topping on the day of eating.

SERVES 6

2 or 3 pheasants

For the stock

Stock vegetables—1 stalk celery, 1 onion, 1 carrot, chopped

10 peppercorns

Flour for dusting

2 tablespoons butter

20 shallots, peeled

1 teaspoon ground cinnamon

2 bay leaves

2 stalks celery, thinly sliced

1 tablespoon red wine vinegar

3 fennel bulbs, roughly chopped

One 500-ml (18-ounce) can Sweetheart stout or 2¼ cups other stout

A handful of roughly chopped fresh parsley

Salt and pepper

3 handfuls button mushrooms

A small basket of small round berries such as huckleberries, blueberries or cranberries

For the topping

3 cloves garlic, crushed

2 tablespoons butter

1 baguette or a thick crusty white country loaf

Dijon mustard

Cut the pheasant into serving pieces and reserve the skin and all the bones. Make a stock with the carcasses, celery, onion, carrot, and peppercorns. Lightly flour the pheasant pieces. Melt the butter in a large frying pan over medium heat. In batches, brown the pheasant on both sides in the butter. Remove to a platter.

Add the shallots and cinnamon to the pan and cook a few minutes, loosening any burnt bits on the bottom of the pan with a tablespoon of the stock.

Add the bay leaves, celery, wine vinegar and fennel. Pour the can of stout into the pan, minus a small glass for the chef. It's a sweet, light-tasting stout. Add the parsley, browned pheasant pieces and enough stock to cover all the ingredients. Season with salt and pepper. Finally, sprinkle the mushrooms and berries on top. Cover and simmer gently for 40 minutes. Either let cool and refrigerate overnight for finishing the next day, or continue with the carbonnade topping.

Preheat the oven to 425°F. Make garlic butter by melting the butter in a pan with the crushed garlic; keep warm. Choose a wide baking dish about 3 inches deep; I use a Spanish earthenware dish. Pour the cooked stew into the dish. The liquid needs to be just poking up around the contents; add extra water if you need to. Cut the bread into ¾-inch-thick slices. Spread mustard on each slice and arrange in a tight layer, mustard side down, over the stew. Brush the top of the bread with the garlic butter.

Bake on the middle oven rack for about 30 minutes. When ready, the breaded top should be golden and crispy with the stew bubbling around the edges. Serve with kailkenny (page 147), and mealie jimmies (onion and oatmeal sausages) or skirlie (page 129).

LAND O' CAKES

On visits to Aberdeenshire I become an explorer and gastronomic detective—on the lookout for differences. Subtle nuances that reveal local character and color. I hunt down vernacular baking, examine packaging, photograph shop architecture, collect cookie typography, buy used books and jars of local produce, gradually building up a body of clues that at first sight appear peripheral. I approach my search as a novelist or set designer would, trying to find everyday items that wholly embody their location but are not parodies of it. Objects that reflect indigenous culture become carriers of its history. It's a slow sifting process, mainly of elimination. A key test requires taking an object *down south*. Removing it from the babble of interference that surrounds an item enables a clearer test of authenticity. Which brand of oatcake makes you want to get straight back on a plane heading north?

Once off the beaten track, away from the ubiquitous marbled shopping malls full of multinational logo-produce, Scotland still has a thriving sense of itself. Look beyond the tartan trappings. Aberdeenshire is crammed with high-quality local producers and delicious foodstuffs and its kitchens produce wonderful meals which often reflect the season or help you enjoy the weather conditions outside.

If you are interested in local vernacular, recipes and produce bakeries offer a good starting place, acting as a barometer for the state and health of a region. The closing of a bakery is a bad omen for a community. As well as preserving indigenous traditions, bakeries often reflect the full cultural mix of a neighborhood and the changing tastes of their customers. For a bakery to add a new cake or variation on a loaf is relatively easy if they produce and sell their own goods. There are few overheads beyond the imagination of creating something new. No special packaging,

Bakeries in Turriff, Stonehaven and Portsoy. Fishmonger and general store at Whitehills. Butcher in Tarves.

distribution or marketing is required. Even in the most brand-conscious, supermarket-driven high streets or shopping malls, bakeries often thrive, preserving traditional recipes and keeping local food available.

Some of Scotland's finest food is baked. Butteries, black bun, bannocks, oatcakes, shortbread, scones, Forfar bridie, ginger cake and Dundee cake. The best bakeries still avoid using the unmentionable hydrogenated vegetable fat, long may they continue. Sadly, many local bakeries around Methlick have closed. Crighton's in Methlick is now a doctors' office. Cumming's in Tarves was a bakery, then a bakehouse supplying local MACE supermarkets—now it's closed. However, Ythan Bakery in Ellon, north of Aberdeen, is thriving and sums up all that I expect from a first-class bakery. The shop is named after the river Ythan, which flows off the hills of Formartine through Methlick, Ythanbank and down through Ellon to the North Sea. Originally the bakery was owned by the Scottish Co-op but it was acquired by John Gillan in 1970 and is now run by his son Michael and his wife. Ellon was expanding in the 1970s to accommodate workers in the oil industry. Ythan Bakery is a well-established family firm with strong community ties. They supply local shops in Balmedie, Newburgh and Mintlaw, as well as local hotels. They're members of the Scottish Association of Master Bakers. At the moment they are gearing up for Christmas. Ellon's festive decorations will be turned on December 1, and the bakery is running flat out to fill orders of Christmas cake and shortbread fingers to firms and local individuals who have placed orders. One entire bake room is dedicated to shortbread at this time of year. Over the years the range of produce has increased considerably. Bread, which was originally either white or brown, is now made in-house and comes in a wide range of styles, flours and finishes. Michael Gillan invested in an electric oven in 1970. New houses have been built in Ellon and locals' requirements have changed. Hotels ask for dinner rolls and croissants. We visit the bakery on our way to the beach at Newburgh when Ellon Academy is turning out for lunch. The school empties onto the streets for its lunch hour. If you are delayed crossing the road the queue inside the Ythan Bakery can grow from three to thirty in as many

Sweetshop and bakery in Stonehaven. Butcher in Methlick. Butchers in Turriff and Oldmeldrum.

seconds—all hungry children. Their holiday specials are always a draw for our daughter, Hannah. Spooky, decorative Halloween buns—a Scottish tradition (All Hallow's Eve comes from the ancient Celtic festival of *Samhuinn)*. Big Easter sponges or frosted Santa pies. This seasonal, festive feel covers all the main holidays during the year. Black bun is the old Scottish Twelfth Cake, which was transferred to Hogmanay after the banning of Christmas and its subsidiary festival Uphalieday, or Twelfth Night, by the reformers. Robert Louis Stevenson called black bun "a black substance inimical to Life." The shape of a brick, it's moist, fruity and, rather like an extremely thick sandwich, it has thin shortcrust pastry as a base and top. Black bun is an expensive cake for a bakery to make, packed with nuts, raisins, currants, candied citrus peel and spices—no hidden filler—and matured for two months. Many large bakeries have ceased making it. I look for a delicate, thin pastry top and a dark, black, dense slab underneath. The best I've eaten was from George Robertson in Stonehaven, perfection.

After buying a bag full of perkin biscuits, buckies biskets, shortbread rounds and butteries at The Ythan Bakery, Hannah and I share a Scotch pie or two en route to meet Jeff and her mother, Mary, in Safeway.

My first taste of Scottish buns was in the 1960s. My Scottish uncle, Alex, was a dairy farmer in Ayrshire. His wife, Irene, was first a potter and later ran the local Robbie Burns Centre. They have four children—twins Alastair and Patrick, and daughters Gill and Shireen. While on visits from Englandshire, my sisters and I played in dusty haylofts on the farm and watched chickens and cows. As we walked back home through the swaying field of wheat, we listened out for the rattling drone of Blacky's mobile shop from Maybole. A small van with a miniaturized shop interior, the van door opened like a giant sweet box, the smell of sugar filling the air. It was loaded with canned foods, unfamiliar brands in bright packets, exotic sweets in strange shapes, butter shortbread and wooden trays of pink pastries. Alex and Irene also had regular deliveries from their local butcher, fishmonger and greengrocer.

Oatmeal crunch.

SCOTCH BROTH

Lunchtime broth wards off a blizzard outside that has brought down power cables and closed roads. The perfect winter soup. Sweet, tasty and filling. Traditionally it would be made with mutton stock. The broth mix contains barley, yellow split peas, dried peas, green split peas and red split lentils.

SERVES 6

One 3½-ounce package Scotch broth mix (look for Kedem Vegetable Soup Mix in the U.S.)

7 cups stock of your choice

3 carrots, finely diced

1 small peeled turnip slice, finely diced

1 leek, finely chopped

Salt and pepper

A handful of frozen peas

A handful of chopped fresh parsley

Soak the broth mix overnight in water to cover. The next day, rinse the mix in a sieve under cold running water and put into a large saucepan. Add the stock, along with water if necessary to cover by 2 inches. Simmer for 15 minutes, skimming off any scum. Add the carrots and turnip, then, after 8 minutes add the leek. Season, unless your stock is already salty. Cook until all the barley is soft, 30 minutes or so. Finally add the peas for the last few minutes.

Serve in deep bowls, sprinkled with the fresh parsley. Serve with oatcakes.

At dinner, Dr. Johnson ate several plates of Scotch broth,
with barley and peas in it, and seemed very fond of the dish.
I said, "You never ate it before?"
Johnson, "No sir, but I don't care how soon I eat it again."

BOSWELL, JOURNAL OF A TOUR TO THE HEBRIDES
WITH SAMUEL JOHNSON, 1786

ANCESTRAL LANDSCAPE

Home for me is both a state of mind and a shifting geographical territory. As a building, home is where family dust settles on accumulated possessions and memories are made. In our street I share a local communal history of building development battles and school runs. The city beyond our neighborhood holds a deeper vision of time, colliding scenes of childhood against college days, layers of professional life and eventually viewing the metropolis as a father. However, feeling at home is not a sensation restricted to where I spend the majority of my year and pay property taxes. Home occurs in a scattering of locations and in varying degrees, forming a personal atlas that acts as an embedded touchstone connecting these disparate locations, expanding my sense of what and where is family and home.

Food and cooking are pivotal to building this sense of identity. Marriage brought extended family connections deeply rooted in the local rural community north of Aberdeen, opening up a rolling genealogical landscape. The family farm perches on the windswept hills of the Formartine area of Aberdeenshire, which butts out into the wintry North Sea. Kodiak Island off Alaska shares the same latitude. Jeff's brother, Ernie, now runs the family farm and also helps manage a second farm in Poland. Their sister, Susie, is married to a vet, Bill, who runs the Laurencekirk Animal Hospital south of Aberdeen.

Driving through the Aberdeenshire farming landscape with Jeff's family is a special experience. Like most city dwellers, I am used to seeing passing, nameless vistas of anonymous fields, unidentified crops and outsized road signs pointing to villages with enigmatic names. Even if I studied local agriculture, geology and history, I would still remain blind to what is visible to them. As the artist Rebecca Solnit said, "Landscape's most crucial condition is considered to be space, but its deepest theme is time." Jeff and her family, like others who live within their ancestral landscape, have the ability to perceive time, past and present. A vast map would be necessary to chronicle their awareness of change—rotating crops, asparagus being tried, flooded fields, crop yield, banks of snow, a snail farm, repossessed steadings, changing businesses, village halls, churches, graveyards and roads that lead to the sea. There is a tale told by the Argentinian writer Jorge Luis Borges of a forgotten republic whose only surviving artifact is a life-size map of their country, drawn in one-mile-square folded sections. Scraps of these actual-size maps are said to blow about our wastelands or lie awaiting rediscovery in musty antiquarian book shops.

Up past the farmstead and grain-dryer beyond the farm and out to the braes stretches a view of staggering beauty. This panorama is in stark contrast to the rolling farmland and stone dike-lined dirt roads with wind-sculpted trees. As with my own

internal vista of mounded, oak mountains in Tuscany, it is a scene that over slow time embeds itself in you. This view across the braes seems to be a physical, inseparable part of Jeff. The River Ythan cuts a winding gorge with craggy grass slopes and rock cliffs through thick woodland disappearing into misted wilderness beyond. The Ythan's spreading floodplain is covered in thick reeds and scattered with silver birch. A scene that conveys daily seasonal change. Jeff's family have lived on their farm since 1953. They farm and breed beef cattle alongside mixed arable crops.

Jeff's father, Ernie, also reared pheasants, constructed ponds for wild duck and planted extensive woodland cover. His parents had been tea planters and farmers in Sumatra.

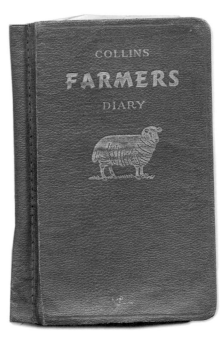

Ernie was an expert animal tracker with an encyclopedic knowledge of the changing bird population and their habitats. He had an intimate understanding of the forbidding nature that he was part of. The land's accretion of history and its wildlife were an integral part of him. He rarely left the pull of Aberdeenshire. To observe him walking through the lower field approaching the dark woodland made me conscious of his astute awareness of the land he worked and the gradual evolution he had witnessed.

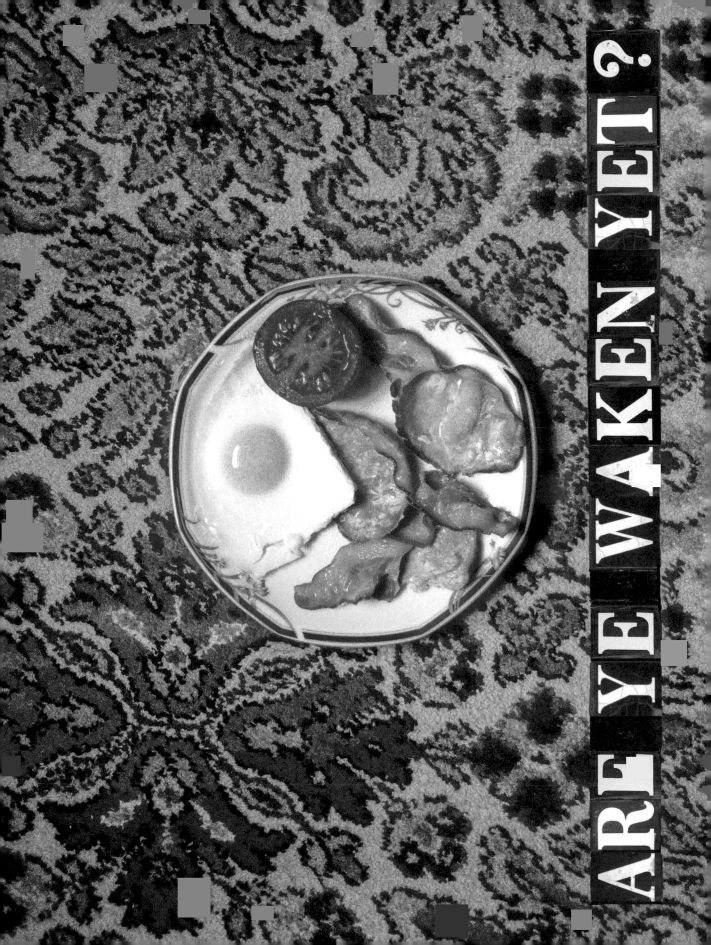

ARE YE WAKEN YET?

CULLEN SKINK

Aberdeen has been a major center for haddock since the thirteenth-century. On the Moray Firth is the small town of Cullen, from which this creamy smoked haddock soup gets its name. It is sometimes called fishwives' stew. Variations on the recipe allow you to make it either like a stew or like a soup. *Skink* means an essence of Cullen or a stew. We have bought finnan haddie and kippers from Downies in Whitehills, along the coast from Cullen. The extraordinary aroma was so strong we had to quadruple-box the fish for our check-in luggage.

SERVES 4

1 pound finnan haddie (smoked haddock)	4 tablespoons butter
2 onions, peeled, 1 chopped	1 pound potatoes, peeled and
1 bay leaf	chopped into bite-sized pieces
Generous 3 cups milk	Pepper
Generous 3 cups water	Finely chopped fresh parsley

Place the finnan haddie, the whole onion and the bay leaf in a wide saucepan with the milk and water. Bring gently to a boil and simmer for 5 minutes, then let cool in the liquid for 15 minutes. Strain the liquid and reserve it. Skin and carefully remove any bones from the finnan haddie.

In a large saucepan, melt the butter and sauté the chopped onion until translucent. Add the strained liquid and the potatoes and cook until they are soft. Some people now puree the mixture in a blender before flaking the fish into it. I prefer the potatoes to have a bit of a bite to them, so I leave most of them whole, mashing a few. Flake the fish into the mixture, season with pepper and heat through. Serve with a sprinkle of parsley. You can also add a little cream. Yesterday's mashed potato can be substituted for uncooked potatoes.

A view of Cullen.

ATHOLL BROSE

Some dishes open up labyrinthine paths back into history, not only revealing previous tastes but also illuminating the lives and circumstances of those who developed and used the recipes. Atholl brose, legend has it, was a drink used against fifteenth-century enemies of the Earl of Atholl in Perthshire. The intoxicating mixture cunningly rendered the enemy unconscious. It was also served to Queen Victoria when she visited Blair Atholl in 1844. The creamy, rich Atholl brose of today, often served as a dessert, stems from brose. Brose was born out of poverty and resourcefulness and consisted of oatmeal, salt and boiling water, with milk if any could be afforded. It was quick to prepare and avoided the usual one-third shrinkage of porridge when it cooled. Another method uses soaked oatmeal, which is pressed to extract a foamy liquid; the oatmeal mush is discarded, and the liquid has heather honey and whiskey added. It's whisked together and bottled for a chilly day or for when you have a cold. The version we serve on Burns Night is a dessert. Sassenachs!

SERVES 4

2 cups whipping cream

2 tablespoons heather honey

7 tablespoons fine oatmeal, toasted

1/2 cup Scotch whiskey

Beat the cream until soft peaks form, then fold in the honey and most of the toasted oats. Refrigerate for 30 minutes.

Before serving, fold in the Scotch. Put the mixture into glasses and top with the remaining toasted oatmeal.

Alternatively, soak the oatmeal in the whiskey and honey, and refrigerate for a week. Serve with a drizzle of honey. Another recipe that uses oatmeal, whiskey and cream is cranachan or cream crowdie. Toast a scant cup of coarse oatmeal until lightly browned. Whisk a cup of heavy cream, a cup of whipping cream, a little superfine sugar and a tablespoon or two of Scotch whiskey until stiff. Layer the oatmeal and cream mix with fresh raspberries in a glass bowl.

Aye since he wore the tartan trews
He dearly lo'ed the Athole Brose.

NEIL GOW, 1727–1807

BLIZZARD DUCK

Aberdeenshire is smothered in snowdrifts, choking all roads. We can't go anywhere. I have a flashback— I'm standing in the small English-language section of an antiquarian bookshop, near the Hortoget Saluhall subterranean market in Stockholm, backpack laden with pancake mix, gherkin sauce and jars of cloudberry jam, as well as audio recording equipment and too many cameras. Wedged in a tight corner of the bookshop propping up a shelf is a heavy tome on ancient Chinese gastronomy. A five-volume set, this is Book 1. I should really be getting back to the hotel, so I flip through the book quickly but manage to read a poetic account of an old custom for cooking wild duck that guarantees succulence. Duck are boiled, then plunged into a deep bank of snow to cool rapidly. The cooked birds are briefly roasted later in the day. It may not be a Scottish dish, but it uses indigenous fowl, local weather and is suited to the Aga. Precooking the duck allows the Aga to recover its heat before roasting and lets the kitchen return to a comfortable humidity level. Requires a slow, snowbound day.

BEING AN OPPORTUNIST IS AN ASSET FOR A COOK, NOT ONLY WHEN TRYING TO DEAL WITH MISTAKES AS THEY OCCUR BUT ALSO TO RECOGNIZE CHANCE AND INTERESTING CULINARY POSSIBILITIES. TODAY I HAVE TWO WILD DUCKS AND A FOOT OF FRESHLY FALLEN SNOW.

SERVES 6

1 or 2 wild mallard ducks	Honey
1 teaspoon salt	
Worcestershire sauce	Freshly fallen snow

Gut and clean your ducks, or buy them from a good local butcher.

Part 1. Boiling and snow-cooling

I certainly don't have a pan big enough at home to boil two large ducks. Luckily Mary has a huge pot that easily accommodates the two birds immersed in water. Bring the water to a gently rolling boil. Put the ducks in, add the salt and simmer for 40 minutes.

Carefully lift the birds out. Discard the greasy gray water. (If someone knows a use for this water, please write to me; I hate waste.) Dry the duck with paper towels and carry them on a tray outside. Mary's kitchen fortunately has a lawn nearby sloping up away from the house that catches snow beautifully. Bury the ducks for 15 to 20 minutes. Choose a stretch of snow that you know to be dog, cat and raccoon free! Tracking pet activity in fresh snow is a cinch. Once cooled, exhume the birds and take them indoors. Store in the fridge for later.

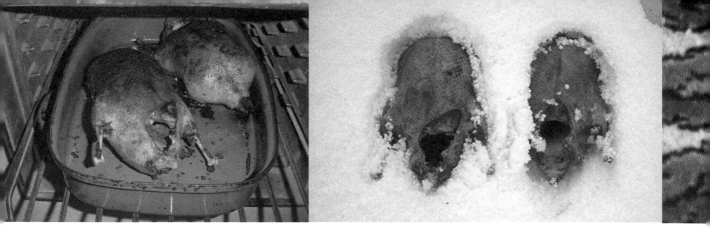

Part 2. Roasting

I use the term *roasting* casually here. Ideally you should now spit-roast the duck in front of a fierce fire in order to heat it through and crackle the skin. Ovens don't really "roast," they "bake"—and few people own a roasting spit!

The succulent boiled birds only require finishing in a hot oven. Preheat the oven to 425°F. Put the ducks in a roasting pan and baste with a little Worcestershire sauce and honey. Roast them for about 20 minutes, to brown the skin but retain the juices inside. Being used to Agas, I check the duck every few minutes after the first 15 minutes—I don't want to frazzle them, undoing all the work of the boiling and cooling. Cover the cooked birds and let them rest for 15 minutes before serving. I use poultry shears and cut them into large portions. I would recommend serving this with a wild fruit sauce (page 224), skirlie (page 129) and kailkenny (opposite).

Variations

The duck can be boiled and cooled and either put in the fridge for the next day or frozen for another day. I froze a few birds and wrapped them in newspaper to take back to London in our luggage—still frozen after five hours' travel.

KAILKENNY

There are many northern British recipes that combine boiled cabbage with potatoes, such as Rumbledethumps (Borders) and Colcannon (Highlands). In Aberdeenshire the variation is called Kailkenny. As F. Marian McNeill notes, it is probably a corruption of Colcannon. It's a great last-minute-assembly dish.

SERVES 6

1 large bowl of just-boiled potatoes

1 cup milk

A large bowl of cooked, finely shredded cabbage

1 cup light or heavy cream

Salt and pepper

Mash the potatoes with the milk in a large saucepan. Mix in the cabbage and heat thoroughly, stirring occasionally. Stir in the cream and season well. Serve with game, grilled kippers, or sausage and egg.

Variations
Add a boiled onion, melted pan drippings, or cooked rutabagas or carrots.

There's cauld kail in Aberdeen
 And custocks in Straithbogie
Where ilka lad maun ha'e his lass,
 But I maun ha'e my cogie.

OLD SCOTTISH SONG

KIPPERS
90p. lb.
£1·99. kg.

BUTTERIES 👉

Bawbee Baps and Buttery Rowies!

OLD ABERDEEN STREET CRY

MAKING BUTTERIES, LIKE OTHER FLOUR-BASED STAPLES SUCH AS ROTIS AND TORTILLAS, CONNECTS ME TO A DIFFERENT SENSE OF TIME AND PLACE. IN ESSENCE THEY RESEMBLE THE FLATTENED BUCHAN PENINSULA BATTERED BY THE NORTH SEA—FOR BUTTERIES ARE LIKE A FLAT, SLIGHTLY SALTY, SOLID CROISSANT.

Perfect with marmalade or local honey. These delights would have been cooked by granny before you awoke, made and tended amid a score of other dawn chores. Today I can cook butteries after Hannah is back from school, between supper, homework, reading and bathtime, as they require small amounts of attention over three hours' proofing time. You'll need a warm spot for the dough to rise. Beef drippings are supposed to create a deep and rich buttery. Can be made in advance and frozen.

MAKES 12 BUTTERIES

Scant 2 1/4 cups bread flour

1/2 teaspoon salt

1 1/2 teaspoons sugar

Two 1/4-ounce packages active dry yeast

1/2 cup plus 1 1/2 tablespoons warm water

4 tablespoons lard (or vegetable shortening or beef drippings)

8 tablespoons (1 stick) butter

Find a large mixing bowl, sift in the flour, then add the salt. In a small bowl, combine the sugar and yeast. Add the water, mix and then pour over the flour. Stir with a wooden spoon until you have a dough. Cover the bowl of dough with plastic wrap or a damp cloth and find somewhere warm for it to rise for 30 minutes, or until it has doubled in size. I use the top of our kitchen gas-fired hot water tank, which is warm but not hot. I might build a small shelf high up in the kitchen to make use of the warm upper air currents.

Take the lard and butter out of the fridge so they can warm up.

When the dough has risen, take another bowl and cream together the lard and butter. Divide this mixture into three in your bowl. Turn out the yeasty, rather sticky dough onto a well-floured board. It needs careful handling. Roll the dough into a long

strip about 12 inches long, 4 inches wide and 3/4 inch thick. Take one of the lard-butter piles and spread it over the surface of rolled dough. Gently pick up one end and fold it over the middle third of the strip, pick up the other end and fold it over to create a slightly heaped square. Let the dough rest somewhere cool for 10 minutes or more. This rests the gluten, which makes flour elastic. I use my wife's ceramic studio next to our kitchen. On a chilly autumn evening, it's like a fridge.

Repeat the rolling, larding, folding and resting twice more using the other piles of lard-butter. Let the dough rest again.

Roll out the dough into a rectangle about 8 inches by 6 inches and 3/4 inch thick. Cut into 2-inch squares, folding under the corners. Place these 2 inches apart on a greased, floured baking sheet. Cover again with plastic wrap or a damp cloth and let rise for 30 minutes somewhere warm.

Preheat the oven to 400°F.

Uncover the butteries and bake on the middle oven rack for 20 to 25 minutes, until slightly golden. Take out of the oven and place on a wire rack to cool.

These freeze well. To reheat, warm them slightly under the broiler. Or, if you have an Aga, put the butteries in a paper bag to warm in the oven.

theCooker

fine foods for the family

Dec 6. 2003

jake@thecooker.com

16 Talfourd Road London SE15 5NY
www.thecooker.com
www.areaatlas.com

Nancys birth & (emmett ?)

Maria & Anthony

GROUSE in at
7·45
8·00 POTS
8.45 BROCCOLI
TOAST +
uncover
9.00 OUT — settle
& eat 9.15

note: bird out at 9·10 — slightly
bloody still — leave in another
10 minutes . .

Recipe name:

ROAST ALLARGUE GROUSE

Head note:

Stuffing — 12 dried apricots
(chopped)

1 teaspoon — pomegranate molasses
& pepper
        mix & leave to stand

stuff birds
strips bacon on top
        butter on pan
        surround with whole
        onion & garlic.

GAS 6. 200C — 400F
1 hour — baste!
(take off bacon.
place thick slice of toast
under each bird —
cook for 10 min — until
breasts are browned.

whole broad
beans —
soaked overnight

boiled — 1 bayleaf
for 30 mins ?

2 clove — garlic
2 onion — cut into
        rings

add 1 cup pigeon
stock — simmer for
five minutes — CUT X
cover. Turn off
can be reheated later

POTS

P W

Faro — boiled — 5 →
1
washed — 30 minutes

cook 2 onion
9 walnuts
15 cashewnuts
5 chopped sage leaves
1 plum

cook for
7 minutes
(a slug of
        whiskey

1 moistened it
with ½ cup of
pigeon stock

beat in 1 egg

I used about 5
large handfuls of
cooked faro

butter an oven dish.
bake for 1 hour

Yield line:

Time for preparation:

Ingredients list:

Allargue — from Erase

Grouse — small but succulent
— they smell sweet when cooking &
pungent ?

wonderful, deep, succulent taste
a great success.

Gravy
½ pint pigeon stock
1 teaspoon cranberry sauce / jelly
combine.
Roasting pan 1 tablespoon
of whisky

ROCK CAKES

Mary Lee's mouthwatering, melt-in-the-mouth rock cakes—perfect for a cup on the fly after a walk on the hill or a drive to the beach. More milk makes them softer—less rocky. Use butter instead of margarine if you wish.

MAKES ABOUT 14 ROCK CAKES

2 cups self-rising cake flour

1¹/₃ cups granulated sugar

Pinch of salt

8 tablespoons (1 stick) margarine

1 cup golden raisins

1 large egg

2 tablespoons milk

Preheat the oven to 375°F.

Combine the flour, sugar and salt in a bowl. Rub in the margarine. Add the raisins. Beat the egg with the milk. Add to the flour mixture and mix together with a fork. Using the fork, put rough heaps onto a greased baking sheet, making about 14 cakes.

Bake for about 12 minutes, until golden.

THE COOKER
Auld Scottish fare

Presents

BURNS NIGHT

we request the pleisure of yir companee for denner at oor hoose.

JAN 25TH

Statue of Robert Burns by Henry Bain Smith, 1892, Union Terrace, Aberdeen.

BURNS

Hosted by the Peckham Burns Club
PECKHAM'S PREMIERE SCOTTISH EATERIE

HAGGIS DENNER

'I wisna fou' but just had plenty.'
Robert Burns 1759-1796

BILL O' FARE

GUSTY KICKSHAWS

Smoked Pheasant on oatcakes Ernie Lee's birds *8.00* €
Smoked Mackerel Pate on brown bread 8.00 €
Formatine Whirlies 8.00 €

BROTH

Scotch Broth 14.00 €

The Address

BURNS' SELKIRK GRACE

Some hae meat, and canna eat,
And some wad eat, that want it,
But we hae meat and we can eat,
And sae the Lord be thankit.

HAGGIS

Ashet of Aberdeenshire Haggis 30.00 €
Findlay & Leiper of Insch,

served with

Chappit Tatties, Bashed Neeps,
Skirlie. Nairns Oatcakes GM free

ITHER ORRA EATTOCKS

Black Bun Robertson of Stonehaven *9.50* €

Atholl Brose, Cranachan Jeff' conglomeration *9.50* €

Buckies Biskets, Shortbread Rounds, Perkins Biscuits
Ythan Bakery, Ellon

A Tassie o' coffee 5.50 €

Rob Roy:
Famous Grouse,
Martini Rosso Vermouth,
Curacao Triple Sec,
bitters, cherry

HAGGIS AND NEEPS

Bashed neeps (mashed rutabaga), *chappit tatties* (mashed potatoes) and haggis are the main trio for our Burns Night *bill o' fare*. Every piece of tartan we can muster decorates the room, along with maps, paintings of the bard, printed menus, kilts, antlers and poetry books—resembling a crazed Scottish tourist board window display. In keeping with a more spartan ethos, we should really strip the dining room bare, reinstate benches, a single candlestick and a plain table on which to eat our humble Burns Night *denner.* First we eat some *gusty kickshaws* (hot savory starters) and a good broth. Whiskey and Scottish beer are drunk. The haggis is brought in accompanied by a video of Hannah's cousin, Grant, playing the bagpipes. Guests take turns to recite from Burns's "Ode to a Haggis," then the Selkirk Grace. These lines were repeated by Burns when he dined with the Earl of Selkirk. The grace was known before the poet's time in south-west Scotland as the Covenator's Grace. Time to eat. Afterwards there may be dancing, we tend not to sing "Auld Lang Syne."

SERVES 12

2 premium-quality haggis

Preheat the oven to 425°F. Wrap each haggis in aluminium foil. Place in a small roasting pan with a little water. Cook for 40 minutes. Leftover haggis makes a hearty breakfast fried in slices.

Neeps

3 rutabagas	Dash of cream
4 tablespoons butter	1/2 teaspoon sugar
Salt and pepper	

Mary told me off for taking a potato peeler to a rutabaga. Use a sturdy sharp knife to remove the skin and fibrous layer, then cut into chunks. Cook in boiling salted water until tender, about 40 minutes. Drain well and return to the pot. Add the butter, salt and pepper, and cream. Mash until creamy and smooth. Add the sugar.

Fair fa' your honest, sonsie face,
Great chieftain o the puddin'-race!
ROBERT BURNS, ODE TO THE HAGGIS, 1786

Marriage definitely refilled my larder—full of Scottish foodstuffs brought south; thick Methlick honey, salty butteries, delicate oatcakes, superb biscuits, Alford oatmeal and Tunnock's snowballs, which are coconut-covered marshmallows. Our freezer is full of pheasant, wild duck, smoked fish, venison and teal. For my birthday, Ernie, my brother-in-law, kindly ships me Shetland lamb or Allargue grouse—bliss. Burns Night, January 25, has become a pivotal date for an annual expatriate celebration of food that connects us to other Scots, thinking of home. The kitchen bookshelf sags with volumes on Scottish cooking and local history—enough to open a small study center. However, any insights into regional cooking gained from reading are brought into sharp focus by talking to relatives, eating their food, and shopping and cooking in their kitchens. Without access to the domestic scenery, any picture of everyday cooking would be incomplete.

AS CHILDREN OUR THOUGHTS ON FOOD DON'T TEND TO STRAY FAR FROM THE PLATE IN FRONT OF US. AS TEENAGERS FACED WITH THE PROSPECT OF LEAVING HOME WE BEGIN TO FLIRT WITH ACTUALLY COOKING FOR OURSELVES. MARRIAGE ADDS A NEW STRATUM OF INGREDIENTS AND RECIPES TO WHAT WE COOK. THEN SUDDENLY THE TABLES ARE TURNED. AS PARENTS WE CAN WATCH THE EARLY INFLUENCE OF FOOD AFRESH, ON OUR OWN CHILDREN—A CLEAN PLATE.

LIKE MY PARENTS, WHERE WE CHOOSE TO TRAVEL AS A NEW FAMILY NOT ONLY WILL AFFECT OUR KITCHEN HABITS BACK HOME BUT WILL BE FORMATIVE EXPERIENCES FOR OUR DAUGHTER. ONE SUCH DESTINATION, WHICH BEGAN INNOCENTLY ENOUGH, WAS A VISIT TO THE COLORADO DESERT IN CALIFORNIA—THINGS SOON TURN CULINARY AS GASTRONAUTS LEARN HOW TO COOK AND TRAVEL AT THE SAME TIME. SLOWLY MOVING UP THE FAMILY FOOD CHAIN.

When death's dark stream I ferry o'er—
A time that surely shall come—
In heaven itself I'll ask no more
Than just a Highland welcome.

ROBERT BURNS

Out of the Frying Pan

LOS ANGELES & PALM DESERT

THIS EERIE AND CONTRADICTORY SETTING PROVIDES A SURPRISING ARRAY OF GASTRONOMIC OPPORTUNITIES

DESERT SUPERMARKETS, SELF-CATERING HOTELS, PARKING-LOT TACO BOOTHS, MEXICAN GROCERS AND USED RESTAURANT EQUIPMENT—TINGED WITH THE CULINARY FOOTPRINTS OF NORTHERN MEXICO. WHAT MORE DOES A FAMILY NEED?

Cholla Cactus Garden, Joshua Tree National Monument, 2000.
A Palm Desert country club, swimming pool number 26, 2002.

This web of civilization is stretched thin over utter desolation.
There is no guaranteeing that it can be maintained. Its stability
is threatened by the Great Powers back on Earth.

PHILIP K. DICK, MARTIAN TIME-SLIP, 1964

Suddenly there you are, a family unit. Looking for new horizons and kitchens to explore. Each successive generation seems to travel that bit farther, following in the wake of mass tourism. I wonder what gap-year backpackers will cook for themselves? We often travel as a family, visiting friends and for work. Food is central to our understanding and enjoyment of a holiday, even somewhere as seemingly inhospitable as a desert. Deserts attract us to them like children to ice cream vans. Having visited Palm Desert for many years, we now feel strangely at home in the grid of interconnected resort communities that cling to Interstate 10 as it speeds through the Colorado desert: Desert Hot Springs, Palm Springs, Cathedral City, Rancho Mirage, Palm Desert, Indian Wells, La Quinta and Indio. Beyond is the eerie vista of the landlocked Salton Sea, with its bleached fishbone beaches and saline orange shoreline dotted with dead tilapia and abandoned modernist motels dropped in the sand like slabs of pie. Wild palm tree oases lie hidden in the arid mountain canyons. These unexpected eruptions of green mark out the shifting continental plates where uplifted layers of rock push water to the surface, creating small oases. Earthquake country. Amid the sagebrush are cultivated date palm groves where large, succulent Medjool dates are grown. This cultivation explodes south into Imperial Valley, where vast swaths of alfalfa and other fruit and vegetables are grown year-round, aided by little rain and almost no frost. Surrounding all this human activity are millions of acres of desert. After Imperial, the desert and Chocolate Mountains cross into Mexico.

Architectural leftovers ✺

Before reaching the arid haven of Palm Desert we pass through Los Angeles. For the curious culinary traveler there is much to investigate. Border cooking, fresh masa, hotel kitchens and a Pompeii-like vision revealing the architectural shadows of early self-service shopping. Connoisseurs of supermarket history seem to be divided as to where and when the supermarket was actually born. The 1930 King Kullen store in New York is often referred to as being the first. Another contender is Piggly Wiggly in Memphis, opened by Clarence Saunders in 1918. Saunders patented the first self-service retailing system. However, Ralphs, founded in 1873 at Sixth and Spring Streets in Los Angeles, is considered to be the first major chain to develop and proliferate in a metropolis. The sprawling grid of Los Angeles and its car-oriented culture had already created a breeding ground for supermarket precursors such as the drive-in market. Early vestiges of this one-stop-shopping architecture are still visible as we drive out from Los Feliz. The first drive-in market was developed nearby in 1923, the idea of C. L. Peckham, the head of an insurance adjustment company.

Drive-in markets today: Hillhurst Kafco Plaza, 1908 Hillhurst Avenue; Venice McLaughlin Center, 11614 Venice Boulevard; King Plaza, 103 S. Vermont Avenue; 11275 Venice Boulevard; San Marino Plaza, 2800 San Marino Street—all 2005.

It was named Ye Market Place. Carefully placed at road intersections, drive-in markets allowed cars to turn in off the street into a parking lot and park with their noses facing a continuous U- or L-shaped shop frontage. This was architecture truly determined by and for the automobile, a blurring of street and forecourt, with no curbside parking. These one-stop shops weren't built by grocery chains but by intuitive developers. Drivers often called in without having to leave their cars at all, slippers still on as a clerk dealt with their order. The multiple tenants of these markets shared management and marketing but operated separate cash registers. Signs on the façade identified the various departments, such as meat, fruit and vegetables, baked goods and delicatessen. Many had shaded, colonnaded façades with fold-back doors, thus the entire shop interior was open to view from your car. The side entrance to the existing Fairfax Farmers' Market retains a similar frontage. An important aspect of their development was location. Unusually they were sited in outlying residential neighborhoods away from existing commercial centers of business. Aimed at passing motorists, the fusion of car and shopping had arrived. The design was often Hispanic, although some local modernist architects such as Richard Neutra designed drive-in markets. Today these L-shaped lots are still in use and often referred to as markets or plazas; some are branded 7-Elevens or have become a parade of Mexican shops.

Ensuite kitchen ✳

Our Santa Monica hotel turns out to be a converted square apartment block on two stories with an interior courtyard that houses a pool and two towering palm trees. Our "suite," which overlooks the courtyard, has a combined living-dining room, bedroom, hall, bathroom and joy of joys—an ensuite kitchen. I wonder if it's a Californian trend. The East Coast is a tougher destination for a cooking family in search of a kitchen. Aimed perhaps at budget-minded families, hotel suites provide a richer Californian experience; connections with supermarkets, local produce, brands, typography, store layout, the smell of shopping and the conversation of street markets. It's about choice, which type of tomato to buy, how many and at what cost. As at home, you begin to compare and a whole slew of new data enters the shopping-comparison node of your brain. Marketing departments back home would love to mine your enriched brain cells for all that valuable data. Like the Sainsbury's supermarket team that came to the U.S. in 1949, store designers and owners today look elsewhere to gain an edge on their competitors. I wonder when we'll see a fully fledged outdoor Asian market, complete with caged fowl and penned pigs, in a supermarket forecourt to promote the latest Pacific rim imports.

Our Californian hotel kitchen turns out to be a temporal gastronomic laboratory. Bare bones 1950s style, straight from the pages of *Family Circle* 1958. Carefully re-created and sourced with skill from a movie prop warehouse perhaps? A culinary challenge. Could I survive in a twelve-utensil kitchenette and feed a family of three without sneaking out to buy cappuccinos and frozen enchiladas? Although the swimming pool glistens through the white frilled curtains, I am happier in our clean, white adopted kitchen. No piles of school letters or years of accumulated *kibble* (as Philip K. Dick called it) to get in the way of cooking. Not a fridge magnet or private view card in sight. However, the fridge is empty, so we need to shop.

✸ Culinary sightseeing

Luckily for us Santa Monica is surprisingly pedestrian focused—we're within easy walking distance of supermarkets. These blocks are easier to navigate for a European visitor than most of LA. All the familiar identifiers are here. Ordered rows of shops along pavements, most things you'd need within a few streets. Shopping abroad is relaxing. Slowly pushing a juggernaut-sized shopping cart around overdesigned gondolas of produce. Rather expensive. I'm even getting the hang of North American milk varieties after thirty years of practice and instinctively pick up the correct carton first time. I'll look elsewhere for fruit and veg. Los Angeles County hosts a staggering 80 certified farmers' markets, many with organic sections. Produce is sold to you by local farmers whose stalls are erected along temporarily closed streets or in parking lots. I'm up early to photograph one of the four Santa Monica markets, the Saturday Downtown Farmers' Market at Arizona Avenue and Third Street. Later we return to do some shopping from some of the 50 farmers. I buy green almonds grown in Lucerne Valley (peel, soak in salt water, then puree to make a pesto), also Chandler pummelos, Oroblanco grapefruits, cara cara pink navels and strawberries from San Diego County to accompany our buttermilk pancakes back at the hotel. The intensity of citrus fruit flavor makes you fall over with pleasure. As intoxicating as fresh basil in Italy or smoked kippers on a bracing Scottish beach. Back in our time-warp kitchen, we have the pleasure of filling an empty fridge, all the fun of moving into a new house.

In California the word *market* is used liberally on corner convenience stores, wholesale warehouses, trendy organic supermarkets, airport chocolate shops and the occasional street market. Offering a Blade Runner grocery experience downtown is the bustle of Grand Central Market on South Broadway, the oldest indoor market in LA. Billowing smoke from the Mongolian BBQ grill and Roast to Go chicken stands are tinged with buzzing neon. Somewhere below the trailing mass of lighting cables

MOVIE PROPS

In a hotel kitchen you start cooking in good faith, hoping everything you need will be to hand—but what does a hotel consider the minimum kitchen requirement to be?

1 large General Electric fridge, 1 large Sunray 4-burner gas stove with Flame Master oven, electric filter coffee maker, electric toaster, small microwave oven, twin sinks with garbage disposal, wire draining rack, overhead cupboards and sideboard with pull-out chopping board, swing bin, twelve-inch nonstick frying pan, 2 ten-inch stainless steel saucepans, 2 glass-lidded 10-inch saucepans, nine-inch nonstick omelette pan, teakettle, nine-inch stainless steel mixing bowl, wire mesh sieve, 4 glass dinner plates, 4 glass side plates, 3 glass dessert bowls, 1 glass serving bowl, 4 glass soup bowls, 4 ceramic mugs, 4 glass coffee cups and saucers, 2 stemmed wineglasses, 4 glass tumblers, 4 tall beer glasses, 4 forks, 4 knifes, 4 dessert tablespoons, 4 teaspoons, square-ended wooden spoon, slotted serving spoon, paring knife, kitchen knife, serrated bread knife, metal grater, plastic skillet, plastic ladle, corkscrew, plastic water jug, 60 coffee filters, pump-action dishwasher detergent, Morton salt, McCormick pepper, paper towels, 2 dishcloths, oven glove.

Grand Central Market, Los Angeles.

are groceries on offer, revealed in slanting sunlight from the glass roof high above. This mix of produce stalls and small restaurants with metal counters and fixed swivel stools originates from 1917. Frank Lloyd Wright once had an office above the market. I seek out Stall D-6 and E-7, Valeria's Chiles & Spices, run by Ruben and Angel. A spectacular array of overflowing bins packed with whole dried chiles and other Mexican ingredients—dried, canned or bottled. I can visualize the British Airways luggage scales at LAX showing that I've exceeded my weight allowance as I order another ten cans of chipotle chiles in adobo sauce and three pounds of dried *pasilla* chile powder.

Elsewhere in the Florence area of Los Angeles is the incomparable Mexican supermarket-deli, Amapola. An Angeleno friend warned me if he broke down on the nearby freeway he would call the police first and then the tow truck—however, we live in Peckham so weren't deterred. I knew we'd found a gem of a store when I smelt that unmistakable aroma of fresh tortillas wafting from their *tortelleria* at the back of the store. They also sold fresh *masa* for making your own tamales and tortillas—*masa dulce*, *masa preparada*, *masa por tortilla* and *nixtamal*. I could have spent all day exploring the *panadería* and *carnicería*—bakery and butcher. Until now I have always prepared my own *mole* sauce, avoiding preparations in jars and cans—even the *mole* sold in bulk in Grand Central Market. However, shops like Amapola exude confidence in their carefully restricted choice of produce—so I bought several tubs of *mole rojo* and *mole verde* made in Teloloapan, Mexico. The *rojo* resembles a tub of rich, dark chocolate but with a heady spice-market aroma. I couldn't resist a bag of 30 hot, fresh tortillas, a pack of fresh *masa* and a dozen *nopales*, prickly pear cactus paddles, to grill. Back in London our fridge has the scent of corn and lime.

Other must-go gastronomic destinations before we head for the desert include a browse around Sur la Table at the corner of Third and Wilshire for kitchenware and then on to The Cook's Library bookshop on West Third Street and Orlando Avenue. It's organized by category, Africa to Yucatán, artichokes to zesters—through corn, chocolate, vegetarian, soups and salads. America by region. I staggered out, relieved our car was close by.

Museums are a great source for hard-to-find, independently produced cookbooks, books that open up and help you explore the locale. The Southwestern Museum has a great range of cookbooks with local themes such as border cooking, native American recipes and what to eat in deserts.

Tamales

Pre-Columbian stuffed corn-dough dumplings

TAMALES ARE FIRM, MOIST, STUFFED CORN DOUGH—WRAPPED IN CORN HUSKS, THEN STEAMED, OR GENTLY GRILLED. A SUBTLE FLAVOR OF CORN, CHICKEN STOCK AND A WICKED HINT OF LARD ALONGSIDE WHATEVER YOU CHOOSE TO STUFF THEM WITH. THE INNERMOST CORN HUSK IMPRINTS A DELICATE TRACERY OF TEXTURED LINES ON THE COOKED TAMALE.

My first taste of tamales was in the Tesuque Pueblo Flea Market outside Santa Fe. They were served up from the back of a matte black pickup truck, huge deer antlers attached to its front fender. I've since found tamale vendors outside the frozen 26th Street flea market in New York. Tamales make delicious snacks but we serve them for supper with different fillings, usually leftovers. They can be steamed without a filling, blind, to serve with a saucy dish such as turkey *mole rojo* (page 183). For husks, I buy large unsprayed ears of corn from our farmers' market. Cut the bottom off each corn ear and carefully remove the individual husks, discarding the silks. The husks can be kept in a bag in the fridge for a while or frozen. Once steamed, tamales can be frozen. Alas, *masa harina* is essential. *Masa harina* (dough flour) is made from corn that has been dried, soaked and cooked with slaked lime or wood ash—a process called nixtamalization. This ancient process magically enhances the protein value of the corn and is believed to have been responsible for the growth of Mesoamerican civilizations. Bags of *masa harina* used to weigh down my transatlantic luggage until I found a source in London. In Mexico and parts of the USA and Canada, you can buy fresh *masa* dough and dried corn husks from supermarkets.

MAKES ABOUT 12 SMALL TAMALES

The tamale mix
A 1-inch slice of lard
1 cup *masa harina,* or as needed
1/2 teaspoon baking powder
1/2 teaspoon salt
About 1 cup cup chicken stock, tepid, or as needed

Filling
2 cups cubed cooked chicken, duck or pork; chopped cooked spinach or chard; or grated or soft cheese

15 flat corn husks, fresh or dried

In a bowl, cream the lard with a fork. Add the *masa harina,* baking powder and salt and rub everything together with your fingers. Gradually add some of the tepid stock. For 1 cup of *masa harina,* I would first add 1/2 cup of stock. It needs to be a sticky dough but not at all runny. You can always add more *masa harina* if you need to.

Assembling tamales is easier than it sounds. If you handle the tamale mix with a spoon, your hands won't be too sticky to tie the knots. First you need to cut ties from a

couple of the longer corn husks. Cut 12 or so long strips ¼ inch wide (or cut 12 pieces of string). Flatten out a corn husk. Place about a tablespoon dollop of tamale mix in the middle, then push a teaspoon of filling into its center. Fold either side of the husk over the filling. To complete the parcel, fold down the top flap and then fold up the bottom flap. Wrap a corn tie (or string) around its waist and make a knot. Place upright in a steamer. Continue making the tamales until your mix runs out or the steamer is full.

Steam the tamales, covered, over boiling water for 30 to 40 minutes. When cooked, take the tamales in the steamer to the table and let your guests unwrap their own parcels.

Tamales can be refrigerated overnight, or frozen, thawed and resteamed. As you become more proficient, try making larger tamales, tied at each end and steamed flat. A thumb-sized piece of salmon makes a great tamale filling. Add sugar and make sweet tamales—the possibilities are endless.

100%
HECHOS
A MANOS

Takeouts for the freeway:
Merkato, Ethiopian Restaurant on Fairfax in little Ethiopia, Los Angeles;
Mexican platter from El Galito in Cathedral City.

El Gallito
EST. 1978
HOMEMADE MEXICAN FOOD

Food without frontiers

California, Texas, New Mexico and Arizona were once part of northern Mexico. In 1848 the treaty of Guadalupe-Hidalgo ended the Mexican-American War, the California Gold Rush followed, and in 1850 California entered the Union. Many culinary commentators would put California in the northwestern edge of an area of shared heritage that stretches east from California through Arizona, New Mexico and Texas, then heads south of the current border into Baja California, Sonora, Chihuahua, Coahuila, Nuevo León and Tamaulipas. This is Border cooking, Southwestern, or as the Mexicans call it *norteño*. The conquering Spanish brought Aztec and pre-Columbian influences, as well as their own, when they eventually traveled north into this arid land. This fusion was further developed by white settlers, ranchers, native Americans, *vaqueros* (cowboys), Anglos and Hispanics. Over a century the resulting mix has produced Tex-Mex, New Mexican, Sonoran and Border cooking, to name a few. Today regional Mexican food from Yucatán to Oaxaca can be eaten in Los Angeles, served from taco-burrito huts in parking lots, takeouts in markets, fast food drive-throughs, to restaurants like Lula's and the upmarket Border Grill, which sports its own successful cookbook. Many of the dishes would be considered street food in Mexico, and some entirely new, with only traces remaining of their southern ancestry. You would expect Californian bookstores to stock dozens of Mexican cookery titles, but there are virtually none. Over the past century northern Mexican cuisine has permeated Southwestern American domestic cooking so deeply that many Californians already understand the basics of Mexican cookery. Their kitchen reading seems to be purist Mexican and regional, including such gems as books by Diana Kennedy or Rick Bayless. However, it's books on Border cooking that reveal the culinary heritage that simmers in Southern Californian kitchens, such as the excellent *The Border Cookbook* by Cheryl Alters Jamison and Bill Jamison.

If I want to cook Mexican food outside Mexico, this is the place to try it. Southern produce abounds. Once I find an interesting ingredient I need to build a whole meal around it and understand its usage from a purist point of view. Many cookbook writers alter and amend recipes from their original source. I tend to collect books that gather recipes from a national or regional perspective, which are researched over many years, accumulating tales and recipes from history and from kitchens of friends and family. Tales of domestic food rather than restaurant-focused cuisine. I will happily buy a cookbook for a single recipe, a set of photographs or even a useful diagram. With domestic recipes in particular, there is obviously no definitive way of cooking a dish, but with the help of several books I can at least understand the origins and parameters of a recipe before amending and changing it myself.

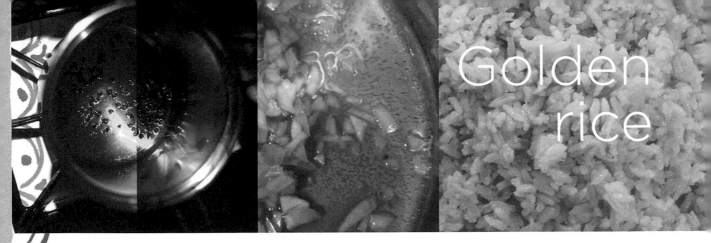

Golden rice

A delicately flavored rice—perfect for any dish requiring a soak-it-up-partner. Achiote is the coloring agent used for orange-colored cheese. In Mexico, it is used for its flavor.

SERVES 4

1 tablespoon corn oil

1 teaspoon achiote seeds *(annatto)*

1 small white onion, finely chopped

1 cup rice, rinsed and dried

Salt

Heat the oil in a medium sauté pan. Add the achiote and cook over low heat for 2 minutes, coloring the oil with a deep orange glow. Remove the achiote seeds with a teaspoon; they've done their work. Sauté the onion in the golden oil for 3 minutes. Add the rice, stir it around and pour in 2 cups water. Stir once, add a little salt and leave to simmer gently undisturbed until the water cooks off and the rice is tender.

Squash with yellow tomatoes
Calabacitas con jitomate

A soft, mellow dish using yellow squash with a nip of chile to complement the acidity of the tomatoes. *Calabacita* means little squash. Use yellow zucchini as a substitute.

SERVES 4

1 small white onion, finely chopped

2 tablespoons olive oil

4 yellow tomatoes, sliced

1 *güero* chile (or banana pepper), finely chopped

3 long thin yellow squash, sliced into rounds (use Mexican *chilacayotes* if you can find them)

Salt

In a large frying pan, sauté onion in oil until translucent. Add the tomatoes and cook until soft. Add the chile, squash and a little salt. Cover. Simmer gently for 30 minutes.

Taco taco taco

If I ate only one meal in Los Angeles ever again it would be a *carne asada* burrito from Yuca's in Los Feliz—the taste of heaven on a paper plate: without doubt the best tacos and burritos in Los Angeles. Everything you expect from a taco: small, fresh, succulent meat and perfectly balanced spices—eaten outdoors in the sunshine holding a beer. A mixture of hunger and gastronomic instinct led us to Yuca's years ago and now we never visit LA without a few trips to their miraculous hut. I made a postcard of their tacos and sent them a boxful, I'm now the postcard-guy. Situated in a small parking lot at 2056 Hillhurst Avenue just before it reaches Los Feliz Boulevard, this little taco and burrito stand draws a regular, adoring crowd, some from across the globe. Friends who live nearby will phone their order ahead to beat the queue. Independent and family owned, they recently won the America's Classic Award from the James Beard Foundation. Yucatán-style fillings such as *machaca* (shredded meat) and *cochinita pibil* (pit-roasted pork) sit inside their perfect tortillas. You can buy a cold Corona or Dos Equis beer from the liquor store next door while you wait for your order. I want to be there now.

Other taco and burrito experiences abound, sometimes out of the blue. As we are about to leave the Laguna Clay Company, my wife, Jeff, spots a blue and white van with a slatted roof lurch into the parking lot. It's a mobile food truck that migrates through the industrial outskirts of Los Angeles. At least I should take a photo of the two women inside, who begin setting up. We start asking if they will open soon— before we even finish our question the side flaps are down, coffee dispensers revealed, ordering hatch propped up and orders being taken. Hannah is already digging through an ice bucket of canned drinks and Jeff is pouring a coffee. She notices Juan from the Laguna laboratory in the line that's forming. We ask him for recommendations. The two women are hard at work: one preparing orders, the other taking money.

Not everything on the menu is available today, which I take as a good sign. Hannah avoids the burger or hot-dog items. We go for a ground beef taco, *asada burrito*, chicken enchilada, thick-cut fries, lemonade, coffees and a pack of Cheetos— all for $11. It tastes good and fresh, a perfect light lunch. We eat it at a wooden table under a shady tree in the 85 degree heat. As they pack up the truck we talk to the driver about her day. She starts work at 5.45 A.M. and finishes up around 1 P.M. Their brief stay in the Laguna car lot lasts about fifteen minutes. Angelenos refer to these gleaming metal trucks unflatteringly as roach-mobiles. My friend Bruce says you need to nurture the required bacteria to eat from them. I think three buttermilk pancakes a day and diner coffee prepares your stomach for almost anything.

Chile, chili or chilli?

One of the great joys of Southwestern cooking is its imaginative use of chiles. The Nahuatl Indians of southern Mexico and Central America named the chile plant in the fifteenth century, although it had been in use as a culinary additive as long ago as 6200 B.C. Most cooks use chiles from time to time, usually to add heat to a dish. In small quantities chili powder can lie unobserved in a tomato *sugo* working hard to enrich other flavors in the sauce. The heat in chile is caused by the chemical capsaicin, 80 percent of which is concentrated along the chiles' veins. Because of their proximity to the veins, the seeds are also hot. Capsaicin triggers the brain to produce endorphins—natural painkillers that give you a sense of well-being. Out in border country chiles are close to their ancestral home.

Many people assume the use of chile to be indigenous to Asian and Far Eastern cuisines. This is not the case. Chiles were introduced by the Portuguese and Spanish along their maritime trade routes only as late as 1550 to western China, the East Indies and Southeast Asia. Chiles were also beginning to be traded in North Africa, along the West African coast, India and Madagascar. It's hard to imagine these cuisines today without the use of chili or chile, and indeed many of the native inhabitants believe them to be indigenous.

The geographical origin of chiles left a strong influence on Mexican gastronomy and Mexico produces the widest range of chiles. Their cuisine regularly uses over half of the 200 chile varieties, often in combinations such as the classic triad of *ancho*, *mulatto* and *pasilla* used in traditional *mole* sauces. Chile is integral to Mexican food, not merely to add a piquant edge to a dish but also to deepen it with broad, complex, spiced flavors. This influence can be tasted in Southern Californian Border cooking.

The word *chile* often refers to the plant itself, *chili* is used for a cooked dish and the spiced powder. In the U.K., the powder is often spelled *chilli*. To confuse issues further, the name of a fresh chile changes when it's dried. This probably arises from a cuisine that needs to differentiate dried from fresh as they perform different tasks in the kitchen. So when you require a dried *chilaca* you would ask for *pasilla*—that is, unless you are in California, where the fresh *poblano* and its dried varieties *mulatto* and *ancho* are mistakenly called *pasillas*. So choosing a pack of chiles by name isn't straightforward. Chiles are often mislabeled. Use a shop or supplier you can trust, such as the Kitchen Market on Eighth Avenue in New York. I would suggest buying Mark Miller's *The Great Chile Book* from Ten Speed Press. The actual-size photographs and descriptions act as a field guide for identifying each of the 86 varieties illustrated. Here are two interesting chiles—a smoked one and a more ubiquitous variety.

ATLAS

EL CAPO CHILLI OIL

Arbol Chili Pods, California
Il Casolare cold pressed
unfiltered olive oil, Italy

Made and packed by
ATLAS of London,
Fine Foods for the Family

Shipped by
CAMEL COURIERS of Peckham,
Don't Get the Hump

Chipotle chiles

Jalapeños are named after the town of Jalapa in the state of Veracruz. These fresh hot chiles are difficult to dry and likely to rot if stored too long. Fortunately for us, as well as developing a system for drying meat, the Aztecs also smoke-dried their jalapeños to store them. Today as much as one-fifth of the Mexican jalapeño crop is dried. These jalapeños are called *chipotles*, pronounced chuh-POT-lay, combining the Aztec words for both *chile* and *smoke*. Different varieties of jalapeño produce various types of *chipotle*—*chile seco, chili ahumado, grande, mora rojo, morita*, the latter of which means little blackberry in Spanish.

I buy *chile ahumado*. This type of *chipotle* has been smoked longer, producing a rich, smoky taste—fiery and chocolatey with a tobacco edge. A well-smoked jalapeño may take several days of smoking to produce a worthwhile *chipotle*. You can buy *chipotles* whole, powdered or canned in adobo sauce—an excellent product.

New Mexico / California chiles

In 1894 Emilio Ortega introduced New Mexico chiles to Anaheim in Southern California. When dried these milder chiles were referred to as California chile or chile Colorado, although when scientists at the National Pepper Conference tried to designate a new type of chile under the name Californian, New Mexican lobbyists won out and the name became "New Mexican chile type" as given in the *Congressional Record*—this may of course change.

California chile is often used in commercially produced salsas, sold as flakes, used dried in chili powder or can be seen in decorative strings of chiles called *ristras*—hung outside Mexican homes to ward off evil spirits.

Rehydrating whole dried chiles

Toast the chiles gently in a dry pan for a few minutes, being careful not to scorch the taste away. Take out of the pan, pull off the stems and discard the seeds. Cut them up roughly, place in a bowl and cover with recently boiled water for 30 minutes—boiling water would scald the taste. Remove the chiles and either cut up fine for a stew or add to a food processor to make a sauce, using a little of the soaking water.

Turkey *mole rojo*

Mole, from the Nahuatl word *molli,* means mixture, or sauce, and is thought to have originated in central Mexico, in Puebla and Oaxaca. There are many varieties of *mole* such as *rojo, negro, amarillo* and *verde.* The triad of chiles used in *mole rojo* is

DISCOVERING AN ARRAY OF DRIED CHILES AND DARK MEXICAN CHOCOLATE AT THE GRAND CENTRAL MARKET MEANS ONE THING—MAKING *MOLE ROJO* FROM SCRATCH, INTRODUCING ONE OF THE KEYS OF MEXICAN CUISINE, MIXING CHILE TYPES.

extended with a vast range of spices, creating a taste of great complexity. Binding these tastes together is chocolate, giving it a dark, velvety richness—not sweet. *Mole* can be used as an accompanying sauce or for cooking something. Prepared *mole* is available in tubs, jars and cans, or sold in bulk at Mexican markets. I would recommend getting some dried chiles and making it yourself—if you can't find them at the market, buy them online. Substitute a 70 percent cacao chocolate if you can't track down Mexican chocolate. *Mole* is a great way to revitalize your post-Christmas or Thanksgiving turkey.

SERVES 8

Turkey breast cutlets, to serve 8

6 *ancho* chiles

4 *pasilla* chiles

4 *mulato* chiles

2 tablespoons lard

1 onion, finely chopped

4 tomatoes, finely chopped

4 cloves garlic, chopped

1 slice toast or old tortilla

1/4 cup sliced almonds

1/4 cup raisins

1 tablespoon fresh cilantro leaves

1 tablespoon sesame seeds

1/4 teaspoon ground cloves

1/4 teaspoon ground cinnamon

1/4 teaspoon ground coriander

1 ounce Mexican chocolate

In a large pot, cover the turkey pieces with salted water and simmer for 30 minutes. Meanwhile, rehydrate your dried *ancho, pasilla* and *mulato* chiles (see page 181). Remove the cooked turkey and pat dry. Simmer the remaining stock for 15 minutes; set aside.

Preheat the oven to 425°F. Brown the cooked turkey in 1 tablespoon lard, and drain on paper towels.

Combine the rehydrated chiles and the remaining ingredients except for the chocolate in a food processor and whizz the ingredients into a thick, coarse paste. In a wide saucepan fry the *mole* paste in the remaining lard for 5 minutes, stirring. Add 2 cups of the turkey stock and the chocolate and cook until the chocolate melts. Place the turkey in a casserole and cover with the *mole.* Bake for 30 minutes. Serve with tortillas.

Hotel-bathroom burritos

On-the-road cooking requires planning—keep your airline cutlery and seasoning packets. At breakfast, take a few extra Concord grape jelly tubs. Half-and-half milk cartons from your midmorning road stop taste better than the nondairy creamer

FRESH, CRISP, MOIST, SWEET AND TART, A BURRITO MAKES THE PERFECT BORDER COUNTRY SELF-ASSEMBLY HOTEL ROOM SNACK, LUNCH OR LIGHT SUPPER. SEMI-SURVIVALIST CUISINE UTILIZING INGREDIENTS CULLED FROM REMOTE GAS STATIONS AND LONE FOOD MARTS.

packet awaiting in the hotel room in your "courtesy coffee pack." (I must attend a commercial food processing fair to find out what nondairy creamer is made from. Maybe it's borax? According to the Death Valley marketing machine, most things seen to have benefited from borax, which used to be mined there.)

I wish Sabatier made culinary penknife sets for off-site cooking: paring knife, serrated-edge kitchen knife, fork and spoon. A mini chopping board would help. Next trip I'll take a nine-inch section of our thin plastic chopping mat to ensure a clean surface free of industrial hotel cleansers. I'm trying to develop a recipe that uses the bedside coffee percolator to make a quick meal—perhaps quick-cook noodles or drip-boiled spinach?

MAKES 4 BURRITOS

Salsa filling
Juice of 1 lime
2 tomatoes, finely chopped with a
   penknife
1 stalk celery, finely chopped

Tortillas
A package of large flour tortillas

Other filling
1 avocado, halved, pitted and scooped out
Some broken tortilla chips
1 green chile, finely chopped
A tub of sour cream
Pepper
Bottled salsa

Combine the lime juice, tomatoes and celery in a spare coffee cup and mix. In the center of a tortilla, place some avocado, fresh salsa, tortilla chips, green chile, sour cream, pepper and bottled salsa. Roll gently and serve. You could also warm tortillas on the coffeepot hot plate.

Palm Springs

Chicken chipotle burritos

What a pleasure it was to find another ensuite hotel kitchen in Palm Springs. A tiled galley kitchen with a small breakfast table and even a backdoor. The door didn't lead to a backyard or

THE "ITO" IMPLIES SMALL. IN ARIZONA, WHERE THEY ARE DEFINITELY NOT SMALL, THESE ARE CALLED BURROS. BURRITOS ARE PERFECT FOR ON-THE-ROAD COOKING.

porch, just a narrow service alley crammed with metal ducting. Long desert drives need a quick and easy supper if you can't face the overindulgence of another super-sized Californian meal. A quick dash to the nearest supermarket in the Chevy Trailblazer for some basic ingredients seemed in order. The aim of the recipe is browned strips of chicken in a thick, bean-filled sauce, highlighted with some chipotle chile smokiness.

MAKES 4 LARGE BURRITOS

3 boneless skinless chicken breasts, cut into long 1/2-inch wide strips

1/4 cup olive oil

1 yellow bell pepper, cut into thin strips

1/2 white onion, diced

1 chipotle chile, rehydrated (see page 181) and finely chopped

1/4 cup Mexican beer

One 15-ounce can black beans, drained but not rinsed

1 tomato, chopped

1 cup cilantro leaves, roughly chopped, plus 1 cup cilantro stems, finely chopped

A package of large flour tortillas

In a large frying pan, sauté the chicken pieces in the oil until golden. Add the bell pepper and onion. Cook for 3 minutes, stirring. Add the chipotle chile. Add the beer, stirring to loosen any browned bits around the pan, then add the beans, tomato and cilantro stems. Cover with water and simmer gently, covered for 40 minutes; stir occasionally.

Heap a few tablespoons of the chicken mix onto each tortilla, add the cilantro leaves and roll tightly to make a burrito. Underfill the tortillas if you want to pick them up and eat with your hands. Serve with a crisp salad, fresh salsa and plain rice.

If you are traveling in serious summer heat, pull over and make use of some hot rocks to warm your tortillas (see page 161), but watch out for rattlesnakes.

247-5443
LA MEXICANA
FOOD PRODUCTS
CORN TORTILLAS
NET WT 9 OZ (253g)
ONE DOZEN
2703 S. KEDZIE AVE.
CHICAGO, ILL. 60623
REFRIGERATED AFTER PURCHASE

Desert shopping

Out of Los Angeles past San Bernadino, through Beaumont and Banning, Freeway 10 sweeps down into the Coachella Valley. This narrow corridor of habitation is squeezed between the desert wilderness of Joshua Tree National Monument to the north and Anza-Borrego Desert State Park to the south. A few isolated wind-powered turbines appear on high ridges like cacti, then the freeway takes a grand turn and a vista of vast windmill farms opens up. Palm Springs is nearing. We take the exit ramp and stop at the traffic lights behind a refrigerated truck from Illinois and then cross over the Southern Pacific Railroad.

Before turning off Cook onto Country Club Drive, we pull into one of the many drive-in shopping courts. A vast parking lot, edged with low, stuccoed Hispanic-style retail stores, an occasional arcade and the inevitable palm trees. It resembles a scaled-up drive-in market from the 1920s. On the northern rim of the lot is my favorite branch of the Ralphs supermarket chain. Our Ralphs loyalty club card still works after three years' inactivity; they probably think we've deserted them for Trader Joe's. This branch sits eerily at the top west corner of the Colorado Desert, 1.5 miles from the Big Bend of the San Andreas fault, where it meets the San Jacinto, Elsinore and Garlock faults. Earthquake central.

As I climb out of our cold, air-conditioned car, the low desert air takes my breath away, intense heat visibly rising off the tarmac. An extraordinary sensation, like being dry-fried. A minute later we're in the chilled, crisp air of an aircraft-hangar-sized store. An astonishing location to push a grocery cart up icy aisles. Buying ten days' grocery supplies for erratic cooking is often problematic, wasteful and expensive. A late air-conditioned lunch in the high heat of the day doesn't leave us hungry in the evening. Salad, salsa, blue corn chips with West Coast chardonnay or a cold local beer is usually enough. So it's not always a vacation full of days spent cooking—but with so much tempting produce I have to try.

Ralphs' inventory reflects Americans' necessity for wide choice at low cost. Even staple purchases such as bread, milk and butter assault me with a baffling array of subset choices and bizarre categories to foil the uninitiated visitor. How much olive oil can we use in only ten days? My mind goes into overdrive—it's too much, fantastic. I want to try it all, vainly hoping to fill our cart with ingredients rather than snacks.

Like Sainsbury's in Britain, Ralphs has enjoyed a long history as a premier grocer since 1873. Sainsbury's had opened in similar fashion in 1869. Both businesses grew with changing markets, although it took diplomatic passports from the Ministry of Food in 1949 to enable Sainsbury's directors to visit and study North American supermarkets firsthand.

In Ralphs I'll munch on a corn dog as we methodically traverse up and down each aisle, taking it all in, still camera poised, video camera whirring. In this age of unerring globalization I am glad to report that some of the produce still remains new to us. Fifteen types of tortilla to test. Having a design-led brain makes me ponder the shop layout as I wander. I examine packaging typography, looking for trends in letterspacing or font choice. My organic intentions soon waver when confronted with the graphic imprint of my youth. It's the advertising I saw in imported DC and Marvel Comics I read in the 1960s that draws me to the Nabisco-type Trix packaging design. Food was also glimpsed in imported television series and at the cinema. I know David Hockney was drawn to the sunlit Californian streets in black and white Laurel & Hardy movies long before he visited LA. I liked the look of the pickle shops. In Ralphs I'm like a child again. Luckily our daughter, Hannah, requests a breakfast cereal multipack so I can try some of the brands that still exist, graphics fairly intact, forty years on. As we leave I wonder if Ralphs ever makes use of its spacious capacity—a glorious emptiness, as if the store was cleared of other customers just for us.

Sixty years ago Palm Springs and Indio were separated by desert along the Coachella Valley. Our country club kitchen resides in Palm Desert, part of the urban infilling south of the freeway, which created a string of interlocking towns. On the north side property speculators are fast developing the land adjacent to the Coachella Valley Preserve. The 1000 Palms oasis boasts naturally occurring sand dunes and is home to the endangered fringe-toed lizard, western yellow bat, burrowing owl, Palm Springs pocket mouse and a diminishing population in McCallum Pond of the beautiful diminutive pupfish. At the small visitor center beneath the beautifully ragged, wild, skirted *Washingtonia* palm trees, I am shown an aerial map that illustrates sand migration through the entire valley system. The map depicts loose sand. The preserve is trying to buy additional land so they can maintain the dunes, allowing a channel of mountainside to continue to feed and replenish the dunes with new sand. Without a continual source of sand the existing dunes will blow away and vanish.

The view from our kitchen should be of a parched desert landscape, dotted with mesquite trees and the occasional prickly pear cactus. In the hazy distance we should see the graceful curves of sand dunes. Wide, plate-glass windows instead invite a view beyond manicured lawns to shimmering lakes ringed with purple flowers, palm trees and bungalows. The air conditioning is working so hard it sounds as if a small airplane is revving up on our roof. Ducks sit outside waiting for us to eat breakfast. It really is like reclaimed land on Mars. Hidden sprinklers silently rise out of the grass each night to keep the desert at bay and to surprise any lurking, unsuspecting raccoons.

On a practical level, to live in an air-conditioned gardened city with full amenities twenty minutes away from serious desert wilderness is perfect for a family with limited time. We are used to being mindful of water usage as family homes in both Scotland and Italy rely on wells for their supplies. However, the communal level of water consumption here is hard to ignore and is affecting the delicate ecosystem of the desert—but as a nonresident it's difficult to rally against. Perhaps the only way to protest is by not going there—reverse tourism, as it were. However, we are like camels drawn to the desert and the fringe communities along its edge. The area is also like a architectural national park for midcentury modernist buildings, so we spend as much time hunting down gems by John Lautner and Alfred Frey as we do trekking among the Joshua trees and cooking Border cuisine.

Vacation kitchens often develop a time warp appearance because they avoid the slow incremental tweaking caused by everyday life. Our blissful desert kitchen is no exception—it seems to have been born in 1980, a good vintage—well-equipped, tiled and spacious, with acres of fridge for groceries.

Mango salsa

All Southwestern Border meals benefit from a fresh salsa to add a little crisp, tart bite and a touch of heat. The chile should only open up the other flavors in the salsa—not sear them.

SERVES 4

½ white onion, finely diced

1 firm but ripe tomato, seeded and diced

1 firm but ripe yellow tomato, seeded and diced

½ firm but ripe mango, diced

1 cup chopped fresh cilantro

Juice of 1 lime

1 *güero* chile (or banana pepper), finely chopped

Salt and pepper

Combine all the ingredients in a bowl and toss gently. Let infuse for half an hour.

Green chicken with dates

At a Mexican farmers' market stall in Palm Springs, I spy tomatillos bundled in red mesh sacks. Driving back home on Route 111, in need of a respite from the air-conditioning, we pull up in the parking lot of Shields Date Shop. I buy Medjool dates, a date shake and a date ice cream cone. We don't watch the instructional film about dates in the rickety corner cinema. Back in the country club, as I watch a roadrunner darting fervently past swimming pool number 48, I spot a line of large grapefruit trees—several fruits lie on the grass. Chance and a foraging eye has brought together the ingredients.

COOKING ON VACATION WITHOUT THE AID OF COOKBOOKS, YOU HAVE TO TRUST YOUR CULINARY INSTINCTS. THIS RECIPE WAS CONCOCTED FROM SOME SUPERMARKET SHOPPING, A FORTUITOUS FARMERS' MARKET, A ROADSIDE CURIOSITY AND SOME WINDFALL FRUIT. ALL BROUGHT TOGETHER IN THE COOL OF OUR COUNTRY CLUB KITCHEN.

SERVES 3

Juice of 1 medium grapefruit

3 cloves garlic, crushed

1/4 teaspoon dried oregano

Salt and pepper

1 pound boneless, skinless chicken breasts or thighs

1 pound tomatillos

1 white onion, finely chopped

1 stalk celery, finely chopped

2 tablespoons olive oil

3 Medjool dates, chopped

1 *ancho* chile (optional)

Sour cream

In a shallow bowl, make a marinade from the grapefruit juice, 2 of the garlic cloves, the oregano and salt and pepper to taste. Marinate the chicken in the refrigerator for 2 hours.

Remove the tomatillo husks, best done near running water, as the skin is slightly sticky. Blanch the tomatillos in boiling water for 5 minutes. From a vivid bright green, they will turn a soft dull green. Coarsely chop the tomatillos and puree in a blender or food processor.

In a medium frying pan, sauté the onion, celery and remaining garlic clove in a little of the olive oil until the onion is translucent. Add the tomatillo puree and dates and cook 3 minutes.

Remove the chicken from the marinade, reserving the marinade, and pat dry. Brown the chicken on both sides in the remaining olive oil in a large frying pan. Add the tomatillo mixture, half the marinade and a little water if it's looking dry. Normally I would add an *ancho* chile, but our daughter, Hannah, doesn't like chiles. Simmer gently for 40 minutes, adding dribbles of water if the sauce dries out, then letting it thicken toward the end of cooking. Serve with sour cream.

Outpost oasis

We find ourselves at a road junction that leads to the landlocked Salton Sea. The sea is artificial, reliant on agricultural drain water. Its origin was an accidental overflow from the Colorado River bursting through a levee in 1905 and flooding Salton Sink, 228 feet below sea level. Now the sea is the center of a water war—a struggle between senators, farmers, private water corporations and environmentalists. The 400 species of bird that migrate and use the sea each year are at risk from a possible buy-off by the City of San Diego to pay tens of millions of dollars to farmers in the arid Imperial Valley. The water they currently use from the Colorado River would go to urban use instead. This would reduce the water runoff into the Salton Sea, which at present keeps its salinity just above toxic levels. Brown pelican, Yuma clapper rail, great blue herons, cormorants and snowy egrets all thrive on the fish here.

At this small junction crossroad is a small run-down community called Mecca. Single-story cinder-block buildings punctuate the crisscross of dusty roads, dispersing any sense of street and sidewalk. Slow-cruising cars and youths hanging out make parents with a seven-year-old in the backseat of their rental car slightly nervous. We're soon woken from this paranoia by what looks like a grocery store. Rising from the dust is a solitary, long, squat building—Leon's Mercado Tortilleria. Worth exploring. Next to the central entrance is the *tortilleria* itself, a small factory-like production line of people making fresh tortillas. There's also a takeout taco shop. We place our orders through a small sliding-glass hatch. I have a 99-cent *asada taco*. Hannah and Jeff order *enchiladas*. Second orders seem obligatory. Fresh and simple served in Styrofoam cartons. We buy tubs of fresh salsa to take home. The green salsa tastes mellow and deep, with none of the acidity that store-bought salsas often have. The red salsa is smooth and slightly pasty, made from chiles that apparently grow in trees and are incredibly hot. The supermarket inside doesn't disappoint: lurid cakes, stacks of fresh warm tortillas, spice and herb bins full of tamarind and fresh chiles and a glazed meat aquarium full of thick marbled cuts of beef. I select achiote seeds, *pinole*, *menudo* mix and *piloncillo* (cane sugar) which looks like jaggery. Next stop, the fishbone beach on the north shore of Salton Sea.

Used
restaurant
supplies

After supermarkets, the other must-go location on a gastronomic odyssey is kitchenware suppliers. On this Californian trip my wanted list had two items— a tortilla press and a cast-iron waffle iron. I had bought a flimsy aluminum waffle iron in Paris the week before. I was now seeking out the cast-iron variety. Preferably a Griswold heart-shaped iron such as I'd seen on an eBay auction for $49—the shipping price for a hunk of iron is anyone's guess! There isn't a supplier of new, non-electric waffle irons in North America that I could find, except for a camping specialist offering awkward, long-handled campfire irons and a few ugly reproductions from a Midwest heritage center. So this gap in the market is still filled by the ongoing competition between two cookware manufacturers of the 1800s—Griswold of Erie, Pennsylvania, and Wagner from Sydney, Ohio. Wagner eventually took ownership of Griswold's molds. True collectors don't buy from this "double-stamped-logo" era.

Thrift shops and swap meets are good hunting grounds for old kitchen utensils. I spotted a Griswold frying pan in the Yucca Valley Angel View Thrift Mart and a Wagner frying pan in the vast Cathedral City Angel View Thrift Mart, but no waffle irons. Tortilla presses were equally scarce.

The tarmac expanse of the Indio Swap Meet was bubbling and warping in late afternoon heat. These glowing rectangles didn't conjure up anything culinary. However, hidden among the glamor-cookware in the Upper Crust Cooking Company on the immaculate El Paseo Drive in Palm Desert, I found the generic cast aluminum tortilla press I had been looking for, *hecho en Mexico* cast into its base.

Driving along Route 111 through Cathedral City past Galito's Mexican restaurant, we hit real pay dirt! Paoli's Restaurant Supply—restaurant, bakery and bar equipment— with the magic word *used*. Nirvana. A low, squat frontage hid a cavernous depth of delights. The contents of dozens of diners, restaurants and bars had been dismembered and laid out on racks, bins and shelves to pick through—from ducting and deep-fryers down to napkin rings, menu holders and fake plastic cane baskets. Room after packed room—it was like that famous scene in Martin Scorsese's *GoodFellas* (walking through the kitchen), an endless stream of stainless steel and aluminum. My brain almost short-circuits with the possibilities. Perhaps we should open a bar, bakery or combined diner—just to make use of such glorious gastronomic equipment.

So we buy: stainless steel countertop cake stands, battered aluminum pizza trays, measuring ladles, blank menu holders, stainless steel coffee jugs, barbecue tongs, large slotted spoons, a gigantic stainless steel colander, muffin tins, frying pans, U.S.-size measuring cups, stainless steel sauceboats and so much more. They kindly gave us two huge packing boxes for the return air journey home.

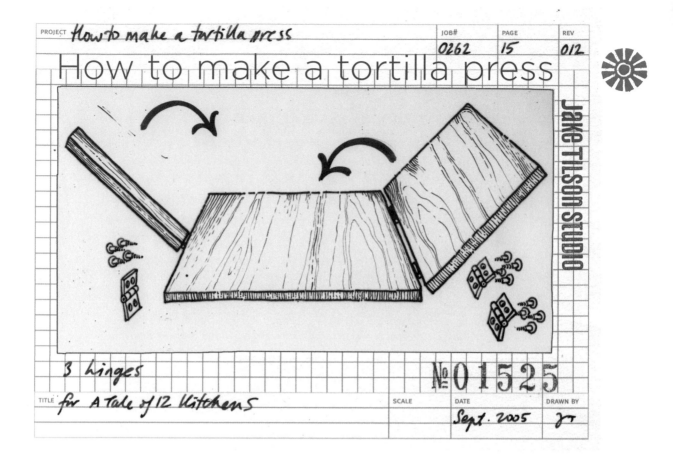

How to make a tortilla press

3 hinges

№ 01525

TITLE for A Tale of 12 Kitchens   SCALE   DATE Sept. 2005   DRAWN BY JT

Jake Tilson Studio

To make a cooking implement from scratch takes time, spare time. During busy, work-filled, school-focused life it's out of the question. At such times having a fridge full of food is a minor miracle, requiring time and constant planning. So for certain culinary projects I wait for a holiday. My Mexican cookbooks tell me how easy it is to make my own tortilla press. They provide all the culinary details—but no diagrams, and I need diagrams. Several search engines later, a fuzzy JPEG hums out of my laserwriter with a rudimentary drawing of a tortilla press in elevation and plan views. I already have the hinges, bought in Paris in the hardware-heaven basement at BHV on Rue de Rivoli, but that's another book—*Hardware Observed*.

You'll need three pieces of sturdy wood—handle, base board and top board. Although you don't exert a great deal of pressure when operating the press, you wouldn't want it to break on your first ball of dough. The wood doesn't have to be scrupulously clean, since the uncooked tortilla never touches it—a plastic carrier bag is used to protect the tortilla dough from sticking to the boards of the press. Three hinges: one to attach the handle to the base board, and another two to attach the base board to the top board. Pre-drill the holes to avoid splitting. Use long screws for added strength. The press is easy to use—the handle presses the top board onto the bottom board, between which is your ball of dough.

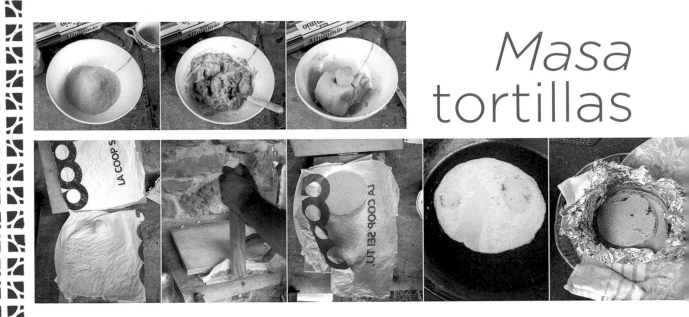

Masa tortillas

Making bread, chapatis or tortillas reminds me of the thumbprints you find fired into ancient ceramic pots, marks left by their maker. Cooking tortillas is another of those grounding culinary practices—rooting you back in time to past civilizations and generations of cooks stretching back thousands of years.

In California corn or flour tortillas of all sizes are available in most supermarkets. Better still are fresh tortillas available from *tortellerias*. If there isn't a handy *tortelleria* nearby, tortillas are easy to make yourself. Although some tortillas are made from wheat flour, they are traditionally made from *masa* (see page 172). For ease you can use *masa harina* (flour), which is becoming easier to find. Tortillas are cooked on a *comal*—a thin disk of steel that, unlike a griddle, cooks very quickly indeed—similar to an Indian *tava*, or *tawa*, used for cooking chapatis. A sturdy frying pan can work nearly as well. Make tortillas in advance, wrap in a towel and aluminum foil to keep warm—they can be reheated later.

MAKES ABOUT NINE 5-INCH TORTILLAS

2 cups *masa harina*, or as needed	Plastic bag, cut in half
Scant 1 cup lukewarm water	Tortilla press

Mix the *masa harina* and water in a bowl until a soft dough forms. For each tortilla, take a small ball of dough—1 inch in diameter—and place on a halved plastic bag on the base of your tortilla press. Cover the ball with the other half of the bag. Gently pull the handle down to flatten the ball into a tortilla—5 inches wide, 1/8 inch thick. If it is too sticky, add more *masa harina* to the mix; if crumbly, add a little water.

Remove the tortilla from the press and cook on your griddle, *comal* or *tava*—no oil, moderate heat for 1 minute on each side. Stack the cooked tortillas inside a clean dish cloth to keep them warm.

Calabaza enmielada
Pumpkin with piloncillo

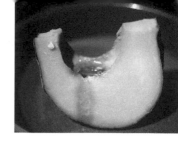

A strange and wonderful Mexican dessert that tastes like hot sweet chestnuts. It uses *piloncillo*, a hard cone of unrefined cane sugar that is sold either *blanco* (white) or *oscuro* (dark). It used to be sold wrapped in yucca or palm leaves. Also called *panela* or *panocha*, it's used in chocolate drinks and baking too. You may need a small hammer to break the *piloncillo*. Demerara sugar can be used as a substitute. The pumpkin wedges need to be wide enough to sit firmly in a pan.

SERVES 4

4 wedges pumpkin, seeded but skin left on
1/2 cup crushed *piloncillo* or demerara sugar

Make the concave dip in each pumpkin wedge deeper with a sharp teaspoon. Pack with the *piloncillo* or demerara sugar.

Pour 1 cup of water in a pan and stand the pumpkin slices upright in the water. Bring to a boil, cover and simmer slowly for 15 minutes, or until the pumpkin is soft and cooked—test with a skewer. Take out of the pan, turn up the heat and reduce the liquid to a syrup, then pour over the pumpkin. Serve with crème fraîche or ice cream.

CANE SUGAR PILONCILLO 99¢ L B

IT'S NOT ONLY TRAVEL THAT AFFECTS WHAT I COOK—
IT'S ALSO THE TIME OF LIFE SUCH INFLUENCES
OCCUR, BE IT IN AN ITALIAN FARMER'S KITCHEN
WITH MY PARENTS, A LONE NEW YORK DINER AS A
STUDENT, A SCOTTISH BAKERY WITH MY WIFE OR A
FAMILY OUTING IN THE DESERT TO A SECONDHAND
RESTAURANT SUPPLY SHOP. BACK HOME, CHOOSING
WHAT TO PREPARE FOR A FAMILY MEAL IS USUALLY
DETERMINED BY WHAT HAPPENS TO BE FRESH IN
THE FRIDGE.

THE VEGETABLE BASKET, KITCHEN DRAWERS
AND CONTENTS OF OUR FRIDGE OVERFLOW WITH
PRODUCE FROM ACROSS THE GLOBE, BUT HOW
DOES OUR LONDON NEIGHBORHOOD ADD TO THIS
CULINARY AND CULTURAL FUSION? SHOP LOCAL.

Drying banana leaves in our Peckham kitchen.

Culinary
Collage

THE ART OF NEIGHBORHOOD EATING. FOOD EMPORIUMS RUN BY SIERRA LEONESE, JAMAICAN, CHINESE, VIETNAMESE, IRISH, KENYAN, IRANIAN, ENGLISH, INDIAN, NIGERIAN, COTE D'IVOIRE, GHANAIAN, INDIAN, ETHIOPIAN, GREEK, CYPRIOT AND TURKISH.

CULINARY RECONNAISSANCE IS THE TOOL FOR UNEARTHING ANY EPICUREAN DELIGHTS HIDDEN IN YOUR NEIGHBORHOOD. EXPLORE, SHOP, CHOP AND COOK.

FLOTSAM AND JETSAM

Just when I thought our kitchen couldn't soak up any more influences, we moved to Peckham—one of the most ethnically diverse neighborhoods in London, brimming with culinary potential. When setting up a new home, epicurean nomads like to explore their unfamiliar surroundings. Peckham in 1987 was *terra incognita*. Some pioneering friends, like artist Tom Phillips, had lived here for years. To us it was an unused page in the *London A-Z*. Local food stores and restaurants reflected a poor neighborhood. As a break from the back-wrenching work of gutting our terraced Victorian house we would wander across to Jumbo, a large, crumbling warehouse on the Peckham Road, which sold products precariously close to their sell-by dates. Vast industrial shelving, which used to hold pallets of sand and cement, were stacked with 5-kilogram cans of army-surplus mashed potatoes, 20-liter bottles of unspecified cola, Thai beer that frothed more than it should and tall elegant cans with the word *frankfurters* roughly stenciled on the bare metal. More dip-and-dare than cash-and-carry. At the back of the eerie warehouse I found a case of Thunderbird wine—straight out of the pages of *On the Road* by Jack Kerouac. Our "open road ahead" was a new kitchen, full of brick-rubble and unhinged, broken glass doors. The sweet wine dispelled the taste of London soot from our mouths as we hammered off the flaking Victorian plaster.

For an Edwardian lunch diversion I walked to Manze's, a traditional pie and mash shop, opened in Peckham by Michele Manze in 1927, his fifth shop (the first one opened on Tower Bridge Road in 1902). Stewed eels, jellied eels, meat pies and liquor—a thin parsley sauce. Otherwise there were the Paris Café, and Bolu Kebab, both introduced to us by Tom. Seated by the steamed-up windows of the Paris Café, I ate fried egg, sausage, bacon, beans and toast and drank tea. Coaches passed noisily along the Peckham Road, en route to central London from Europe and the Channel ports. None of them stopped for lunch in Peckham. Over a few months I test-drove every Indian restaurant within walking distance. Dimly lit, optimistically large premises with vast menus Scotch-taped to their windows. Often I was the sole customer, seated at a grubby table sunk in curled-up carpeting as I sampled a *bhuna ghost* and *roti*. Thankfully those restaurants evolved into minicab offices, décor left intact.

The local Nigerian community knew how to eat well. From a converted caravan in an unused parking lot sat the fabulous Suya Spot. Real street food. Telltale sweet-smelling smoke billowed up from the lot, visible several blocks away. I ordered delicious slices of grilled goat wrapped in a paper bag, served with sliced onion and tomato and liberally dusted with an almost lethal-hot mix of earth-colored spices. The Turkish and Cypriot communities also dined well. Stepping off a number 12 bus I would call by Tadim's for a *lahmacun*, Turkish pizza—rather like a burrito; round flatbread covered in a thin layer of minced lamb, rolled, heated, filled with salad and cut in half. Bliss.

A self-help experiment to prevent the giddying effects of jet lag from an impending trip to Japan meant waking at 3 A.M.—lunchtime in Tokyo. I wandered out into the quiet snow-covered streets of Peckham with my video camera (*Vulture Reality* VHS, Atlas, 1999). To my amazement the Bolu Kebab at Camberwell Green was open, coping with late-night, early-morning trade. The secret back room was empty, reached through louvered swing doors. For breakfast I ate sizzling shish kebab in pita bread, with lashings of chili sauce. Such warming Mediterranean fare set me up to explore the transformed London streets, deep in snow, lit by sodium orange streetlights, a marshmallow wonderland.

Our kitchen in Peckham has a resonance of the old Notting Hill Gate dairy I lived in as a child. A cobbled-together installation/collage of found furniture and fittings: a cast-iron sink from a skip, hanging utensil racks made from large wire-mesh bread baskets, a replacement eye-level grill discovered in a front garden for our 1950s Cannon gas cooker, cupboards, table and chairs discarded by the Royal College of Art and display cabinets that once housed a beetle collection, retrieved from the trash at the Science Museum. All detoxed, scrubbed and reinvented for use in the kitchen.

Like many urban kitchens, it resembles a ship's galley—rather small and seemingly detached from nature and season, far from autumnal orchards or hot swaying fields of wheat. Instead we seem to moor at different ports each week to take on new cargo and supplies. Fortunately, amid the urban squall, a connection to a seasonal and regional food chain has returned to London life—farmers' markets. Most Sundays I cycle down to Peckham Farmers' Market to buy produce farmed locally in Kent or fished from the English Channel. There's always a long queue of faithful customers at Lillah's truck from Thrognall Farm—long trestle tables laid out with boxes of well-tended fruit, vegetables, free-range eggs and their own fruit juice. I ask which crops are coming along and mention how tasty last week's bagful was. The fare on offer is a mirror to the season. From their orchards come apples such as Elstar and Laxton,

Comice and Conference pears. Over the year we buy squash that sit in our cellar to be eaten months later, varieties such as New Zealand blue, acorn, butternut, spaghetti and uchiki kuri. After eating their corn I save the husks for making tamales (page 172). We look forward to purple sprouting broccoli, rainbow chard, wild fennel and tomatillos. Thrognall is the only farm I know that grows huckleberries in the U.K. Their soft fruit is a treat—Edward, Reeves, Victoria and Marjorie Seedling plums and an old English variety of greengage, which are divine. Damsons are hand picked from hedgerows. Wild garlic, elderflower and nettles—a foodie kitchen garden on our urban doorstep.

We rarely bake bread. Instead we buy whole wheat organic and Tuscan loaves from the Cheese Block on Lordship Lane, sesame-seeded loaves from Sophocles and Iranian flatbreads from our favorite shop in Peckham, Persepolis—a Persian delicatessen. An exceptional shop. Rather than establish a showroom for their spice-importing business, Sally and Jamshid opened a high-street shop that has become both a mecca for local gourmets and a catalyst for the local Iranian community. Their store embraces ingredients used across the Middle East, including Iraq, Iran, Syria, Lebanon, Egypt and Turkey. Our spice drawer is packed with their hard-to-find wares. Many London restaurants shop there too, such as Moro, whose owners, Sam and Sam Clark, had a book signing of *Casa Moro* at Persepolis.

Sadly, the best local butchers have closed over the past eighteen years, so having William Rose butchers move to Lordship Lane is like having an international football star transfer to your local team. They deliver, but I prefer to visit—courting temptation. When only supposed to be picking up a guinea fowl I leave instead with Scottish ground beef, Welsh lamb, Suffolk pork sausages, merguez, organic chicken livers and a stack of unsmoked bacon—a meat week. They stock mainly British produce which is sourced on a seasonal basis. So lamb may come from Wales or Orkney, depending on the time of year. Venturing into central London, I explore Soho to buy Italian gourmet delights in Lina Stores—hand-made *tortellini*, Parmesan and pancetta. A visit to Neal's Yard Dairy, then a hunt for Poilâne bread. Jeff buys kilos of cheap fruit and vegetables from Berwick Street Market in Soho; her record is 24 kilos, carried home on the bus! But one tends to rely on what's local. It was an art project which opened up the full breadth of exotic, international stores that we have on our doorstep. The renowned South London Gallery invited me to contribute to a themed

exhibition, "Independence." As an artist who lives locally I decided to consider the neighborhood aspect of independence—something culinary. I decided to cook lunch for the gallery staff. The meal would use produce sourced exclusively from local independent suppliers and shops—no chain stores. Unless I am planning a festive meal, I tend to buy ingredients first and deal with recipes later. A cookbook might get consulted; otherwise I trust to memory or concoct something on the spot. I usually start with chopping onions, crushing garlic, sautéing in olive oil—a daily occurrence in our kitchen. The project shifted into party-catering territory when it was decided to serve the meal in the gallery itself rather than at home.

Amid our frantic urban life it was a wonderful diversion to create a celebration feast—weeks of planning, shopping, writing, photographing, cooking, testing, publishing online and finally delivering a meal. My self-imposed rule to shop local and independent opened up new views of the neighborhood in which we had lived for fifteen years. Recipes mirrored the ethnic mix of Peckham. Some dishes were developed from single ingredients discovered in local stores; others from talking to fellow shoppers who would suggest using strange items such as *ogbono* or *fufu* flour. Often the shopkeepers themselves didn't know how to cook their products and would point out a regular customer to help me. Cookbooks also aided the research.

Shopping and cooking become instinctive acts. When confronted with a vegetable stall or supermarket aisle our foremost thoughts tend to be of quality, quantity, price and sell-by date—something to cross off the shopping list and stick in the fridge. To shop in an exploratory, unplanned fashion felt liberating. Neighborhood shopping can be fun, especially if you're inquisitive and allow extra time to enjoy it. Your hard-earned money also remains invested in your community, showing some resistance to the dominance of chain stores. I talked to shopkeepers, some grumpy and focused on trying to make a living, others enthusiastic and friendly, fully engaged with the goods they were selling. Each shop was an assault on the senses. No brand-conscious marketing placement or focus-group led displays. Day-to-day, hand-to-mouth shopkeeping. Some stores were clean, well-stocked and organized; others shambolic, dusty and anarchic. At times I felt I was shopping in Tehran, Lagos, Hanoi or Istanbul. The checkout girl at the Wing Tai, where I bought banana leaves and fresh mint, helped translate a recipe title for my chicken package (page 219). I found *yufka* to make *börek* in Yesil Irmak. My fusion store cupboard expanded.

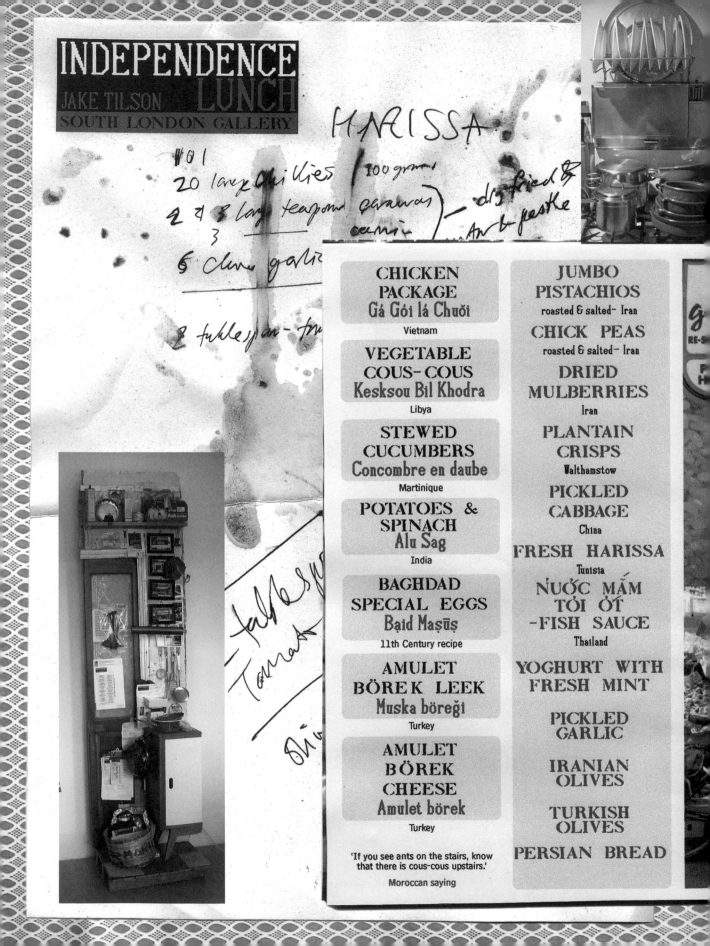

INDEPENDENCE LUNCH

JAKE TILSON

SOUTH LONDON GALLERY

HARISSA

#01
20 large chillies (100 grams
2 & 3 large teaspoons caraways) — dry fried &
3 _____ cumin) — Mortar & pestle
6 clove garlic

2 tablespoon — fresh

CHICKEN PACKAGE
Gà Gói là Chuối
Vietnam

VEGETABLE COUS-COUS
Kesksou Bil Khodra
Libya

STEWED CUCUMBERS
Concombre en daube
Martinique

POTATOES & SPINACH
Alu Sag
India

BAGHDAD SPECIAL EGGS
Baid Maṣūs
11th Century recipe

AMULET BÖREK LEEK
Muska böreği
Turkey

AMULET BÖREK CHEESE
Amulet börek
Turkey

'If you see ants on the stairs, know that there is cous-cous upstairs.'
Moroccan saying

JUMBO PISTACHIOS
roasted & salted- Iran

CHICK PEAS
roasted & salted- Iran

DRIED MULBERRIES
Iran

PLANTAIN CRISPS
Walthamstow

PICKLED CABBAGE
China

FRESH HARISSA
Tunisia

NƯỚC MẮM TỎI ỚT
-FISH SAUCE
Thailand

YOGHURT WITH FRESH MINT

PICKLED GARLIC

IRANIAN OLIVES

TURKISH OLIVES

PERSIAN BREAD

Up at 6:45 A.M.—1 P.M. deadline. Weather lurches from dark, torrential, streaking rain to hot blue sky. Much to learn about catering—preparation and timing. Everything out of the fridge to reach room temperature—pack it around the busy cooker, banana leaf chicken baking inside. Print out new labels for additional dishes. Stuff, fold and fry the *börek*—five at a time after perfecting the pastry folding—keep warm, not covered to avoid sogginess. Set up video camera to catch cooking action, check batteries, film supplies. Getting hot. Windows open, rain pours in, heat escapes. Soak couscous, it's reassuring to have one dish I'm completely confident with and have cooked hundreds of times. Make an additional pint of emergency couscous stew, store in a large thermos. Today was the beginning of national vegetarian week. Independence Lunch was vegetarian except the chicken package. No lurking meat stocks.

Note: left chicken in for three hours, it was fine. Don't use plantains under the chicken again, revolting.

Sunshine breaks through the rain. We load the car for a 200 yard journey—by accident I leave the pickled garlic in the fridge. Twenty-five for lunch, a mixture of gallery staff, trustees, artists, contractors and helpers. The chicken package remains hot. Each dish has a label which lists ingredients and where they were bought—encouraging discussion on nationality and produce in Peckham. A small pamphlet containing recipes and photos of the shops provides further context, revealing planning and recipe sources. I talk with Jacqui Poncelet, a local friend and artist, about difficulties we've had trying to make West African dishes tasty using *fufu* flour. We need help! A Mexican contractor tells me that the *epazote* I've used, a herb from his homeland, can be bought locally in Elephant and Castle. It grows wild by the roadside in Mexico. Both Margot and Donna from the gallery have their newborn babies with them, which adds to the relaxed atmosphere. The catering panic seems over. The dried mulberries from Persepolis provoke much tasting and talk, as does the wrapped chicken. We wash up—an important part of making a meal—and drive the single block home. Hot sunshine, dark slate-blue sky, in the distance rain awaits. After unpacking I attach a trailer bike to my bicycle and collect Hannah from after-school orchestra, where she plays the solo trombone. It's warm enough to wear a T-shirt, and the cool wind is fresh, clearing my head, blowing out the steam and heat from the kitchen.

Independence Lunch—diorama by Jake Tilson, 267 x 71 x 56 cms, 2003. Made from fly-tipped materials found within half a mile of the South London Gallery.

BAGHDAD SPECIAL EGGS
BAIḌ MAṢŪṢ

For Independence Lunch I sought a tempting recipe to spark culinary discussions on nationality and conflict. Considering current political events, an Iraqi dish was needed. An expansive gem, *Medieval Arab Cookery* (Prospect Books), opens a kitchen door to Baghdad's gastronomic past, containing translated medieval manuscripts and essays by Maxime Rodinson, A. J. Arberry and Charles Perry. It was exciting to try out recipes from thirteenth-century Baghdad. In particular I was drawn to the English translation of al-Baghdadi's manuscript *Kitab al-Tabikh*, 1200, translated in 1939 by Professor Arberry. A recipe for fried eggs on a bed of spiced celery and onion sounded intriguing. I had eaten a spicy egg dish in Los Angeles recently, *huevos rancheros*, and although different, it made the *Baid Masus* recipe say "try me." Thank goodness I did—it's an Arabic triumph. Perfect for a Middle Eastern brunch.

SERVES 6

For the sesame oil
3 tablespoons olive oil
1 teaspoon sesame seeds

4 large stalks celery, finely chopped
2 cups chopped fresh cilantro

1 teaspoon ground cumin
1/2 teaspoon ground cinnamon
1 teaspoon wine vinegar
Several saffron threads
Pinch of salt
6 large eggs

To make the sesame oil, heat the olive oil in a small frying pan, add the sesame seeds and lightly sauté for a few minutes. Allow to cool, then strain out the seeds.

Pour a little of the sesame oil into a wide frying pan. When it's hot, add the celery and cook until translucent. Add the cilantro, cumin, cinnamon, wine vinegar, saffron and salt. Stir well and cook for 2 minutes. Spread the mixture evenly over the bottom of the pan, then break the eggs carefully over the mixture leaving them whole. Cover the pan and cook slowly. When cooked, remove eggs from the heat and let cool a few minutes, then cut into wedges. I serve it with spicy merguez sausages and flatbread.

INDEPENDENCE LUNCH

JAKE TILSON

SOUTH LONDON GALLERY

BEST BEFORE > **19.05.03**

INGREDIENTS BOUGHT AT >
PECKHAM FARMERS MARKET
CHOMERT ROAD MARKET
PERSEPOLIS, Peckham Road
ZARAS TROPICAL FOODS, Peckham Road

BAGHDAD SPECIAL EGGS

Baid Masūṣ

from al-Baghdádi's medieval manuscript
Kitāb al-Tabīkh
1200

**VEGETARIAN –
CONTAINS NUTS**

INGREDIENTS >
eggs, celery, sesame oil, cinnamon, cumin, saffron, vinegar, pepper, salt.

RED CHICKEN PACKAGE
GÁ GÓI LÁ CHUOI

A spectacular banana leaf parcel opens to reveal a succulent chicken encased in a rich blanket of red spiced sauce. A fair amount of preparation, but once wrapped, the parcel just needs baking and taking to table.

SERVES 6

For the marinade

Juice of 1 lime

Pinch of salt

1/4 teaspoon chili powder

1/2 teaspoon turmeric

1 tablespoon muscovado or
   dark brown sugar

1 large free-range roasting chicken

For the red paste

1 stalk lemongrass, finely sliced

3 large red chiles, seeded and chopped

3 red bell peppers, cored, seeded
   and chopped

1 large onion, chopped

4 cloves garlic

A handful of cashews

One 2-inch cube of fresh ginger,
   peeled and chopped

Salt and pepper to taste

Olive oil

Enough banana leaves to wrap
   the chicken, washed and dried

A small bunch of fresh cilantro

Marinade

In a small bowl, combine put the lime juice, the salt, chili powder, turmeric, sugar and a little water. Place the chicken in a large bowl. Cut a few deep incisions across the back of the chicken and rub some of the marinade into the cuts. Turn the chicken over and make deep cuts across each breast and the legs, wings and thighs. Apply the remainder of the marinade, rubbing it well into the cuts. Refrigerate for 1 hour.

Red paste

Puree the ingredients in a food processor until you have a smooth paste. Sauté the paste in a little olive oil over medium heat, until it takes on a dark red color, about 10 minutes.

Making the parcel

Preheat the oven to 375°F. The aim is to wrap the entire chicken in a double parcel of banana leaves, sewn together at the edges. Lay 2 long banana leaves side by side, with a slight overlap, across a shallow roasting pan and check that they will cover the chicken with a good overlap. Spread some red paste onto the underside of the chicken, set in it in the center of the banana leaves and smear the remainder of the paste over the chicken. Stuff the bunch of cilantro into the cavity. Carefully fold additional leaves over the chicken, tucking some under, then sew the top pair together. Cook for 3 hours, turning the pan occasionally. Place the whole package on your table so guests can help themselves.

BÖREK

Amulet börek: triangular
Sigara börek: cigar-shaped
Ceviz börek: walnut-shaped
Peynirli börek: with cheese
Kiymali börek: with meat

OUR NEIGHBORHOOD HAS HAD A TURKISH COMMUNITY FOR MANY YEARS—RESTAURANTS, BAKERIES AND FOOD SHOPS, ALL BRING A WELCOME TASTE OF THE MIDDLE EAST TO SOUTHEAST LONDON.

Digging in a refrigerated case in a local shop, Yesil Irmak, I find a packet of *yufka*—triangular sheets of pastry. I ask the shop keeper what they're for—she says *börek*. *Yufka* are Turkish, rather like *phyllo* in Greece, called *brik* or *malsouka* in Tunisia. For anyone interested in making the dough themselves, or to explore the wider story of these savory pastries, read the seminal *A New Book of Middle Eastern Food* by Claudia Roden.

MAKES 22 *BÖREK*

14 ounces feta cheese

2 large handfuls fresh mint leaves, finely chopped

1 tablespoon chopped pistachios (optional)

One 14-ounce package triangular *yufka* (sheets of paper-thin dough; about 25 sheets)

1 egg beaten (for *siagara börek*)

Crumble the feta into a bowl with the chopped mint and chopped pistachios, if using, and mix evenly together.

Amulet börek—triangular

Divide the filling into 22 flattened balls, 1 inch in diameter.

Take a sheet of *yufka*. Place a feta-mint ball in the middle and fold the *yufka*, brushing the edges with water as you fold—see the diagram opposite. The folding method creates *börek* with three layers of *yufka* on one side and one layer on the reverse side. Assemble all the *börek*.

Fry them in batches, starting with the three-layer side down, until golden, about 3 minutes. Flip them over and fry the other side briefly. Drain on paper towels. Keep warm and eat as soon as possible. They remain delicious even if left at room temperature, although they lose their crispness. Triangular *amulet börek* can also be baked; see below.

Sigara börek—cigar-shaped

Preheat the oven to 425°F. Divide the filling into 22 long finger shapes.

Take a sheet of *yufka*. With the thin point of the triangle at the top, place a finger of feta-mint filling at the bottom—see diagram opposite. Brush some water along the edge of the *yufka*. Fold the bottom of the *yufka* up over the filling, fold the two small flaps into the center, then continue to roll it like a cigar.

Assemble all of the *sigara börek*, place on a greased baking sheet and brush the *börek* with beaten egg. Bake them for 20 minutes, or until golden.

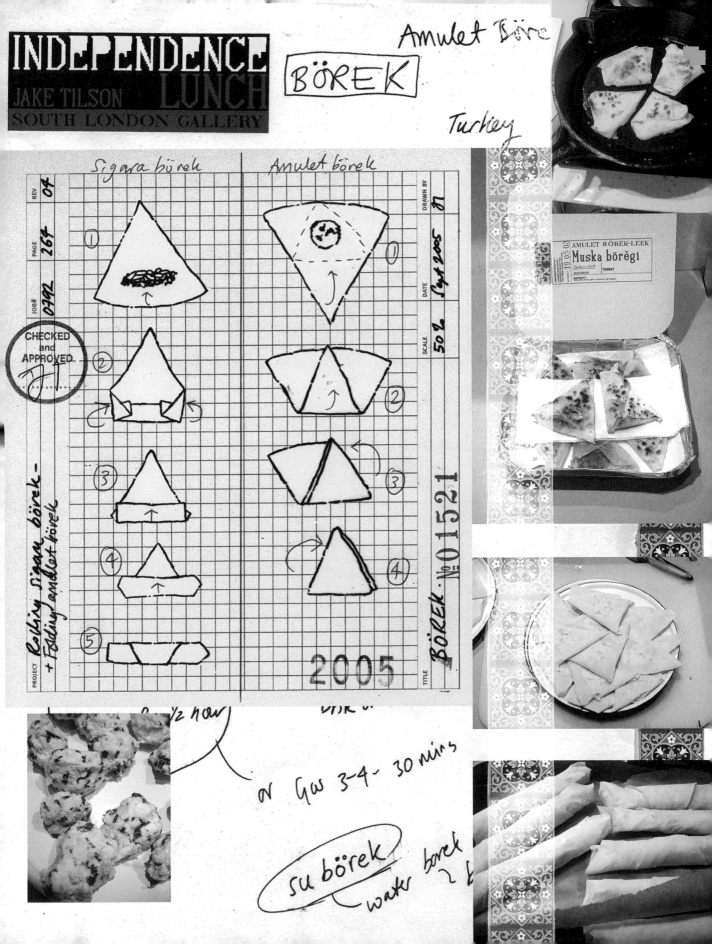

STEWED CUCUMBERS
CONCOMBRE EN DAUBE

After slicing cucumbers into salads, cutting julienne strips to accompany Peking duck or eating paper-thin slivers between white bread with salt, cooking cucumbers is a revelation (also see page 118, Fried Cucumbers). This simple French-Caribbean dish from the island of Martinique is a subtle delight. When cucumbers are cooked, they reveal a world of new tastes.

SERVES 6

Olive oil

1 onion, finely chopped

3 cucumbers, peeled, cut in half
   lengthwise, seeds scraped out and diced

3 tomatoes, peeled and chopped

1 teaspoon sugar

Salt and pepper

Heat some olive oil in a heavy frying pan and sauté the onions until translucent. Add the cucumbers, tomatoes, sugar, salt and pepper to taste. Simmer gently for 30 minutes. You may need to add an occasional tablespoon of water to prevent the cucumbers from burning.

   Serve hot.

SECRET GARDEN MULBERRY SAUCE

A rare chance for some urban foraging, mulberries make a perfect sauce for game. We love this with roast duck. Walking in our neighborhood, you can tell you're nearing a mulberry tree as the bird droppings on the sidewalk become distinctly mulberry in color. Many people miss these telling stains. Squeezed between three converging rows of Victorian gardens is a large rambling secret garden. It can be entered through gates at either end with a key. You buy the key—it's a semi-public community space, and a careful sense of wilderness prevails. In the late summer we often visit, keeping an eye on the concealed mulberry trees within. We go armed with plastic containers and damp paper towels to clean our stained hands and arms. Mulberries are tricky to pick without getting completely covered in their blood-red juice, making it look as if you've been butchering something.

SERVES 6

8 ounces mulberries
1/4 cup white wine
1/2 cup chicken stock

A generous splash of white wine vinegar, or to taste
2 teaspoons sugar
Salt (optional)

Place the mulberries, white wine, chicken stock, vinegar and sugar in a saucepan, bring to a simmer and simmer gently for 20 minutes. Sometimes I add the juices from a roast duck and cook it a little longer.

Put the mixture through the very fine blade of a food mill, or puree in a food processor. If your stock was unsalted, you may wish to add salt. Serve with game, accompanied by couscous or rice.

ALBONDIGAS
MEATBALLS

I used to either fry meatballs in a heavy cast-iron frying pan, smoking up the kitchen, or grill them as long, thumb-sized kebabs. However, while researching Mexican recipes for this book, I discovered a new meatball variation—poaching in tomato *sugo*. The results are always moist and reminiscent of those small earthenware tapas dishes full of *albondigas* eaten in Plaça Reil, Barcelona. To satisfy the tastes of most meatball lovers, I simmer half the meatballs in *sugo* while roasting the rest, which adds a caramelized crispness. Try both and decide which you prefer.

MEATBALLS ARE ANOTHER DISH THAT ENCOURAGE EXPERIMENTATION AND VARIATION. ENDLESS COMBINATIONS AND MIXTURES OF VEGETABLES, MEATS, FILLERS, HERBS AND SPICES—WHICH DON'T ALWAYS HAVE TO BE FRIED, GRILLED OR BARBECUED.

SERVES 6 (MAKES ABOUT 44 MEATBALLS)

9 ounces ground beef

9 ounces ground lamb

9 ounces ground pork

1/2 cup bread crumbs

1/2 cup rolled oats

1 egg, slightly beaten

1 onion, finely chopped

4 cloves garlic, finely chopped

1 teaspoon sweet Spanish smoked paprika

Salt and pepper to taste

3 handfuls cooked spinach or chard, finely chopped

5 cups tomato *sugo* (page 60)

Preheat the oven to 425°F. In a bowl, mix together the ground beef, lamb and pork with your fingers. Don't use a food processor, as that would turn the meat to mush. Mix in the bread crumbs, oats, egg, onion, garlic, paprika, salt and pepper and spinach. Keep mixing with your fingers. The mixture should be firm and hold together well.

Take a tablespoon of meatball mix at a time and roll it in the palm of your hand. The balls need to be just smaller than a golf ball. Place them on a plate.

Pour the tomato *sugo* into a large deep frying pan. Bring the *sugo* to a strong boil, reduce the heat slightly and and gently add half the meatballs—make sure they are covered by *sugo*. Add extra water if the sauce is looking too thick. Cover and simmer gently for 30 minutes, stirring occasionally.

Place the remaining meatballs on a generously oiled rimmed baking sheet and roast in the center of the oven for about 30 minutes.

I like to add the roasted meatballs to the *sugo* for a few minutes, then empty the pan into a hot earthenware dish. Serve with spaghetti for a New York City experience, in pita bread with shredded lettuce or with couscous.

16 TALFOURD ROAD LONDON SE15 5NY

JAKE TILSON

theCookerCooks

How to make a

TORTILLA PRESS ATLAS

BYZANTINE BAZAAR
OTTOMAN
MIX NO.1 &
SUMAC

OTTOMAN MIX NO.1

Succulent mix of Pul Biberi
Source: Peckham & Turkey
Produce of: Turkey

SUMAC

Source: Peckham
Produce of: Iran

CHECKED and APPROVED

THIS SMALL PACK OF SPICE IS BROUGHT TO YOU BY JAKE'S CHILLI SHOP

theCooker
Fine Foods for the Family™
in association with Culinary Planet Distribution

BIBERI NOTES

...of the *Solanaceae*... ...are a close cousin ...tomato, potato, ...Capsicum contains ...min C; this ...lated from ripe ...ngarian chemist ...o later won the ...ck. Don't grow ...t trees because a ...r is prone to can

...ul Biberi is *Marichi-*... ...un. For those of you ...ic Dosha is KV-P+.

...family for bringing ...m Datça. *Biberi =*

SUMAC

A sour, lemon flavoured spice from the Eastern Mediterranean. Sumac belongs to the genus *Rhus. Rhus coriaria*. Elm-leaved sumac or Sicilian sumac. Sold in souks as a coarse powder, sumac is made from the hairy berries that cluster on sumac trees in southern Italy and the Eastern Mediterranean. The berries are gathered before maturity, then sundried and ground. Their hairs are high in malic acid which is also present in apples and grapes. Sumac was used by the ancient Romans as a souring agent and used medicinally by Native Americans as it has diuretic properties and can relieve digestion problems and reduce fever. Sumac powder is used to make a drink, often called Indian lemonade. It is also an important and preservable source of vitamin C.

§ SOME SUMAC RECIPES §

In Turkey, Egypt, Lebanon and Syria sumac is used to season grilled meat and fish, add tang to salad dressings and as a table condiment. Levantine cooking often uses sumac to replace lemon juice or vinegar. It adds colour to fried onions or raw sliced onions and dishes of potato or beetroot. Add it to hummus instead of lemon juice for added colour and flavour.

BEETROOT
SUMAC SALAD §

A Middle Eastern winter salad. Serves 6.

3 large beetroot
2 tsp sumac, or more
1 large red onion, thinly sliced
2 handfuls rocket leaves
   Dressing
   1 cup natural yogurt
   2 tsp tahini
   2 tbsp lemon juice
   2 garlic cloves, crushed
   salt and black pepper

Cook the whole beetroot in a large pan of water until tender – about 30-40 minutes. Drain and cool. Peel, cut into quarters, slice thinly. In a serving bowl put the onion, sumac, rocket and beetroot slices. Mix the dressing ingredients in a cup and pour over the beetroot. Serve with flat bread and marinated olives.

FIRAKH MASHWIYA BI-L-SUMMA'S
BREAD PARCELLED
WHOLE BAKED CHICKEN

A subtle, lemon flavoured whole chicken wrapped in Arabic fl...

1 large ...
2 large ...
2 tbsp s...
1 tbsp o...
salt and ...
3 large A...

Make a ...
salt and ...
inside a...
bread in...
if you ne...
of a 350...
the brea...
brick bre...
brown th...

...and onions before encasing them in bread and baking. Some recipes boil chicken pieces first, others pan fry them until browned. *Musakhkhan* literally means *'something that is heated.'*

Serves 6.

1 chicken, cut into serving pieces
3 tbsp sumac
6 tbsp olive oil

...becoming brick ...last 5 minutes to ...x. Serve with pilau

SUMAC is available by post from *Persepolis* - tel 020 7639 8007.

PUL BIBERI, from which the Ottoman Mix is made, is available from good Turkish supermarkets.

THERE YOU ARE IN CALIFORNIA

LOOKING AT DESERT DANDELIONS

SUDDENLY YOU FIND YOURSELF AT GRAND CENTRAL MARKET BUYING DRIED CHILLIES, THEN ON TOWARDS EAST LA IN A PICKUP TRUCK IN SEARCH OF A FAMED MEXICAN DELI. AS EVER I BUY TOO MUCH FOR OUR KITCHEN. JAKE'S CHILLI SHOP REDISTRIBUTES OUR GLOBAL CULINARY FINDS TO YOU.

HAPPY COOKING.

§ **BRUSCHETTA TRADIZIONALE**

Imported, mixed and packed by TheCooker
Fine Foods for the Family™

MIX NUMBER 4

These chillies are brought to you by

SPRING TIME BORDER COOKING FROM SOUTHERN CALIFORNIA AND NORTHERN MEXICO

BEET & SUMAC SALAD

A Middle Eastern winter salad with a creamy, nutty taste and a delicious bite of onions, flavored with sumac and lemon. A great addition to a *mezze* supper.

SERVES 6

3 large beets, trimmed

1 large red onion, thinly sliced

2 teaspoons sumac, or more to taste

2 handfuls arugula leaves

Dressing

1 cup yoghurt

2 teaspoons tahini (sesame paste)

2 tablespoons lemon juice

2 cloves garlic, crushed

Salt and pepper to taste

Cook the beets in a large pan of gently boiling water until tender, about 30 to 40 minutes. Drain and cool. Peel, cut into quarters and thinly slice. Put the onion, sumac, arugula and beets in a serving bowl. Mix the dressing ingredients in a cup, pour over the salad and toss gently. Serve with flatbread and marinated olives.

SUMAC

A sour lemon-flavored spice from the eastern Mediterranean, sumac belongs to the genus *Rhus, Rhus coriaria*. Also called elm-leaved sumac or Sicilian sumac. Sold in souks as a coarse powder, sumac is made from the hairy berries that cluster on sumac trees in southern Italy and the eastern Mediterranean. The berries are gathered before maturity, then sun-dried and ground. Their fibers are high in malic acid, which is also present in apples and grapes. Sumac was used by the ancient Romans as a souring agent and medicinally by Native Americans as it has diuretic properties, relieves digestive problems and reduces fever. Sumac powder is used to make a drink, often called Indian lemonade. It is also a preservable source of vitamin C.

In Turkey, Egypt, Lebanon and Syria, sumac is used to season grilled meat and fish, adding tang to salad dressings and as a table condiment. Levantine cooking often uses sumac to replace lemon juice or vinegar. It gives color to fried or raw sliced onions and dishes of potatoes or beets. Add it to hummus instead of lemon juice for extra color and flavor.

When I was at a book signing of *Casa Moro* by Sam and Sam Clark at Persepolis in Peckham, I asked Sam (husband) which produce from the shop they used in their restaurant, Moro. He kindly pointed out the hard-to-find items and suggested how to use them. Sumac was one of the spices he recommended: "Use liberally in place of lemon or vinegar—by the handful!"

WATERMELON & FETA SALAD

This simple, unusual summer salad makes a surprising start for a meal—or a refreshing end. The magic is that the watermelon seeds are cunningly replaced with roasted pumpkin seeds, the sweetness of the melon is cut through by vinaigrette and feta and it's finished off with a glossy sheen of dark green pumpkin seed oil. Fabulous, sweet, bitter and salty.

SERVES 6

5 tablespoons olive oil

1 tablespoon balsamic vinegar

Pepper to taste

1/2 small round watermelon, seeded, and cubed

9 ounce feta, cut into small cubes

3 tablespoons hulled pumpkin seeds, roasted

Roasted pumpkin seed oil

Make a vinaigrette with the olive oil, vinegar and pepper. In a salad bowl, combine the watermelon and feta. Just before serving, sprinkle on the pumpkin seeds, pour over the vinaigrette and drizzle with pumpkin seed oil. Toss gently and serve in bowls.

SPINACH LEMON & TURMERIC SOUP

I have no idea where this delicious, easy soup originated—other than from a beautifully written note in my wife's recipe file. It sounds rather Lebanese or perhaps Syrian, although they add lentils to their spinach soup. It can be eaten rich and thick in the autumn with wedges of bread or thinned with extra stock for a cold light soup. Leftovers can become the base for a lemony vegetable curry—just add potatoes, onion, garlic, cumin and a little chili powder, then simmer for 20 minutes.

SERVES 4

2 onions, finely chopped

4 tablespoons butter

2 1/4 pounds spinach, trimmed and finely chopped

Juice and grated zest of 1 lemon

1 tablespoon turmeric

5 cups stock, chicken or ham, or as needed

Salt and pepper

1/4 cup yoghurt

In a large pot, sauté the onions in the butter until translucent. Add the spinach and let it wilt, then add the lemon juice and zest, turmeric and stock. Season, cover and simmer for 30 minutes. Let the mixture cool, then puree in a food processor until smooth. Reheat, adding extra stock if needed. Serve with a swirl of yoghurt in each bowl.

FIRAKH MASHWIYA BI-AL-SUMMA
MUMMIFIED CHICKEN

Researching the use of sumac for a Jake's Chilli Shop mailing sent to friends, I discovered Egyptian and Palestinian recipes that encase chicken, onions and sumac in a parcel of flatbread before baking. I hope food historians will forgive me naming it mummified chicken—not an etymologically correct name, but one that my wife described it as. The final baked parcel does look ready for a museum showcase, but it tastes divine.

I SEEM DRAWN TO DISHES THAT ENCASE CHICKENS IN PARCELS. THIS MIDDLE EASTERN RECIPE USES FLATBREAD RATHER THAN BANANA LEAVES, WITH KEY INGREDIENTS SUMAC AND ONION—CREATING A DELICATE PURPLE CASE.

SERVES 6

2 large onions, grated

2 tablespoons sumac

1 tablespoon olive oil

Salt and pepper to taste

1 large free-range roasting chicken

3 large Lebanese *lavash* flatbread
   (often 2 feet long) or a bag of pita bread

Preheat the oven to 350°F. Make a coarse paste with the onions, sumac, olive oil, salt and pepper. Cover the chicken with the paste, inside and out. Grease a baking dish and drape some flatbread over it. Place the chicken on the bread, then wrap the bread over it to form a neat parcel; add more bread if required. Cover loosely with aluminum foil. Bake in the center of the oven for about 3 hours, depending on the size of your chicken. Brush the bread occasionally with water to keep it from burning. Remove the foil for the last 5 minutes. Serve with pilaf rice.

Musakhkhan

Musakhkhan literally means "something that is heated." This Palestinian recipe precooks the chicken and onions before encasing them in bread by either sautéing the chicken pieces or braising them for 30 to 45 minutes. Sauté 2 grated onions in olive oil with 1 teaspoon ground allspice, salt, pepper and 3 cardamom pods until the onions are cooked. In another pan, sauté 1 tablespoon pine nuts in olive oil until browned. Add the nuts and 2 tablespoons sumac to the onions. Encase the chicken pieces, as in the recipe above, wrap and bake for 1 hour.

خبز مرقوق
LAVASH BREAD
ݬݦ ܬ݂ܒ

DAD'S ROAST BEEF LUNCH

MY MOTHER CALLED ME ON HER CELLPHONE FROM THE SUPERMARKET TO ASK IF A 2.6 POUND ABERDEEN ANGUS ROAST WOULD BE ENOUGH TO ADD TO THE 2.4 POUND ROAST WE HAD BOUGHT THE DAY BEFORE AT THE FARMERS' MARKET. I HAD ASKED MY MOTHER-IN-LAW, MARY, IN SCOTLAND IF 2.4 POUNDS WAS ENOUGH FOR 6 ADULTS AND 6 CHILDREN—SHE HAD LAUGHED AND SAID IT WAS ALMOST A SINGLE PORTION.

It was my father's birthday. As a present I would cook a Sunday roast beef lunch for the family and then fall asleep on the sofa as the kids watched Laurel & Hardy DVDs. The day before, Hannah and I went with my parents to their farmers' market, buying too little beef and too few potatoes. A fringe benefit of having two roasts is that one can be medium rare, the other almost well-done, catering to all tastes. We did buy decent quantities of carrots and beets—small mercies. Like Christmas lunch, roast beef requires rather military timing, an ordered sequence of roasting, veg preparation and the final glory of a risen Yorkshire pudding signaling the time to eat.

SERVES 12 (6 ADULTS, 3 TEENAGERS, 3 CHILDREN)

One 10-pound beef top round roast

1 tablespoon all-purpose flour

1 teaspoon dried mustard powder

A knob of butter

2 tablespoons goose fat

6 1/2 pounds potatoes, peeled and cut into small cubes

1 tablespoon fine polenta flour

Salt

2 beets, peeled and cut into small cubes

10 carrots, cut into rounds

Yorkshire pudding

6 large eggs

1 3/4 cups plus 2 tablespoons milk

Salt and pepper to taste

1 3/4 cups plus 1 tablespoon all-purpose flour

Gravy

1 onion, finely sliced

Olive oil

1 teaspoon all-purpose flour

1 1/4 cups beef stock

Let the beef reach room temperature. Preheat the oven to 475°F. Mix the flour and mustard and rub over the beef. (Do not add salt, as that would draw out the moisture from the roast.) Place the beef in a roasting pan with the butter.

Roast for 30 minutes, then reduce the heat to 325°F and cook for a total of 15 minutes per pound. Baste every half hour with the pan juices.

While the beef is roasting, prepare the vegetables and make the Yorkshire pudding batter. We make a version of Jane Grigson's wonderful recipe from *English Food*. In a bowl, mix the eggs, milk, salt and pepper, then let rest for 15 minutes.

Preheat a rimmed baking sheet, then add the goose fat. Parboil the potatoes for 5 minutes and drain in a colander. Knock them around until they become rather flaky, then slide onto the hot baking sheet. Shake on the polenta flour and salt to add extra crispness to the potatoes. Add the beets at one end of the tray. Roast the vegetables for 1 hour, the last half of which can be when the beef is out of the oven resting.

While the potatoes are roasting make the gravy. In a medium saucepan sauté the onion in olive oil until translucent. Add the flour, stirring well. Add the beef stock, stirring to prevent lumps, then cook for 5 minutes.

Before the beef comes out, finish making the Yorkshire pudding batter. Sift the flour into the batter and whisk together. Remove the beef, cover and leave somewhere warm to rest. Use the roasting pan, with its juices, for the Yorkshire. Reheat the pan in the oven; turn the oven up to 425°F. When the pan is very hot, pour in the batter. Cook the Yorkshire pudding for 20 to 25 minutes. While the roasted veg and Yorkshire finish cooking, steam the carrots. Strain and reheat the gravy, carve the beef. Laurel & Hardy, here I come!

DINNERS

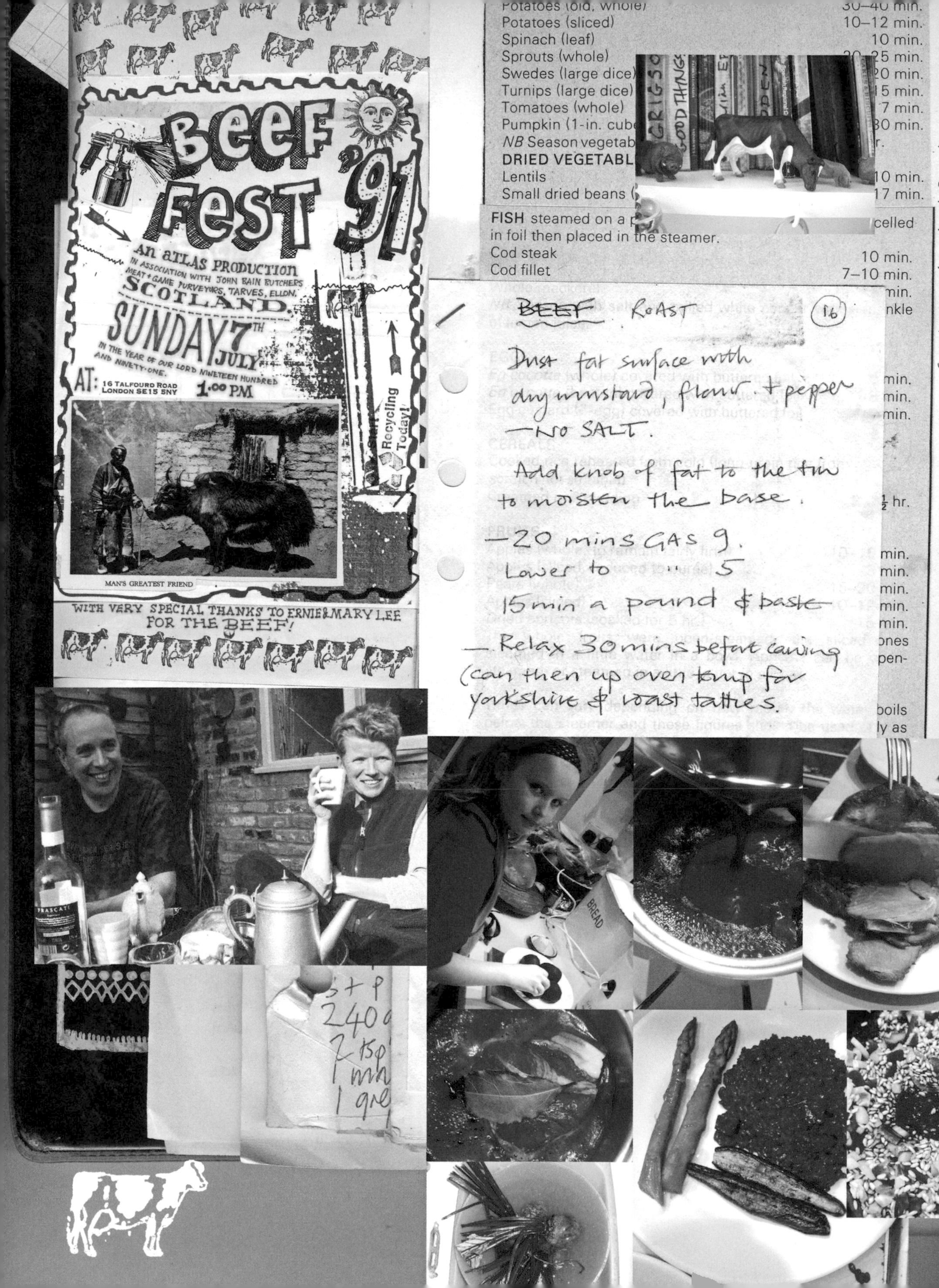

Potatoes (old, whole)	30–40 min.
Potatoes (sliced)	10–12 min.
Spinach (leaf)	10 min.
Sprouts (whole)	20–25 min.
Swedes (large dice)	20 min.
Turnips (large dice)	15 min.
Tomatoes (whole)	7 min.
Pumpkin (1-in. cube)	30 min.

NB Season vegetable

DRIED VEGETABL

Lentils	10 min.
Small dried beans	17 min.

FISH steamed on a ...celled in foil then placed in the steamer.

Cod steak	10 min.
Cod fillet	7–10 min.

BEEF FEST '91

AN ATLAS PRODUCTION
IN ASSOCIATION WITH JOHN BAIN BUTCHERS
MEAT + GAME PURVEYORS. TARVES, ELLON.
SCOTLAND

SUNDAY 7TH JULY
IN THE YEAR OF OUR LORD NINETEEN HUNDRED
AND NINETY-ONE.

AT: 16 TALFOURD ROAD
LONDON SE15 5NY   1.00 PM

Recycling Today!

MAN'S GREATEST FRIEND

WITH VERY SPECIAL THANKS TO ERNIE & MARY LEE
FOR THE BEEF!

BEEF ROAST (16)

Dust fat surface with
dry mustard, flour + pepper
— NO SALT.

Add knob of fat to the tin
to moisten the base.

— 20 mins GAS 9.
Lower to 5
15 min a pound & baste

— Relax 30 mins before carving
(can then up oven temp for
yorkshire & roast tatties.

s + p
240g
2 tsp
1 mh
1 gno

Hannah's Beetroot Ham

Ingredients

776 grams of raw beetroot (1 pound, 11 $\frac{1}{4}$ ounces)

882 grams of ham (1 pound, 15 $\frac{1}{8}$ Ounces)

Juice the beetroot in a juicer. It should taste sort of frothy and beetrooty. Put the ham into a pan and pour in the beetroot juice. The ham must be covered with the juice, add some water if you need to. Add a bay leaf, then simmer gently for forty minutes. Take the ham out of the pan and roast it in the oven for fifteen minutes, gas mark seven.

Recommendation

The stock makes a wonderful red risotto.

by Hannah T

VEGETABLES

DESERTS

OTHER

FROM A LONDON KITCHEN

As a domestic cook, not a chef, I can avoid the worrying notions of consistency and standardization—lunches and suppers may vary in quality from occasionally sublime to rather plain. Whether cooked from scratch or from an ad-hoc mix of leftovers it's rarely inedible—unless I'm feeling experimental, in which case pasta awaits as an instant substitute. Second-rate meals usually fail due to poor timing—too much chat while the chicken sits ignored in a 400°F oven. One aspect of cooking I do share with chefs is that I rarely cook alone—it's a family sport, something shared. Although during the week I cook alternate suppers, there is still collaboration—my wife makes a salad, our daughter cuts zucchini, cutlery needs to be found. There may be an occasional disagreement about how thin to cut the onions but that's rare. Not being the sole cook avoids the splinters of monotony setting in and relieves any sense of obligation.

The food we cook at home draws upon a complex blend of influences that aren't concerned with gastronomic trends, reflecting personal history and circumstance rather than national identity. Like language, cooking evolves slowly from generation to generation, picking up international inflections while hopefully retaining a local dialect. So-called fusion cooking is often just the natural state of affairs in many homes, a gastronomic evolution.

My mother took our neighbors in Tuscany, the Antolinis, a box of couscous from Màscari in Venice, one of the oldest spice shops in Europe. They'd never tasted it before but loved it. Maura is a superb cook and will by now be an expert couscous cook. A small Tunisian influence in Tuscany.

The quandary of many gourmands was expressed well by the chef Rick Stein, whose roving television series *Food Heroes* (BBC) helped rediscover and celebrate regional British producers and ingredients. Like many of us, he can't resist cooking the occasional recipe from Thailand, Provence or Puglia alongside local regional dishes—a moot point if you are reading this in Bangkok, Marseille or Brindisi! Our appetite for assimilating foreign dishes seems unstoppable. We want to try it all. As more vacationers shake off their "playing it safe with chips" attitude and instead appreciate and relish the nuances of regional food abroad, their views change on returning home. We become thankful for local differences which have survived at home, as well as taking delight from the self-imported produce spilling over from our carry-on luggage.

LOOKING BACK AT THE INFLUENCES FELT FROM CHILDHOOD KITCHENS, WHILE TRAVELING AND FROM SETTING UP A HOME, I AM STRUCK BY HOW CENTRAL COOKING IS TO OUR NOTION OF WHO WE ARE. AS DOMESTIC COOKS WE HAVE THE HEALTH OF OUR LOVED ONES AT STAKE, BUT CHOICES IN THE KITCHEN ALSO DRAMATICALLY AFFECT THE WORLD AROUND US—NOT ONLY OUR LOCAL COMMUNITIES BUT ALSO DISTANT FARMS, FORESTS, SHORELINES AND BUSTLING CITIES; WE TRY TO BECOME RESPONSIBLE CONSUMERS. MY OWN CULINARY IDENTITY APPEARS TO BE IN A BLISSFUL STATE OF FLUX AND IS AIDED BY INQUISITIVENESS AND A NEED FOR EXPLORATION. LONG MAY IT CONTINUE. I SUSPECT I'VE WRITTEN THIS BOOK FOR OUR DAUGHTER, HANNAH, AS A GUIDE TO THE SIGNIFICANCE OF COOKING, SHARING AND EATING IN OUR LIVES, A DEEP ENGAGEMENT WITH ALL THINGS CULINARY, ROOTED IN A SENSE OF RESPONSIBILITY BUT EXPERIENCED WITH JOY AND LOVE. HAPPY COOKING.

BEAUTY PACKAGE

I can't deny it: I often buy produce solely because of seductive packaging. A particular typeface may catch my eye—perhaps some curious decorative lettering derived from 1800s American wood block type. Shops and market stalls reach out to all our senses—the sound of fruit, the taste of canvas, the feel of pasta, the smell of paper and the color of freshness. Repetition and quantity—stacked, piled, fanned out, formed into a pyramid—all touch a shopper's visual instinct. Would you buy the last dented can of tomatoes from an empty shelf? I've only ever seen two empty supermarkets, one in 1980s Russia and one in London during a delivery strike. It's an unsettling experience to see the end of the urban food chain laid bare, empty and exhausted. Supermarkets, by definition, should be fully stocked at all times. I'm less bothered by a farmers' market running out of purple sprouting broccoli. Empty supermarkets appear vaguely apocalyptic. These days supermarket chains try to look more like a farmers' market attached to a delicatessen—that carefully studied dishevelled look, handwritten signs, wicker baskets full of apples. We're not fooled.

Although I have read books on Slow Food, chemically grown produce, food politics, and even *Farmers Weekly*, all this wisdom seems to vanish when confronted with a beautiful package—a rectangular yellow box, its die-cut hole revealing the contents through a delicate, cellophane window. An elegant line drawing sits next to bold red typography. In the corner, reversed-out white lettering billows in a red flag shape. Long lines of minute text cluster on the back of the box—calming and authoritative, informative and reassuring. It all whispers "buy me, buy me," so I do. The design of packaging used to be restricted to a few colors by cheap printing technology—in some countries it still is. However, new printing techniques and software have evolved and changed the vocabulary and possibilities offered to packaging designers. Today you can print full-color photographic quality images on almost any surface imaginable at little extra cost—full color has become endemic. Ironically it's now gourmet products which use single-color printing to elevate them from the surrounding full-color babble—utilizing old associations of quality—muted and discreet, simple and restrained. Other than in speciality aisles, the only use of simple color combinations you'll find in a supermarket will be in the own-brand economy range.

Packaging often lingers in the home. Biscuit cans of nails, harissa cans of paper clips—I even spotted a 1976 Sainsbury's oregano jar hiding in my spice rack.

On recent travels I sought out possible contenders for what I consider to be exquisite food packaging. I delved into shops as far apart as Venice, New York, Stockholm, Aberdeen, Los Angeles and locally in Peckham. As promising items were discovered a set of rules slowly evolved. I needed subcategories. For instance, the properties that make a tin can special are different than the qualities required by a box to be a beautiful box. Old packaging favorites that I remembered as stunning had since become dreary and infested by poorly placed bar codes, EEC logos, reduced-salt stickers and low-fat labels. Few classic packages deal well with this onslaught of food regulation labeling. Over the years manufacturers tweak their logos, remodel jars and fit safety lids, often eroding a good design. A successful example of a design that has evolved well is the Marmite jar, whose front label beautifully displays the graphic history of the product, leaving the label at the back to keep up with the current legislation of ingredients and bar codes. A successful and appropriate design creates a sense of wholeness—producing a box-like box or can-like can. This is achieved by recognizing its inherent qualities and by using a sympathetic graphic language to enhance and assert the form. There are many generic types of design that are effective, from the handed-down intricacies of Victorian packaging and the bold and simple beauty of 1950s layout, to the eclectic designs of today. Attention to detail is essential. Each facet should declare itself clearly. When you pick up a rectangular box it needs to be obvious which is the top, bottom, face, back and sides. This is still not enough to guarantee beauty—a certain rightness is required which harnesses the graphic language of usage created over centuries. A delicate balance of simplicity and careful ornamentation.

The power of association is something that designers and advertisers have utilized since the first labels and packages were devised. Form is another key signifier for selling or identifying food products, from Roman amphorae being piled on a dockside in fourth-century Ostia to the classic Coca-Cola bottle. Many ingredients have such a deeply rooted generic form of packaging associated with them it's hard to separate the package from the produce—egg boxes are a good example. I remember seeing my first flat-lidded, rectangular, vacuum pack of eggs, with a full-color photograph of fields on it. Even though I was looking for eggs, I walked past it several times! Shopping abroad reveals that other cultures have their own generic forms, colors, images and word play that are associated with specific produce. Doing a family shop in Gotëborg, New York, Tokyo or Delhi can be disorientating.

Hannah Tilson
Marmite, 2004
pastel on paper, 44 x 36 cm.

BELL'S
ALL NATURAL
SALT FREE
THE WILLIAM G. BELL CO.
Since 1867
NET WT. 1 OZ.
SEASONING

MILK CHOCOLATE
TUNNOCK'S EST. 1890
STILL A FAMILY BUSINESS
6 TEA CAKES
ONLY 91 CALORIES
4 GRAMS FAT PER TEACAKE

BISCUITS UDDINGSTE
K CHOCOLATE MA
TUNNOCK'S TEA CAKES

AMERICA'S FAVORITE
Quality and Value since 1930
"JIFFY"
corn muffin
mix
add egg and milk
SEE BACK PANEL FOR
OTHER JIFFY MUFFINS
NET WT
8½ OZ (240 g)

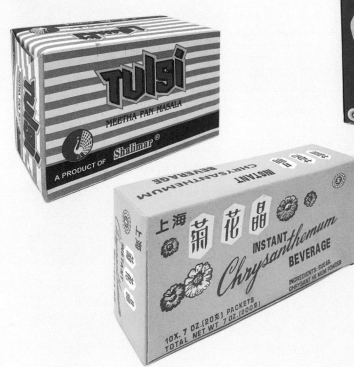

TULSI
MEETHA PAN MASALA
A PRODUCT OF Shalimar®

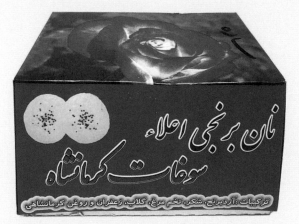

نان برنجی اعلاء
سوغات کرماشاه
ترکیبات: آردبرنج، شکر، تخم مرغ، گلاب، زعفران و روغن کرمانشاهی

上海
菊花晶
INSTANT
Chrysanthemum
BEVERAGE
INGREDIENTS: SUGAR,
CHRYSANTHEMUM POWDER
10X. 7 OZ.(20%) PACKETS
TOTAL NET WT 7 OZ.(200%)
INSTANT CHRYSANTHEMUM BEVERAGE

شاي الوزة
سيلاني خالص
شاي الوزة

BOXES

Opposite

A small comparative survey of boxes, cans, bottles and jars I have bought while traveling over the past few years. Measurements are given in centimeters as height, width and depth. Unless otherwise stated, all packages were bought and photographed between 2003 and 2005.

Bell's seasoning, The William Bell Co., E. Weymouth, Mass.—8 x 5.5 x 2.5 cm, 1 oz. *Tea Cakes*, Tunnock's, Scotland—11 x 17 x 4 cm. *Jiffy corn muffin mix*, Chelsea Milling Co, Chelsea, Michigan—14 x 7.5 x 4 cm, 240 g. *Tulsi meetha pan masala*, Shalimar, Karachi, Pakistan, 9 x 14 x 6 cm. *Instant chrysanthemum beverage*, China National Native Produce & Animal By-Products Import & Export Corp., Shanghai, China, 15 x 8 x 4 cm. *Rice bread*, Ali Seeahboni, Kermanshah, Iran, 12 x 20 x 13 cm. *Alwazah Tea*, Swan Brand, Sri Lanka, 15 x 11 x 9 cm, 500 g.

This Page

Medium couscous, Ferrero, Vitrolles, France, 15.5 x 9.5 x 4.5 cm, 500 g. *Organic cheddar cheese crackers, organic round saltine crackers, organic peanut butter classic rich sandwich crackers, organic cheddar cheese classic rich sandwich crackers,* Late July, Hyannis, Mass. *Zucchero*, Riseria Toscana, Vecchiano, Italy—18 x 10 x 6 cm, 1 kg, 1999. *Anchoas del cantábrico en aceite de oliva*, Conservas Ortiz, Ondárroa, Spain, 10 x 5 x 2 cm, 47.5 g. *Amido di mais*, Maizena, Milan, Italy—16 x 10 x 4 cm, 250 g. *Kak*, Kermanshah, Iran, 17 x 17 x 4 cm.

FOODMARKET FOCUS

This Page

Harvey Nichols Foodmarket packaging. Extended patterns are created when viewing multiple packets on the Foodmarket shelves.

Columbian coffee beans, Harvey Nichols, London— 16.5 x 9 x 4.5 cm, 227 g. *French raspberry vinegar*, Harvey Nichols, London— 21 x 4.5 x 4.5 cm, 25 cl. In-store views at Harvey Nichols Foodmarket.

PACKETS

This Page

Riso semifino vialone nano, Riseria Zanini, Cologna Veneta, Italy—21 x 8 x 7 cm, 1 kg. *Risotto rice*, Ferron Carnaroli, Verona, Italy—19 x 8 x 7 cm, 1 kg.

Opposite

Polenta svelta, Carluccio's Ltd., London—21 x 10.5 x 7 cm, 500 g. *Shri Mahila Griha Udyog Lijjat Papad*, Mumbai, India. *Lievito*, 18 x 15 cm, 64 g, *Vanillina*, A. Bertolini, Champdepraz, Italy—18 x 15 cm.

Bitter chocolate, Luker, Casa Luker, Manizales, Colombia— 8 x 12 x 2.5 cm, 250 g. *Corn tortillas*, Pinata, Don Miguel Mexican Foods, Anaheim, Calif.—22 x 19 cm, 254 g. *Flour tortillas*, Pinata, Don Miguel Mexican Foods, Anaheim, Calif.—27 x 23 cm, 354 g. *Traditional whole rye crisp bread*, Korsnäs Knäcke; Siljans, Vaasan & Vaasan, Helsinki, Finland—27 x 5 cm, 480 g. *Sweet chocolate*, Sol Casa Luker, Bogotá, Colombia— 9 x 18 x 2 cm, 469 g. *Roasted and salted sunflower kernels*, Bazzini, New York—13 x 24 x 2 cm, 340 g. *Rams head pistachio nuts*, Bazzini, New York— 22 x 5 x 9 cm, 454 g.

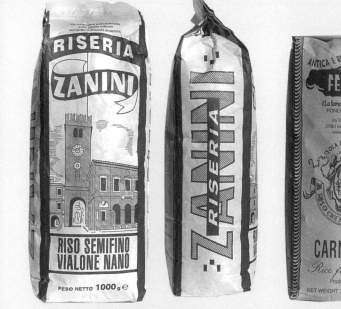

TIN CANS

This Page

Lyle's Golden Syrup, Tate & Lyle, London, 8 x 8 cm, 454 g. *Lyle's Black Treacle*, Tate & Lyle, London, 8 x 8 cm, 454 g. *Bonito de norte en aceite de oliva*, Conservas Ortiz, Ondárroa, Spain, 9.5 x 4 cm, 265 g. *Bonito de norte en aceite de oliva*, Conservas Ortiz, Ondárroa, Spain, 10.5 x 6.5 x 2.5 cm, 112 g. *Portuguese sardines in olive oil*, Sainsbury's, London, 2.5 x 10.5 x 6 cm, 120 g. *Fillets of mackerel in tomato sauce*, Sainsbury's, London, 2.5 x 10.5 x 6 cm, 125 g. *Crabe royal au naturel*, Chatka, Russia. *Chiles chilpotles adobados*, La Morena, Puebla, Mexico, 7 x 6.5 cm, 200 g. *Flat fillets of anchovies in olive oil*, American Roland Food Corp., New York, 25 x 4 cm, 56 g. *Spiced Portuguese sardines*, Pinhais & Co., Matosimnos, Portugal, 10 x 5.5 x 2 cm, 90 g. *El Pato jalapeño salsa*, La Flor del Sur Empacadores, Los Angeles, 7.5 x 6.5 cm, 220 g. *Broad beans*, Ma Ling Jiangsu Cereals, Nanjing, China, 10.5 x 7.5 cm, 397 g.

TIN CANS

This Page

Harissa, Le Phare du Cap Bon, Nabeul, Tunisia, 7 x 5 cm, 135 g. In-store photographs of cans in London and New York.

Pickled cabbage, Narcissus Brand, China, 5 x 7 cm, 198 g. *Vermont grade fancy maple syrup*, Axel Blomberg, Vermont, USA, can made by New England Container Co., 8 x 7.5 x 6 cm, 8.45 fl. oz. *Honey roasted peanuts*, Bazzini, New York, 7 x 9 cm, 170 g. *English mustard*, 8 x 4.5 cm, 100 g jar, and *Dried mustard*, 11 x 6 x 4 cm, 113 g, Colman's, Norwich, England. *Hungarian hot paprika*, Szeged Spiceco, East Newark, NJ, 12 x 7 x 4 cm 142 g. *Black pepper*, McCormick & Co., Hunt Valley, Md, 8 x 5.5 x 3 cm, 56 g.

NOTES ON RECIPE DESIGN

The starting points for the recipes in this book are the same as they were for generations of family cooks stretching back centuries—handwritten, handed-down recipes. As well as kitchen manuscripts, the old, used books in our house tend to be recipe books or volumes on typography. Over the years they have become unique objects—browned, splattered, annotated and patched, looking more like old manuscripts again. Utilitarian, for reference and inspiration. I can happily be transported to Vienna by either a recipe for Sachertorte or by curvy Art Nouveau typography.

Published recipes are like small poems. The literary and typographic rules that apply to them today have developed slowly. Over the centuries, surprisingly few approaches to structuring a recipe have been tried.

When writing out a recipe for a friend, it seems unnatural to separate the ingredients as a list in the order they are to be used. For a domestic cook it's also counterintuitive to translate the unmeasured handfuls, teacupfuls and dodgy oven temperatures into a more universal form. If an ingredient is missed, you can annotate the recipe later, and your friends can call you up if a procedure isn't crystal clear. Equally strange would be to write an informative description or anecdote after the recipe title.

Published recipes today tend to adhere to a descending order of structured parts—title, headnote, servings (yield line), ingredients list, method (instructions) and variations.

Some recipes also state the preparation time. Within each section lingers a minefield of grammatical rules and typographic conventions that need to be addressed. A recipe title should be short, seductive and work well in an index. Headnotes are for bedside reading, providing background material and somewhere for a writer to place an anecdote or to display his or her knowledge of artichoke varieties. Many nuts-and-bolts cookbooks do away with headnotes altogether. Beware the yield line—a friend visiting from San Francisco bought the ingredients to cook us a rich chocolate dessert from a book she found in our kitchen. It called for 24 eggs and many pounds of chocolate. We were four for supper, but the yield line on the recipe was for 16! Our freezer was happy for months, as were we. The ingredients list should be typographically separate from the headnote above and the instructions below. To save space, the lists often appear as two columns. The method (instructions) should be concise and use single paragraphs to break up the procedures in the recipe. Variations are for additional practical considerations, alternatives and add-ons.

These factors are merely the foundation for a successful recipe from which nuances of form can progress. A reference book, *Recipes Into Type: A Handbook for Writers and Editors* (HarperCollins, 1993), by Joan Whitman and Dolores Simon, stretches across 258 pages to help with the other intricacies involved in getting a usable recipe onto someone else's kitchen counter. How did we arrive at such a compact literary form?

Cookbooks were printed as early as 1474—*De honesta voluptate et valetudine* (*On Right Pleasures and Good Health*) by Platina (1421–1481). The book contained many recipes from the earlier Tuscan manuscript by the cook Maestro Martino de Rossi (1450–1475), *Libro de arte coquinaria*. Another early cookbook is by Marcus Gabius Apicius, 1st century—*Apicius de re quoquinaria*, printed in 1498 in Milan by Guillermus le Signerre from recipes dating from A.D. 14. Earlier recipes were carved on Egyptian stone tablets, written on ancient Roman kitchen walls or handwritten as manuscripts.

For centuries a rather haphazard approach to collecting recipes by families and professional cooks developed as they recorded and passed on their recipes. This rather unstructured, unplanned and disorganized approach was carried forth into early printed cookbooks—resulting in books that read like novels whose pages had been shuffled and rebound out of sequence. Ingredients quantities were often missing, no alphabetical order was applied, cooking times and temperatures were unable to be specified or often not mentioned at all. Most early printed cookbooks would have been of use only to an experienced cook. A name and short text, with ingredients mentioned as required, was often all you were given.

As cookbooks began to sell in greater quantities to a domestic market in the 1700s, their recipe structure became more organized. However, the common practice of borrowing, stealing or adapting recipes, or using entire sections of another author's book, meant that some recipes may have been written in the previous century. The origins of these might stretch back even further, as manuscripts. Confusion still reigned. Looking at books from the early 1800s, there are inklings of organization. Separate ingredients lists appear, as do paragraphs for each major part of the method, and even a yield line. There are indexes, chapters and alphabetical order. With authors such as Mrs. Rundell, Eliza Acton and Mrs. Beeton, the recipe format we are familiar with today matured and settled down. Typographic conventions for structuring a recipe on a page also became set, as did much of the language for describing culinary procedure.

After the general adoption of a headnote, ingredients list and method, it's interesting to see cookbooks today that use other approaches. The wonderful, evocative works of Elizabeth David use recipes that appear as tight, well-formed gems—not an ingredients list in sight.

Cookbooks that bring together recipes from a wide range of sources occasionally bear the structure of the original recipes—echoes of the varied hands which wrote them—if the editor allows it. Good examples of this approach are the seminal cookbooks on seafood by Alan Davidson—some recipes have separate ingredients lists, others incorporate them into the method.

For *A Tale of 12 Kitchens*, I chose a structured recipe system. I wanted the recipes to be visually separate from other text. I hope they are clear. Please write and let me know if they are not.

contact @ jake tilson.com

SUPPLIES

CO-OP CAMUCIA
Centro i Girasoli (on SS71)
Camucia (AR), Tuscany, Italy

Eat, drink and shop at
IMOLA MONACCHINI
Enoteca
via Nazionale (eastern end)
Cortona (AR), Tuscany, Italy

Eat, drink and shop at
TAMBURINI
via Caprarie, 1 - 40124
Bologna, Italy

Venetian spice merchant
ANTICA DROGHERIA MÀSCARI
San Polo 381, Ruga del Spezier
Venice, Italy

Covered fresh food market
MERCATO DELLE ERBE
near via Ugo Bassi
and via Belvedere
Bologna, Italy

ZABAR'S
2245 Broadway
New York NY 10024

JEFFERSON MARKET
450 Avenue of the Americas
New York NY 10011

BALDUCCI'S
81 8th Avenue
New York NY 10011

CITARELLA
424 Avenue of the Americas
New York NY 10011

BAZZINI
339 Greenwich Street
New York NY 10013

ELI'S MANHATTAN
1411 Third Avenue
New York NY 10028

DEAN & DELUCA
560 Broadway
New York NY 10012

FAIRWAY MARKET
2127 Broadway
New York NY 10023

FAIRWAY MARKET UPTOWN
2328 Twelfth Avenue
New York NY 10027

MURRAY'S CHEESE
254 Bleecker Street
New York NY 10014

WHOLE FOODS
Time Warner Center at
Columbus Circle
New York NY 10019
*(and many other stores
throughout USA)*

Chiles (ground and whole) from
KITCHEN MARKET
218 8th Avenue
New York NY 10011

Inverurie's specialist butcher
DAVIDSONS
Unit 1, Burn Lane, Inverurie
Aberdeenshire AB51 4UZ
Scotland
shop@davidsons.plus.com

Buy butteries and black bun
ROBERTSON'S OF STONEHAVEN
68-72 Allardice Street
Stonehaven
Aberdeenshire AB39 2AA
Scotland

Fresh and smoked fish
DOWNIES OF WHITEHILLS
40 Low Shore, Whitehills
Aberdeenshire AB45 2NN
Scotland
www.downiefish.co.uk

OATMEAL OF ALFORD
Montgarrie Mill, Alford
Aberdeenshire AB33 8AP
Scotland
www.oatmealofalford.com

YTHAN BAKERY
54 Bridge Street, Ellon
Aberdeenshire AB41 9AA
Scotland

J. DONALD BAKER
4 Seafield Street, Portsoy
Aberdeenshire AB4 2QL
Scotland

**MACKIE'S OF SCOTLAND
ICE CREAM**
www.mackies.co.uk

PAOLI'S RESTAURANT SUPPLY
68-484 Highway 111
Cathedral City CA 92234

GRAND CENTRAL MARKET
317 South Broadway
Los Angeles CA 90013

AMAPOLA MEXICAN DELI
7223 Compton Avenue
Los Angeles CA 90001

LOS ANGELES FARMERS' MARKET
6333 West Third Street
Los Angeles CA 90036-3154

Italian provisions in London
LINA STORES LTD.
18 Brewer Street
London W1F 0SH
020 7437 6482

Persian provisions in London
PERSEPOLIS
28-30 Peckham High Street
London SE15 5DT
020 7639 8007

WILLIAM ROSE BUTCHERS
126 Lordship Lane
London SE22 8HD
020 8693 9191

Tradecraft and organic foods
SMBS FOODS
75 Lordship Lane
London SE22 8EP

COOKBOOK SHOPS

KITCHEN ARTS & LETTERS
1435 Lexington Avenue
New York NY 10128
www.kitchenartsandletters.com

BOOKS FOR COOKS
4 Blenheim Crescent
London W11 1NN
www.booksforcooks.com

THE COOK'S LIBRARY
8373 West Third Street
Los Angeles CA 90048
www.cookslibrary.com

OLD COOKBOOKS

JOANNE HENDRICKS COOKBOOKS
488 Greenwich Street
New York NY 10013
212-226-5731

BONNIE SLOTNICK COOKBOOKS
163 West 10th Street
New York NY 10014
bonnieslotnickbooks
@earthlink.net

COOKS BOOKS (BY CATALOGUE)
34 Marine Drive
Rottingdean
Sussex BN2 7HQ
01273 302707

RESTAURANTS

SAN LORENZO
22 Beauchamp Place
London SW3 1NH

SHREE KRISHNA
192-194 Tooting High Street
London SW17 0SF

CHEZ OMAR
47 rue de Bretagne
75003 Paris

PORTOLE
via Umbro Cortonese, 36
52044 Cortona (AR), Italy

CASTEL GIRARDI
via Umbro Cortonese
Castel Girardi
near Cortona (AR), Italy

CAFAGGI
via Guelfa, 35r
Florence, Italy

VESELKA'S
144 2nd Avenue
New York NY 10003

NATIONAL CAFE CUBAN CUISINE
210 1st Avenue
New York NY 10009

WESTSIDE
323 Church Street
New York NY 10013

YUCA'S TACO BOOTH
2056 North Hillhurst Ave
Los Angeles CA 90027

EL GALLITO RESTAURANT
68820 Grove Street
Cathedral City
CA 92235

**MERKATO ETHIOPIAN
RESTAURANT**
1036 S. Fairfax Avenue
Los Angeles CA 90019

FOOD SYMPOSIUM

The only place to be in
September is the **OXFORD
SYMPOSIUM ON FOOD AND
COOKERY**
www.oxfordsymposium.org.uk
An annual conference on
food history, its place in
contemporary societies,
and related scientific
developments.

BEDTIME READING

Here are some books I was reading while preparing *A Tale of 12 Kitchens*. Some were old friends, others became entire adventures in themselves, leading me deep into specialized fields. Kafka said we all create our own precursors—as a cook I choose writers such as Elizabeth David, Claudia Roden, Madhur Jaffrey, Dorothy Hartley, Alan Davidson and Jane Grigson. Their combined works would keep me happy on a desert island and provide a wonderfully food-orientated history of our past. Recent kitchen-stained books include those by Sam & Sam Clark and Nigella Lawson. rom the tiny television on top of our fridge blast Keith Floyd, Hugh Fearnley-Whittingstall, Rick Stein and Jamie Oliver. Crackling from the radio is BBC Radio 4's Food Program with Derek Cooper, an unsurpassed media gem. Our color-supplements folder brims with recipes by Nigel Slater and Mark Hix. I'm definitely a bookaholic and would buy a new or used cookbook at the drop of a scone. I buy from yard sales, thrift shops, specialist shops, or from abe.com—an armchair researcher's dream. I subscribe to two food journals: *PPC: Petits Propos Culinaires* (www.prospectbooks.co.uk), edited by Tom Jaine and published by the wonderful Prospect Books; it includes essays and notes on food, cookery and cookbooks. It has appeared three times a year for the past twenty-two years. The journal was founded by Alan Davidson, author of *The Oxford Companion to Food*. The other must-have journal is the beautifully produced *The Art of Eating*, a gastronomic quarterly by Edward Behr, published in Vermont since 1986 (www.artofeating.com).

SIXTIES POTS AND SEVENTIES PANS

The Resource Guide for Food Writers, Gary Allen, Routledge, 1999.

Getting Permission: How to License and Clear Copyrighted Material Online and Off, Richard Stim, Nolo, 2005.

The Physiology of Taste, Jean-Anthelme Brillat-Savarin (1825), Penguin Classics, 1980.

The Essence of Cookery, Karl Friedrich von Rumohr (1822), Prospect Books, 1993.

A History of Cooks and Cooking, Michael Symons, Prospect Books, 2001.

On Food and Cooking: The Science and Lore of the Kitchen, Harold McGee (1984), Scribner, 2004.

The Best Butter in the World: A History of Sainsbury's, Bridget Williams, Ebury Press, 1994.

Traditional Foods of Britain: A Regional Inventory, Laura Mason and Catherine Brown, Prospect Books, 1999.

British Tastes: An Enquiry into the Likes and Dislikes of the Regional Consumer, D. Elliston Allen, Hutchinson, 1968.

The Art of Eating, M. F. K. Fisher (1937-1990), John Wiley, 2004.

The Man Who Ate Everything, Jeffrey Steingarten, Knopf, 1997.

Snail Eggs and Samphire: Dispatches from the Food Front, Derek Cooper, Macmillan, 2000.

The Whole Earth Catalog: Access to Tools, Stewart Brand, journal, fall 1969; book, Point, 1981.

Grow Your Own Fruit and Vegetables, Lawrence D. Hills, Faber & Faber, 1971.

How to Have a Green Thumb Without an Aching Back, Ruth Stout (1955), Simon & Schuster, 1987.

Companion Plants and How to Use Them, Helen Philbrick and Richard B. Gregg (1966), Shambhala, 1976.

Food in England, Dorothy Hartley (1954), Warner, 1999.

The Cookery Book of Lady Clark of Tillypronie (1909), unabridged, Southover Press, 1994.

The Pauper's Cookbook, Jocasta Innes, Penguin, 1971.

Poor Cook, Caroline Conran and Susan Campbell, Macmillan, 1971.

A Book of Middle Eastern Food, Claudia Roden, Vintage, 1974.

South East Asian Food, Rosemary Brissenden, Pantheon, 1969.

Indian Cookery, Dharamjit Singh, Vintage, 1975.

An Invitation to Indian Cooking, Madhur Jaffrey, Vintage, 1975.

Old Polish Traditions in the Kitchen and at the Table, Maria Lemnis and Henryk Vitry (1979), Hippocrene, 1996.

North African Cookery, Arto der Haroutunian, Century, 1985.

Cooking at the Kasbah: Recipes from My Moroccan Kitchen, Kitty Morse, Chronicle Books, 1998.

LIGHT AND DARK

A Book of Mediterranean Food, Elizabeth David (1950), New York Review Books, 2002.

Italian Food, Elizabeth David (1954), Penguin, 1999.

Talismano della Felicità: The Talisman Italian Cook Book, Ada Boni, Crown Publishers, 1950.

La Cucina Romana, Ada Boni, Newton Compton Editori, 1983.

Mediterranean Cookery, Claudia Roden, Knopf, 1987.

La Scienza in cucina e l'Arte di mangiar bene, Pellegrino Artusi, Giunti, 1891. Translated by Kyle M. Phillips III as *The Art of Eating Well*, Random House, 1996.

The Good Food of Italy, Claudia Roden, Knopf, 1990.

The Classic Italian Cook Book, Marcella Hazan, Knopf, 1973.

The Cooking of Tuscany, Valentina Harris, Sainsbury's, 1992.

Cucina Fiorentina, Aldo Santini, Franco Muzzio, 1992.

Flavors of Tuscany, Nancy Harmon Jenkins, Broadway Books, 1998.

Before the Palio, Martin Attwood, Arti Tipografiche To, 1998.

Vino: The Wines and Winemakers of Italy, Burton Anderson, Papermac, 1980.

EAST VILLAGE VENDOR

The Silver Palate Good Times Cookbook, Julee Rosso and Sheila Lukins, Workman, 1984.

The Silver Palate Cookbook, Julee Rosso and Sheila Lukins, Workman, 1982.

The New Basics Cookbook, Julee Rosso and Sheila Lukins, Workman, 1989.

New York Eats (More), Ed Levine, St. Martin's Griffin, 1997.

America Eats, Nelson Algren, University of Iowa Press, 1992.

WHIRLIES AND SKIRLIE

The Lure of the Local: Senses of Place in a Multicentered Society, Lucy R. Lippard, The New Press, 1997. An expansive discourse for anyone interested in the idea of what is local.

My first Scottish cookbook find is still my favorite: *The Scots Kitchen: Its Traditions and Lore with Old-Time Recipes*, F. Marian McNeill, Blackie & Sons, 1929, and Mayflower Books, 1974. Her expansive footnotes often outweigh the body text and push up the page, sometimes brimming to the top. This comes from an anthropologist's point of view.

Hallowe'en: Its Origin Rites and Ceremonies in the Scottish Tradition, F. Marian McNeill, Albyn Press, 1970.

The baton for Scottish cooking was then taken up by Catherine Brown—untainted by *nouvelle cuisine* or the temptation to make haggis roulade with a whiskey coulis. I would buy any book by Catherine Brown. She also cowrote *Traditional Foods of Britain* (see above).

Scottish Regional Recipes, Catherine Brown, Penguin, 1981.

Scottish Cookery, Catherine Brown and Richard Drew, Mercat, 1985.

Broths to Bannocks: Cooking in Scotland, 1690 to the Present Day, Catherine Brown, John Murray, 1990.

A Scottish Feast: An Anthology of Food and Eating, Hamish Whyte and Catherine Brown, Argyll, 1996.

A Year in a Scots Kitchen, Catherine Brown, Neil Wilson, 2002. This truly remarkable book carefully lays out many of the historic recipes. For example, there are four recipes for Atholl brose: nineteenth century, mid-twentieth century, late twentieth century and a quick and easy recipe. All the information an inquisitive cook needs, grounded in fascinating historical, seasonal and festive detail.

Feeding Scotland, Catherine Brown, National Museum of Scotland, 1996.

North East Farming Life, Banff and Buchan District Council, 1987.

Onward and Upward, extracts (1891–96) from a magazine founded by Lady Aberdeen, selected by James Drummond, Aberdeen University Press, 1983.

A Taste of Scotland in Food and Pictures, Theodora Fitzgibbon, Pan, 1970.

The Pot and the Girdle, Muriel Clark, n.d.

The Aberdeen Cookery Book, The Press and Journal, 1948.

The Observer Magazine Guide to Food from Britain. Part 8, Scotland, Jane Grigson, 1984.

Grampian Cookbook, Gladys Menhinick (1984), Mercat, 1999.

Jamie Fleeman's Country Cookbook, Northern Books, 1972.

Hand to Mouth: The Traditional Food of the Scottish Islands, Jane Cheape, Acair, 2002.

Scottish Cooking, Sue McDougall, Domino Books, 1997.

The Escoffier Cookbook, Escoffier (1907), Crown Publishers, 1989.

The Poacher's Cookbook: Game and Country Recipes, Prue Coats, White Lion, 1993.

OUT OF THE FRYING PAN

Whenever I fly into the chaos of Los Angeles, one book helps me reset my mind and prepare me for such a special and unique city: *Los Angeles: The Architecture of Four Ecologies,* Reyner Banham, Penguin, 1971.

I also consider the retail landscape—will it provide answers to why, what and how Safeways was and is? why supermarkets took over? Richard Longstreth's *The Drive-In, the Supermarket, and the Transformation of Commercial Space in Los Angeles, 1914–1941* came as a relief—in particular, for Longstreth's exacting street photographs of the 1920s through 1940s, which Dick Whittington unearthed. A comprehensive study indeed: MIT Press, 1999. It's a follow-up to the expansive *City Center to Regional Mall: Architecture, the Automobile, and Retailing in Los Angeles, 1920–1950,* Richard Longstreth, MIT Press, 1997.

Food Nations: Selling Taste in Consumer Societies, edited by Warren Belasco and Philip Scranton, Routledge, 2002.

For an artist's photographic view of Los Angeles in the 1960s, look at works by Ed Ruscha: *Every Building on Sunset Strip,* 1966; *Some Los Angeles Apartments,* 1965; *Thirty-Four Parking Lots,* 1967.

For such a mobile society I also used *The Thomas Guide, Los Angeles County Street Guide & Directory,* 1991 edition. One of the few city maps I've seen showing only roads and no buildings.

For the desert outside Los Angeles the perfect companion book is Reyner Banham's *Scenes in America Deserta* (1982), MIT Press, 1989. One of the best books written on a contemporary experience of deserts and perhaps Banham's most personal book. I love it.

While in the desert I'm drawn to other books that consider otherworldly colonization, in particular *Martian Time-Slip,* Philip K. Dick, Ballantine, 1964.

Out in border country, I need to consider Border food: *The Border Cookbook: Authentic Home Cooking of the American Southwest and Northern Mexico,* Cheryl Alters Jamison and Bill Jamison, Harvard Common Press, 1995.

And digging farther south, beyond the border: *My Mexico: A Culinary Odyssey,* Diana Kennedy, Clarkson Potter, 1998.

The New Complete Book of Mexican Cooking, Elizabeth Lambert Ortiz, Ecco, 2000. Perhaps an easier first-time Mexican cookbook than Kennedy's.

The Great Chile Book, Mark Miller, Ten Speed Press, 1991.

Coyote Cafe, Mark Miller, Ten Speed Press, 1989.

Tamales 101, Alice Guadalupe Tapp, Ten Speed Press, 2002.

For background on the early settlement of the Palm Desert region, pick up *Nellie's Boarding House: A Dual Biography of Nellie Coffman and Palm Springs,* Marjorie Belle Bright, ETC Publications, 1981.

And referring to the local newspaper: *Desert Editor: The Story of Randall Henderson and Palm Desert,* J. Wilson McKenney, Wilmac, 1972.

CULINARY COLLAGE

To help with the weekly abundance from the farmers' market, here are two classics:

Jane Grigson's Fruit Book, Penguin, 1982, and *Jane Grigson's Vegetable Book,* Penguin, 1978. Both are arranged alphabetically by ingredient—genius.

Eastern Vegetable Cooking, Madhur Jaffrey, Penguin, 1983.

Ethnic Cuisine, Elizabeth Rozin (1982), Penguin, 1992.

The Art of Persian Cooking, Forough Hekmat, Doubleday, 1961.

Medieval Arab Cookery, essays and translations by Maxime Rodinson, A. J. Arberry, and Charles Perry, Prospect Books, 2001.

Egyptian Cooking: A Practical Guide, Samia Abdennour, Hippocrene, 1984.

Moro: The Cookbook, Sam and Sam Clark, Ebury Press, 2001.

Casa Moro, Sam and Sam Clark, Ebury Press, 2004.

The Art of Turkish Cooking or Delectable Delights of Topkapi, Neset Even, Doubleday, 1969.

Turkish Cookery, Inci Kut, Net Books, 1992.

A West African Cook Book, Ellen Gibson Wilson, M. Evans, 1971.

Ghana Recipe Book, Mrs. E. Chapman Nyako, Dr. E. Amarteifio, and Miss J. Asare, Ghana Publishing, 1970.

Nigerian Cookbook, Miriam Isoun and H. O. Anthonio, Riverside Communications, 2002.

Madhur Jaffrey's Far Eastern Cooking, Madhur Jaffrey, BBC, 1989.

Chinese Food, Kenneth Lo, Penguin, 1972.

The River Cottage Meat Book, Hugh Fearnley-Whittingstall, Hodder & Stoughton, 2004.

The Cookery Year, Reader's Digest, 1973. A good place to start for many dishes.

APPENDIXES

For Notes on Recipe Design, the following books were invaluable reading:

The British Housewife: Cookery Books, Cooking and Society in Eighteenth-Century Britain, Gilly Lehmann, Prospect Books, 2003.

Old Cook Books: An Illustrated History, Eric Quayle, Studio Vista, 1978.

Great Cooks and Their Recipes From Taillevent to Escoffier, Anne Willan, Elm Tree Books, 1977.

CLOSING CREDITS

Special thanks for this edition to—Ann Bramson at Artisan for her understanding of my book and her gastronomic and bibliographic passion. Also to Nicki Clendening for her gracious introduction to the U.S. media. Thanks to Trent Duffy and Judith Sutton for clarifying the culinary methods so skillfully, to Jan Derevjanik for her expert artwork direction and to everyone at Artisan's office, where Jeff, Hannah and I shared a delicious breakfast of smoked sturgeon, salmon and bagels.

Special thanks to: Susan Haynes, Michael Dover and David Rowley at Weidenfeld & Nicolson for their continual support, vision and belief in the project. Michael Mack, my agent. Thank you, Michael, for everything—your help, advice and support. Having an agent who is also a publisher is invaluable. Also deserving of my immense gratitude are: Jinny Johnson, who edited the recipes; my wife, Jeff, for her editorial advice as I prepared the manuscript; my parents for reading the text to check my sense of family history; and Elizabeth Wiggans, who prepared the index for the British edition.

Kitchens abroad I have either observed or messed up—in particular, love to Bruce Johnson, Mildred Thompson and Georgia, Peter Goodrich, Linda Mills and Ronnie, Susan Shopmaker and Chris McCann, Critch de Sanctis, Tony and Avril Wilce, Larry Green.

North London qualifies as being abroad from where we live, so thanks to Steve Tompkins, Kate Tyndall, Danny and Joe, Dillwyn, Lynn, Aneurin and Maxima Smith, Claudio, Giuliana, Max and Maya Silvestrin, Gill Scott and Sue Hunter, Anita Besson.

From the kitchen garden of Suffolk and farther north—Crawford and Jean Balch, Ruth, Andrew, Mollie and Sarah Ruck, Mary Lee, Bill, Susie, Philippa and Grant Robson, Nick, Non, Henry, Llewelyn and Arthur Cross.

Childhood and student kitchens I sat in—Betsy and Richard Smith, Ela and Mac MacDonald Machnick, Julia and Howard Hodgkin, Mita, Bruno Arnaldo and Maura Antolini, Peter and Chrissy Blake, Ed and Louise Durdey, Deborah Butler.

Supper and lunch recipe guinea-pigs—Maria Chevska and Anthony Downey, Tom Phillips and Fiona Maddocks, Nick and Non Cross, Andie Cowie and Viktoria Kallinina, Gwyn and David Miles, Nicola Hicks and Dan Flowers, Jacqui Poncelet, Ruth and Michael Dover, Nigel Sherman and Cecilia Aguilar, Karen Livingstone, Amanda Fielding, Stephen Farthing, Ann Gallagher and David Batchelor.

On the road thanks to Critch de Sanctis, Frank Lloyd, Nancy Harmon Jenkins, Ellie Irons, Dan Phiffer, Gabriella Bassano, Pam Pfiffner, Adam Levy and Cindy Chastain, Sam and Tara Seawright, Burt and Nancy Anderson. Special thanks to Jeff for driving me everywhere.

From a Scotch-taped inkjet manuscript to a printed book requires a generous thread of people. I am indebted to Liz Farrelly, who liked the idea of the cookbook in the first place and kindly introduced me to my literary agent, Michael Mack. Considerable help came from Sarah Wedderburn, Amelia Thorpe, Fiona MacLeod, Kate and Nicholas Vineall, Carole Lalli, Aimée Brown and Monroe Price. Thank you all. Particular thanks also to Mark Rusher and Elizabeth Allen at Weidenfeld & Nicolson for their support and help.

Thanks also to Tom Jaine at Prospect Books for his invaluable culinary advice and for letting me use the Baid Masus recipe from *Medieval Arab Cookery*.

Software, digital advice and support abounded from Pam Pfiffner, Alan Milosevic, Iestyn Walters, Bruce Fraser, Jen Haas.

Extra special thanks—I am indebted to Claudia Roden for kindly offering her generous support; her books are an inspiration. And to Keith Floyd for the term *gastronaut*.

CERAMICS

Every kitchenware buyer should have a potter with them who will happily insist on looking through a pile of forty Catalonian earthenware dishes for the right one—thank you, Jeff. Hidden under the food are some great plates and platters. P. 47: earthenware by Jennifer Lee. Pp. 59, 61, 64, 69, 74, 83, 85: Zwiebelmuster Czechoslovakia. P. 62: Duomo by Joslyn Tilson, 2004, Imolarte Cooperativa Ceramica d'Imola. P. 105 (second from top): plate, Raymor Roseville by Ben Seibel; cup and saucer, Russel Wright, Los Angeles. P. 105 (lower right): Veselka's side plate, New York. P. 120: Pentole. P. 141: Royal Doulton Juno, 1988.

PATTERN

Pattern is another great signifier of place. Each chapter uses various patterns to help build a sense of place. P. 42: Victorian garden path tiles, Clapham. P. 55: a linocut re-creation of an Etruscan roof design from the Villa Giulia in Rome. Pp. 63, 79: Victorian paper shelf edge decoration from Cortona, by Fiorentina Parva, 1972. Pp. 64, 69, 80: stencilled door surround, Tuscany, 1976. P. 67: cast concrete fake-log fencing from Camucia, 2004. P. 75: square Portuguese blue and white bathroom tiles, 1970. P. 84: rectangular Portuguese blue and white bathroom tiles, 1970. P. 97: American black-and-white composition book cover, 2003. Pp. 104, 105: glass sidewalk paving, New York, 2004. P. 105: tablecloth by Cath Kidston. P. 106: pressed tin ceiling tiles, New York, 2004. P. 107: fire escapes in SoHo, New York, 1980. P. 114: sidewalk tiling, New York, 2005. Pp. 124, 125, 141: Axminster carpet. P. 133: Scottish upholstery. P. 143: family tartan and a fireplace carving. P. 154: haggis packaging, 2001. P. 156: tartan rug. P. 166: re-creation of tortilla packaging design, 2001. Pp. 172, 177, 181, 185: hand-painted wall decoration, Los Angeles, 2005. Pp. 189, 193, 199, 200: Alfred Frey concrete wall screen, Palm Springs, 2005. P. 219: double-yellow no-parking lines, Peckham, 2005.

PHOTOGRAPHY

All photographs are by the author except for the following. Roger Mayne: p. 9. Joe and Jos Tilson: pp. 11, 16 (center; lower left; lower right), 17, 21, 22 (all except ducks), 26, 27, 34, 36, 53, 56, 57. Ian Yeomans: p. 16 (top). Anna Tilson: pp. 22 (ducks), 38 (large photo). Alan Spain: p. 38 (inset of book cover). Robert Golden: pp. 39, 40 (book covers). Jennifer Lee: pp. 60, 86, 104 (third from top), 111 (rightmost photo in second row), 131, 144, 186, 199, 231 (middle photo in second column). Giorgio Lamentini: p. 70 (top). Hannah Tilson: p. 104 (second from top). Joachim Ackersohn: p. 212 (diorama). Cindy Chastain: p. 232 (lower left).

Pp. 97, 100 and 111 use images by the author available from fstop photo library (www.fstopimages.com).

Warning: All photographs are 100 percent natural. There is no styling of food photographs in this book. Every plateful was eaten seconds after being photographed—sometimes before. All crockery was used as-is and as-found, lighting was used as-available. Shot on a hand-held manual 35mm Nikon FM2, Sony Cyber-shot P120, Super cine8, Sony video8 and Sony Hi8.

DEVELOPMENT

The project originated as an idea for a website. Thanks to Steven Bode at Film and Video Umbrella and Lucy Kimbell, on whom I tested that idea during some digital art seminars in 2002. Early manuscript development made possible by the New Geography Federation and Matilda Dritch at the Institute of Gastronomic Arts, Boston.

RECIPES

Early versions of *salsa di pomodoro, panzanella* and *tortellini in brodo* all appeared in my book *3 Found Fonts* (Atlas, 2003).

Baghdad special eggs, harissa, stewed cucumbers and red chicken package appeared in my PDF book *Independence Lunch* (Atlas, 2003; www.thecooker.com/ independence/).

BOOK DESIGN

Structural engineering help from David Blamey, Gill Scott, Michael Mack and Stephen Kirk. Thank you all.

DESIGN

Jake Tilson Studio

www.jaketilson.com

Made on a PowerMac G4 using QuarkXpress, MS Word, Adobe Photoshop, Extensis Portfolio, NikonScan, VueScan,

PhotoKitSharpener and NeatImage.

TYPOGRAPHY

The body text and recipes are set in

Century Expanded

Designed by Morris Fuller Benton in 1894.

Cover title and chapter introductions are set in

NIZIOLETO

Developed by Jake Tilson in 2003. The font is taken from Venetian street name signs. The font Nizioleto is available on a CD that accompanies my book *3 Found Fonts*.

What better font for the nuts-and-bolts sections of the book (appendixes and index), set in

Meta

Designed by Erik Spiekermann in 2003. Also used in the chapters' captions, introductory and ending paragraphs.

Each chapter uses a font that is evocative of either the era or location of the chapter.

Chapter 1 uses

Designed by Ronne Bonder and Tom Carnase in 1970. A font

that lingers on the borders of the 1960s and 1970s. The titles were printed twice in inkjet on cheap paper, once for each color, to replicate a slightly off-registered print effect. This gave it a soft edge reminiscent of old food packaging.

Chapter 2 uses

Developed by Jake Tilson from a few characters found on a tin of tomatoes in Tuscany in 2003. For the Tuscany chapter the font was made into a rubber stamp alphabet. Titles were then rubber stamped onto paper and scanned. The Pomodori font is available on a CD that accompanies my book *3 Found Fonts*.

Chapter 3 uses

Designed by David Berlow in 1989–94 from titling capitals by Morris Fuller Benton designed in 1937. A wonderful mix of upper- and lowercase characters can be achieved by combining both bold and small caps, to create a sense of 1930s New York.

Chapter 4 uses

SKIRLIE

Scotland is repesented by the stunning ceramic tiles attached to the gray granite walls of Aberdeen used to name the streets. Developed by Jake Tilson, using photographs taken in 2001.

Chapter 5 uses

Gotham

Designed by Tobias Frere-Jones, based on a study of vernacular building lettering he found in New York. Reminiscent of West Coast metal lettering whose thin outlines remain crisp and legible in the desert heat.

Chapter 6 uses

P22 Underground

Based on Johnston, a typeface designed in 1916 by Edward Johnston for use by London Transport on the London Underground and buses.

NUTRITION INFORMATION

One page provides

Energy	786 kJ
	188 kcal
Protein	7.0 g
Carbohydrate	19.0 g
of which sugars	9.8 g
Fat	9.3 g
of which saturated	0.6 g
Fiber	1.6 g
Sodium	0.1 g

TRANSLATION

Special thanks to Marc Dachy and Cecilia Aguilar for translating my "permissions" letter into French and Spanish.

ACKNOWLEDGMENTS

DISCLAIMER

This book has in no way been endorsed by any of the brand owners featured in it.

The author has endeavored to trace all copyright holders and clear rights in connection with photographs and other illustrations reproduced in this book. Not all could be located. Please contact the author at contact@jaketilson.com to notify rights not acknowledged and the publishers will be happy to correct any omission in future editions.

The author sent 149 letters, 282 emails, made 231 phone calls and visited 570 websites.

Thank you to all the companies and individuals who let me reproduce their photographs, packaging and logos.

Sixties Pots and Seventies Pans

P. 9: Family photograph from 1959 reproduced with permission of Roger Mayne. Pp. 13, 17, 18, 19: the Nestlé trademarks, logos and images Fab, Zoom, Rev, Lyons, Smarties and Motta are reproduced with permission of Société des Produits Nestlé (also p. 73); thanks to George Apaya. P. 16: *The Little Red Schoolbook,* copyright © 1971, reproduced with permission of designer Ian Escott. P. 16: Bird's Custard can, circa 1963, all rights in the packaging for Bird's Custard are owned by Premier Ambient Foods; thanks to Christine Hines. P. 16: Ian Yeomans for *The Sunday Times Magazine,* March 14, 1965, reproduced with permission. P. 16: Bassett's Liquorice Allsorts reproduced with permission of Cadbury Trebor Bassett; thanks to Chloe Haynes. P. 16: *My Learn to Cook Book,* by Ursula Sedgwick, illustrated by Martin Mayhew, copyright © 1967 by the

Hamlyn Publishing Group, used with permission of Egmont UK; thanks to Sundeep Turna. P. 17: Allen Jones quote with permission. P. 19: San Lorenzo matchbox with permission; thanks to Mara and Lorenzo Berni. P. 21: *How to Have a Green Thumb Without an Aching Back,* by Ruth Stout, copyright © 1955, 1968 by Ruth Stout, reprinted with the permission of Simon & Schuster Adult Publishing Group; thanks to Rose Marie Cerminaro. P. 21: *Companion Plants,* by Helen Philbrick and Richard B. Gregg, reproduced with permission of Helen Philbrick. P. 22: Boots jam covers circa 1975 reproduced with permission; thanks to Clare Stafford. P. 22: Elderflower champagne recipe with permission of Laurie Clark. Pp. 31, 33: Manns and 6X reproduced with permission of Wadworth & Co.; thanks to Dick Stafford. P. 34: Les Routiers logo reproduced with permission; thanks to Laurent de Saulieu. P. 36: Road map of Italy, ENIT (1974), reproduced with permission; thanks to Belardo Maria Consolata. P. 38: *The Pauper's Cookbook,* by Jocasta Innes (1971), reproduced with permission of Penguin Books; thanks to Mary Fox. P. 39: *Indian Cookery,* by Dharamjit Singh (1970) and *South East Asian Food,* by Rosemary Brissenden (1969), reproduced with permission of Penguin Books; thank you also to Robert Golden. P. 40: Akash Tandoori menu circa 1979, reproduced with permission. P. 40: *A Book of Middle Eastern Food,* by Claudia Roden (1971), reproduced with permission of Penguin Books; thanks also to Robert Golden. P. 40: Epicure cayenne circa 1977 reproduced with permission. P. 40: Schwarz ginger circa 1977 reproduced with permission of McCormick & Co., Inc., and McCormick (UK)

Ltd. P. 43: RATP Métro ticket and Paris Métro map reproduced with permission. P. 43: *North African Cookery,* by Arto der Haroutunian (1985), published by Century, reproduced with permission; thanks to Catherine Trippett. P. 48: Sweet smoked paprika reproduced with permission of La Chinata Norte Extremena, Spain.

Light and Dark

P. 56: *Italian Food,* by Elizabeth David, reproduced with permission of Penguin Books, cover reproduced with permission of the Archivi Guttuso; thanks to Fabio Carapezza Guttuso and Patrizia Pierangeli. P. 61: La Palma reproduced with permission of Franzese srl. P. 70: Cortona postcard reproduced with permission of Giorgio Lamentini. Pp. 70, 73: Images of Co-op in Camucia, Italy, reproduced with permission. P. 82: Chef Parmalat Panna reproduced with permission; thanks to Valentina Napoli. P. 90: *Italy for the Gourmet Traveler,* by Fred Plotkin, published by Kyle Cathie, reproduced with permission.

East Village Vendor

P. 97: Sabrett logo reproduced with permission of Marathon Enterprises, Englewood, New Jersey; thanks to Boyd Adelman. P. 101: Thomas' English Muffins, copyright © 2005, reproduced with permission of S.B. Thomas, a unit of George Weston Bakeries, all rights reserved; thanks to Celeste Makofske. Pp. 107, 113: Jefferson Market carrier bag and price ticket reproduced with permission; thanks to Mary Anders. P. 108: Gold's Horse Radish reproduced with permission of Gold Pure Food Products; thanks to Stephen Gold. Pp. 110, 113: Bazzini's packaging reproduced with permission (also pp. 241, 243); thanks to Rocco Damato. Pp. 111, 113: images and logo

of Fairway Market reproduced with permission; thanks to Tara McBride. P. 113: Citarella carrier bag reproduced with permission; thanks to Nancy Palmarini. P. 113: Murray's Cheese reproduced with permission; thanks to Robert Kaufelt. P. 113: Zabar's carrier bag reproduced with permission. P. 113: Dean & DeLuca carrier bag reproduced with permission; thanks to Tracey Enright. P. 113: Eli's carrier bag reproduced with permission of Eli Zabar; Susanna Delaney designed this beautiful bag.

Whirlies and Skirlie

P. 125: Throughroutes to and from Aberdeen, copyright © 2005 by Automobile Association Developments, reproduced with permission. P. 127: William Least Heat-Moon cited in *The Lure of the Local,* by Lucy R. Lippard (1997), published by The New Press. Pp. 130, 131: Sweetheart Stout reproduced with permission; thanks to Robert Bruce. P. 132: Lee's reproduced with permission; thanks to Eve Robertson. Pp. 133, 137: Great Scots products reproduced with permission of Whitworths; thanks to Dave Smith. P. 133: Stockan & Gardens Oatcakes reproduced with permission of Stockan & Gardens. P. 133: Mr. McKenzie's Biscuits reproduced with permission of Mr. McKenzie's, Turriff, Aberdeenshire. P. 133: Robertson of Stonehaven Oatcakes reproduced with permission of Robertson of Stonehaven. P. 133: Tunnock's Tea Cakes reproduced with permission of Tunnock's (also p. 238); thanks to A. B. Tunnock. P. 134: Mackie's of Scotland packaging reproduced with permission; thanks to Karin Hayhow. P. 135: Syrup Crunch reproduced with permission of J. Donald Bakery, Portsoy.

Out of the Frying Pan

P. 165: *Martian Time-Slip*, by Philip K. Dick, published by Victor Gollancz, an imprint of the Orion Publishing Group; thank you, Gemma Sainsbury. P. 171: Amapola corn tortillas reproduced with permission of Amapola; thanks to Juan Galván. P. 184: Piñata Tortillas reproduced with permission of Don Miguel Mexican Foods; thanks to Bill Parker. P. 187: La Mexicana Corn Tortillas reproduced with permission of La Mexicana Wraps. P. 194: La Morena Chipolte Peppers reproduced with permission of Productos Alimenticios La Morena (also p. 242); thanks to José Luis Marcos. P. 194: Luker chocolate reproduced with permission of Casa Luker (also p. 241).

Beauty Package

P. 238: Bell's Seasoning reproduced with permission of Brady Enterprises; thanks to Desi Gould. Jiffy reproduced with permission of Chelsea Milling Company; thanks to Jennifer Guenther. Tulsi meetha pan masala reproduced with permission of Shalimar. Rice bread reproduced with permission of Kermanshah. Instant chrysanthemum beverage reproduced with permission of China National Native Produce & Animal By-Products Import & Export. Alwazah Tea reproduced with permission of Swan Brand.

P. 239: Couscous reproduced with permission of Ferrero. Anchovies reproduced with permission of Conservas Ortiz. Late July cracker boxes reproduced with kind permission of Late July Snacks; thanks to Nicole Dawes. Maizena cornstarch reproduced with permission of Unilever Italia—Divisione Foods.

P. 240: Harvey Nichols Foodmarket packaging reproduced with permission; thanks to Simon Kilgour-Miller at Harvey Nichols and Anna Davidson at Peretti. Vilone Nano rice reproduced with permission of Riseria Zanini. Carnaroli rice reproduced with permission of Ferron.

P. 241: Polenta reproduced with permission of Carluccio's, design copyright registered to Carluccio's; thanks to Priscilla Carluccio. Shri Mahila Griha Udyog Lijjat reproduced with permission. Yeast and vanilla flavoring reproduced with permission of A. Bertolini. Sol chocolates reproduced with permission of Casa Luker. Pinata corn tortillas reproduced with permission of Don Miguel Mexican Foods. Korsnäs Knäcke and Siljans reproduced with permission of Vaasan & Vaasan.

P. 242: Lyle's Golden Syrup and Lyle's Black Treacle reproduced by permission of Tate & Lyle; thanks to Marion Veisseire. Tuna in olive oil reproduced with permission of Conservas Ortiz. Sainsbury's sardine and mackerel tins reproduced with permission of J. Sainsbury's; thanks to Parveen Johal. Crab package reproduced with permission of Chatka. El Pato jalapeño sauce reproduced with permission of La Flor del cur Empacadores; thanks to Roland Montano. Anchovy fillets reproduced with permission of American Roland Food Corp. Broad beans reproduced with permission of Ma Ling Jiangsu Cereals. Nuri Portuguese sardines reproduced with permission of Pinhais.

P. 243: Harissa reproduced with permission of Le Phare du Cap Bon. Narcissus pickled cabbage reproduced with permission of Narcissus Brand. Maple syrup reproduced with permission of New England Container Company. Colman's mustards reproduced with permission of Colman's; thanks to Helen Oakes. Szeged Paprika reproduced with permission of Szeged Spiceco. McCormick black pepper reproduced with permission of McCormick & Co., Inc., and McCormick (UK) Ltd.

INDEX

recipes appear in bold